Selling on Amazon®

by Deniz Olmez
Amazon consultant and
Fulfillment by Amazon expert
with Joe Kraynak

for
dummies®
A Wiley Brand

Selling on Amazon® For Dummies®

Published by: **John Wiley & Sons, Inc.,** 111 River Street, Hoboken, NJ 07030-5774, www.wiley.com

Copyright © 2020 by John Wiley & Sons, Inc., Hoboken, New Jersey

Published simultaneously in Canada

For general information on our other products and services, please contact our Customer Care Department within the U.S. at 877-762-2974, outside the U.S. at 317-572-3993, or fax 317-572-4002. For technical support, please visit https://hub.wiley.com/community/support/dummies.

Wiley publishes in a variety of print and electronic formats and by print-on-demand. Some material included with standard print versions of this book may not be included in e-books or in print-on-demand. If this book refers to media such as a CD or DVD that is not included in the version you purchased, you may download this material at http://booksupport.wiley.com. For more information about Wiley products, visit www.wiley.com.

Library of Congress Control Number: 2020938975

ISBN: 978-1-119-68933-1 (pbk); ISBN 978-1-119-68935-5 (ebk); ISBN 978-1-119-8939-3 (ebk)

Manufactured in the United States of America

V10019166_061520

Contents at a Glance

Table of Contents

Introduction

Not so long ago, if you wanted to be a retailer, you had to build a store, buy products from wholesalers to stock the shelves, mark up their prices, and sell them to whatever customers happened to show up and wander through the aisles. Amazon has changed all that. Nowadays, you can become a retailer without having to step foot out of your home or even rise from your recliner. Equipped with no more than a decent computer and an Internet connection, you can source products from China (and other countries), list them for sale on Amazon, and sit back and collect your money as shoppers across the country and perhaps around the world buy your products.

Well, maybe that's a little oversimplified and too hopeful an image of what selling on Amazon really involves, but conceptually it *is* that simple. Anyone can do it. Unfortunately, the fact that anyone can do it is why it has become so challenging. Millions of people have flocked to Amazon, creating what can best be described as a 21st century gold rush. As of this writing, Amazon has more than 2.5 million active sellers seeking their fortune as ecommerce retailers, and they're all competing against one another and often against big-box stores and big brands, including Amazon. To succeed as a seller on Amazon, you really need to know what you're doing and be committed to success.

About This Book

Welcome to *Selling on Amazon For Dummies*, your definitive guide to making money on Amazon. Here we lead you step-by-step through the process of selling on Amazon, from creating an Amazon Seller account to choosing products with high sales and profit potential, sourcing products from around the world, creating effective product listings, managing your inventory, leveraging the power of advertising, delivering superior customer service, and much more.

To make the content more accessible, we divide it into five parts:

>> Part 1 brings you up to speed on the basics. We take you on a tour of the entire process, covering each key topic in a nutshell. Then, we give you a primer on how to create your own Amazon Seller account and how to find

your way around Amazon Seller Central — a web-based platform for navigating the Amazon marketplace.

>> Part 2 examines what you can and can't sell on Amazon, how to research products to find those with the greatest sales and profit potential, and how to source products from retailers, auctions, wholesalers, and other suppliers for the purpose of marking up their price and selling them on Amazon.

>> Part 3 covers everything you need to know to sell on Amazon, fulfill orders, help customers find you and your products, build your own webstore, manage your inventory, and keep your customers happy. You also find out how to keep Amazon happy so that your product listings are ranked high enough in product searches for them to be noticed.

>> Part 4 carries you beyond the basics to master various ways to grow your business and improve sales and profits. Here you discover how to create your own brand and register it with Amazon to reap a host of benefits, how to use certified third-party service providers to outsource some tasks and provide you with the expertise you may be lacking, and how to expand your operations with business-to-business and global sales.

>> Part 5 features ten advertising tips, ten tips for delivering superior customer service, and ten tips for finding products with the most sales and profit potential. Regardless of your level of experience and expertise as a seller on Amazon, these tips can help you improve your game.

We can't promise this book contains everything you need to know about selling on Amazon, because that would be an incredibly ambitious goal. What we do promise is that this book covers everything you need to know to master the basics, along with guidance on how to use Amazon's learning resources to plug any gaps in your knowledge and expertise.

Foolish Assumptions

All assumptions are foolish, and we're always reluctant to make them, but to keep this book focused on the right audience and ensure that it fulfills our purpose in writing it, we make the following foolish assumptions about you:

>> You shop and buy stuff on Amazon. To succeed in selling products on Amazon, you need to know what the shopping experience is like from a customer's perspective.

>> You have some money to play with. You can open a standard Amazon Seller account for free, but you need at least a little start-up capital to buy products to sell and cover packing and shipping costs.

>> You're committed to customer service. Amazon puts the customer first, and if you're going to succeed on Amazon, you need to do the same, or you'll suffer the consequences.

>> You're willing to engage in continuous learning. You can easily list a product for sale on Amazon, take an order, and ship the product to a customer, but if you want to sell a lot of stuff and earn a lot of money, you're going to need to invest some time figuring out how to research products and competitors, build and manage your own store, create your own brand, and develop some other higher level skills.

Other than those four foolish assumptions, we can honestly say that we can't assume much more about you. The people who sell on Amazon represent a diverse demographic. You may be a sixth grader trying to earn money for college, a 35-year-old work-from-home parent supporting a family, or a 75-year-old retiree looking to supplement his social security income. You can be rich, poor, or somewhere in between. Regardless of your demographic, we applaud you for your curiosity, ambition, and eagerness to acquire new knowledge and skills, and we hope this venture is as rewarding and profitable as your wildest dreams.

Icons Used in This Book

Throughout this book, icons in the margins highlight certain types of valuable information that call out for your attention. Here are the icons you'll encounter and a brief description of each.

REMEMBER

We want you to remember everything you read in this book, but if you can't quite do that, then remember the important points flagged with this icon.

TIP

Tips provide insider insight. When you're looking for a better, faster way to do something, check out these tips.

WARNING

"Whoa!" Before you take another step, read this warning. We provide this cautionary content to help you avoid the common pitfalls that are otherwise likely to trip you up.

Where to Go from Here

You're certainly welcome to read this book from cover to cover, but we wrote it in a way that facilitates skipping around. If you're on the fence about whether to sell on Amazon or you're looking for some background information about Amazon rules, fees, account types, and so forth, head to Chapter 1. Chapter 2 provides a bird's-eye-view of selling on Amazon, which touches on key topics and directs you to other chapters for more detailed coverage.

When you're ready to get started, head to Chapter 3, where you find out how to create an Amazon Seller Account, and then turn to Chapter 4 to find out how to navigate Seller Central — the web interface you'll be using as an Amazon Seller to list the products you have for sale, manage orders and inventory, monitor your performance as an Amazon Seller, and much more.

With the basics under your belt, you can proceed through the book according to your needs. If you need products to sell, head to Part 2. If you already have products to sell and need to know how to list them on Amazon, check out Part 3. If you're comfortable with sourcing and selling products, fulfilling orders, and managing inventory, refer to Part 4 for more advanced topics to optimize your success.

Consider Part 5 bonus material. Here, you'll find 30 tips that cover everything from advertising and customer service to product sourcing.

In addition to the abundance of information and guidance related to selling on Amazon that we provide in this book, you get access to even more help and information online at www.dummies.com.

You can also choose to use this book as a reference guide, the way most people use instructions for assembly — head to Amazon Seller Central (sellercentral. amazon.com) and start poking around and doing stuff until you get stuck, and then turn to the index at the back of this book to find guidance for the task that has you baffled.

Note: Although we did our best to ensure that the step-by-step instructions are accurate and complete, Seller Central is in a continuous state of improvement, so please remain flexible. Consult Seller Central's help system and Amazon's Seller University to access the most currently available information and instructions. For more about the Seller Central's help system and Seller University, turn to Chapter 4.

1

Getting Started with Selling on Amazon

IN THIS PART . . .

Find out all you need to know about starting to sell products on Amazon, without getting into the intricate details.

Know what you're getting yourself into in terms of Amazon rules, costs, business types, product categories, and the Amazon marketplace.

Take a quick primer on selling products on Amazon that covers the bare basics, including finding products to sell, choosing a fulfillment method, listing products for sale, and delivering top-notch customer service.

Open an Amazon Seller account, so you can start listing products for sale.

Navigate Amazon's Seller Central to access your product catalog, manage your inventory and orders, and find the information and guidance to build a successful ecommerce business through Amazon.

IN THIS CHAPTER

» **Brushing up on ecommerce basics**

» **Weighing the pros and cons of different Amazon business types**

» **Figuring out the costs of doing business on Amazon**

» **Getting up to speed on Amazon Seller rules**

Chapter **1**

Laying the Groundwork

Prior to engaging in any endeavor, you're wise to pause and consider what you're about to get yourself into. You may be excited by your future prospects, which is good because your eagerness provides the energy and drive required to succeed. However, you also need to consider the likely challenges and potential obstacles that may stand in the way of success. Having realistic expectations going in improves your chances of success when the going gets tough.

Consider this chapter part preparation checklist and part reality check. Here, we bring you up to speed on the basics of selling online and specifically on Amazon, introduce you to the different Amazon Seller business types, inform you of the costs of doing business on Amazon, explain the rules, and present the different product categories and restrictions tied to certain categories.

Getting the Lowdown on Selling Online

Online retailing is the digital version of owning and operating a brick-and-mortar retail store — without the brick and mortar. Online retailing enables you to provide goods and services to consumers across the Internet, removing the traditional physical barriers between stores and shoppers. The Internet has also removed barriers of entry to the retail industry, allowing anyone with a computer and an Internet connection to sell online.

However, online retailing is still a business. As such it requires a certain level of ambition, commitment, and expertise to succeed, especially as competition increases. Before you take the leap into online retailing, examine the pros and cons and develop a general idea of where you want to set up shop. In this section, we provide the guidance for making preliminary decisions.

Weighing the pros and cons of online retailing

Many retailers — from huge companies to individual sellers — have become rich by selling products online. But achieving success isn't always as easy as it may seem. In this section, we draw your attention to the pros and cons of starting and running an online retail business.

Recognizing potential benefits

Selling online has multiple advantages over traditional retailing, including these:

>> **Low start-up costs and overhead:** You can start without having to build a store, hire employees, or develop and maintain complex operations.

>> **Easy access to customers (nationally and globally):** You can sell products to anyone, anywhere who has an Internet-enabled device.

>> **Option to outsource inventory storage:** Products can be stored and shipped from third-party warehouses.

>> **Deeper customer insights:** By analyzing shopper activity online, you gain deeper insight into what they want and the effectiveness of your advertising and promotions.

>> **24-hour sales:** You make your own hours, while customers can shop 24/7. You can sell products in your sleep!

>> **No waiting in lines:** Customers don't have to wait in line, which can boost sales.

Considering potential drawbacks

Although online retailing has numerous advantages over traditional retailing, it does have several potential drawbacks, including the following:

>> **Increased competition:** You're often competing against both big businesses and individual sellers.

- **Lower profit margins:** According to the law of supply and demand, increased competition drives down prices, especially in popular marketplaces, such as Amazon.

- **Higher costs:** Although overhead costs are significantly lower, you can expect other costs, such as the cost of building and maintaining an online store, pay-per-click (PPC) advertising, transaction fees on marketplaces such as eBay and Amazon, and so on. (See the later section "Tabulating the Costs" for details regarding Amazon Seller fees.)

- **Reduced consumer trust:** Until you become an established retailer, some shoppers may not trust you enough to place an order. Selling in a trusted marketplace such as Amazon eliminates these trust issues to a certain degree.

- **Reduced customer loyalty:** Online shoppers are fickle and usually swayed more by prices than by any feelings of loyalty to a particular retailer. However, over time, you can build a more loyal customer base.

Taking a tour of online stores and marketplaces

As an online retailer, you're free to choose where you want to list and sell your products. You have three options:

- **Your own online store:** You can find plenty of ecommerce web hosting services that provide the tools for setting up and maintaining your own store, such as Shopify.com.

- **Pure marketplace:** A pure marketplace, such as eBay, simply brings buyers and sellers together and facilitates and secures transactions between the two. It doesn't carry or sell inventory of its own.

- **Hybrid marketplace:** A hybrid marketplace, such as Amazon, brings buyers and sellers together, facilitates and secures transactions between the two, and sells products, competing with other sellers in the marketplace.

TIP

These choices aren't mutually exclusive. In fact, you may want to build and maintain your own online store and establish a presence on multiple pure and hybrid marketplaces to extend your reach. Having your own store also gives you the opportunity to improve customer trust and loyalty.

Online marketplaces (both pure and hybrid) typically profit by collecting a commission on all sales. In exchange, they offer several advantages, including the following:

>> Diverse product selection at competitive prices, which attracts sellers

>> Secure transaction processing for both buyers and sellers

>> Access to millions of shoppers eager to spend

>> Virtually unlimited scalability to accommodate any level of growth

In this book, we focus almost exclusively on the Amazon marketplace, which has revolutionized the world of ecommerce with its superior technology, universal reach, ability to offer nearly every imaginable product, and the unmatched trust and loyalty it has earned among shoppers.

Exploring How Amazon Works

One of the big draws to selling on Amazon is how easy it is. Here, we break the process down into two stages: before you start selling and selling products. We also explain the basics of how Fulfillment by Amazon (FBA) works.

Before you start selling

Preparing to start selling on Amazon is a simple three-step process:

1. **Figure out what you want to sell.**

   Amazon has 20 product categories open to all sellers and 10 or more additional categories open only to Professional Sellers.

2. **Decide on a selling plan.**

   If you plan to sell fewer than 40 items per month, choose an Individual plan, which charges $0.99 per item. If you plan to sell 40 items or more, go with the Professional plan, which charges a $39.99 monthly fee and no fee per item. (See the later section "Comparing Amazon Business Types" for details.)

3. **Register to become an Amazon Seller.**

   Go to SellerCentral.Amazon.com to register and follow the on-screen prompts.

Selling products

After you're registered, you can begin to list products for sale. Chapter 9 covers the product listing process in detail, but the process basically consists of the following four steps:

1. List the product(s) you want to sell.

You have two options:

1. List products already on Amazon.

Choose products already listed on Amazon and specify the number you have available, their condition (new or used), and your shipping options.

2. List products not on Amazon.

If the product you want to sell isn't being sold on Amazon, you need to specify the item's universal product code (UPC) and stock keeping unit (SKU); write a product title and description, and provide product photos.

2. Sell the item.

Selling consists of waiting for someone to buy the item you listed. When someone clicks your listing and buys the product, Amazon notifies you of the sale. During this time, you can try to improve sales via pay-per-click (PPC) advertising on Amazon and engaging in other marketing and advertising efforts. Chapter 12 discusses ways you can market and advertise your products.

3. Ship the product to the customer.

Upon receiving notification of the sale, you ship the product to the customer or, if you use Fulfillment by Amazon (FBA), Amazon ships it from its warehouse for you. (See the next section for more about FBA.)

4. Get paid.

As you sell products, Amazon deposits payments (less Amazon Seller fees) into your account and notifies you when payments have been made.

Using Fulfillment by Amazon (FBA)

With FBA, you ship inventory to various Amazon fulfillment centers across the country and, if desired, around the world. When someone clicks your listing and orders the product, Amazon picks, packs, and ships the product for you. FBA offers several benefits, including the following:

» You save the time and cost of picking, packing, and shipping the product yourself. (However, you pay for inventory storage and pay Amazon an FBA fee based on the product's size and weight, as explained in the later section "Tabulating the Costs.")

» Shipping costs are potentially lower because you benefit from the rates Amazon negotiates with carriers.

» Your products are eligible for free two-day shipping and, in some cases, one-day shipping (for Amazon Prime customers) and free shipping on eligible orders (for all Amazon customers).

» You increase your chance of winning the Buy Box (the box on the right of the product detail page that enables a shopper to add the product to his shopping cart).

» Amazon processes returns and refunds for you.

AMAZON: BEYOND ECOMMERCE

Founded by Jeff Bezos in 1994 out of his garage in Seattle, Amazon has defined ecommerce and revolutionized the way retailers sell products and consumers buy them. However, Amazon has expanded far beyond the world of traditional ecommerce to penetrate even deeper into people's lives. Here are some of the notable Amazon businesses:

- **Consumer electronics:** Kindle devices, Amazon Fire TV, smartphones, and Amazon Echo

- **Digital content production:** Amazon Music, Amazon Kindle Store

- **Amazon Game Studio:** Game streaming services

- **Amazon Prime Video and Amazon Studios:** Video streaming services and original movies and series

- **Private labels:** Amazon Basics, Amazon Elements, Wickedly Prime, and so on

- **Amazon Web Services:** The world's largest cloud services provider

- **Amazon Fresh and Amazon Prime Pantry:** Fresh foods and grocery delivery services

- **Amazon Books:** Physical bookstore

- **Amazon Home Services:** A marketplaces for professional services for homeowners

Comparing Amazon Business Types

"Selling on Amazon" can carry different meanings, depending how you conduct business on or with Amazon. You may be selling on Amazon as a retailer, selling to Amazon as a vendor, selling professionally or as an individual, and so on. In this section, we explain the different business types and how they operate on Amazon.

Vendor (1P) versus Seller (3P)

Amazon *vendors* and *sellers* differ primarily by their relationship with Amazon and the way they sell in these ways:

>> **Vendors** have a first-party (1P) relationship with Amazon, selling their products directly to Amazon, which then resells the products to shoppers. Vendor status is granted by invitation only.

>> **Sellers** have a third-party (3P) relationship with Amazon, selling their products to shoppers and receiving payment through Amazon. Sellers are responsible for listing, pricing, and marketing their products, and anyone can become a seller through the Amazon Seller registration process.

Being an Amazon Vendor, has its pros and cons.

Here are the pros:

>> Products carry the "Sold By Amazon" label, evoking strong customer trust and hence increased sales.

>> Amazon offers a suit of marketing tools for vendors through Amazon Marketing Services (AMS).

>> Amazon vendors typically don't pay seller fees, such as referral fees, fulfillment fees, and other charges.

Here are the cons:

>> Amazon sets prices, and sometimes prices are set so low that the vendor suffers a loss or may not realize the desired profit margin.

>> Launching new products may be a challenge because Amazon is often reluctant to issue purchase orders for products that have no sales history.

Meanwhile, being an Amazon Seller also has its pros and cons.

Here are the pros:

>> More control over the listing, pricing, and delivery options

>> More analytics and customer performance metrics for improving business

>> Direct connection with buyers to gather feedback and information on buyer preferences

And the cons:

>> Seller fees, including commissions and referral fees

>> Not having the "Sold by Amazon" label to instill the consumer trust that leads to increased conversions, which is especially valuable when competing head-to-head with vendor products

Individual versus Professional

When you register to become an Amazon Seller, you must choose from the following two plans:

>> **Individual:** You pay $0.99 per item sold, no monthly fee, and you pay only when an item sells. Amazon provides access to a basic set of listing and order-management tools. As an Amazon Individual Seller, you have the option to create listings one at a time by matching your products to existing listings or by creating new listings. Amazon sets the shipping rates for orders and determines which shipping service levels sellers can offer to buyers.

>> **Professional:** You pay $39.99 per month whether you sell nothing or a million items. You pay no per item sold fee. Amazon provides its Professional Sellers with access to additional features and tools and removes some selling restrictions.

REMEMBER

These aren't the only fees you pay to sell on Amazon. Other fees include referral fees and shipping fees. See the later section "Tabulating the Costs" for a complete accounting.

Do the math, and you quickly conclude that anyone who sells more than 40 items a month will save money with the Professional plan. However, costs are only one difference between the two plans. When choosing a plan, consult Table 1-1 for a side-by-side comparison.

TABLE 1-1   **Comparing Professional and Individual Seller Plans**

Seller Plan	Individual	Professional
Monthly subscription	N/A	$39.99
Per item closing fee	$0.99	N/A
Use of feeds, spreadsheets, and other tools to facilitate multiple listing creation and updates	No	Yes
Access to order reports and order-related feeds	No	Yes
Earn top placement on product detail pages	No	Yes
Sell in 20+ open categories	Yes	Yes
Apply to sell in 10+ additional categories	No	Yes
Customized shipping rates	No	Yes

REMEMBER

If you're selling fewer than 40 items per month and don't need to upload and frequently update diverse inventory, the Individual selling plan is probably the logical choice. You can always upgrade to the Professional plan as you grow your business.

Arbitrage versus private label

As an Amazon Seller, you're responsible for procuring products to sell. Two common product sourcing options are arbitrage and private label, as we explain in this section.

Arbitrage

Retail arbitrage (or simply *arbitrage*) is an easy, low-cost approach to sourcing products, which involves buying discounted products from other retailers, marking up the price, and reselling them. Many sellers get their start on Amazon through arbitrage. Chapter 7 discusses some stores where you may be able to find discounted and clearance items.

Experimenting with arbitrage on Amazon enables you to develop the knowledge and experience of selling on Amazon without risking huge sums of money.

However, arbitrage does have potential drawbacks, including the following:

>> Arbitrage requires considerable time and energy in terms of finding deals and listing and marketing new products that may not be listed on Amazon already.

>> You run the risk of buying substandard, counterfeit products of popular brands and getting into trouble with Amazon for selling them as the real thing.

>> The brand owner may file a complaint, result in Amazon requiring you to remove the product from your listings, in which case you get stuck with the unsold inventory.

Private label

A *private label product* is a product that's manufactured by a third party and sold under a retailer's brand name. Examples include Amazon Essentials, Target's Mainstays, and Walmart's Great Value brand. To create private label products, you have two options:

>> Invent a new product, patent it, manufacture it (or have it manufactured), label it, and sell it as the manufacturer.

>> Contact a manufacturer of a product you want to sell, have the manufacturer label the product with your brand, and start selling it as your own branded product.

Selling private label products offers several advantages, including the following:

>> Reduced competition. You're not selling the same brand-name products as everyone else on Amazon.

>> Greater control over pricing.

>> Improved changes of winning the Buy Box.

>> Greater ability to expand sales in the future and beyond the Amazon marketplace.

Creating and selling under your own private label does have some drawbacks, including the following:

>> Creating a private label can be expensive in terms of manufacturing, branding, labeling, and marketing new products, in addition to manufacturing and inventory costs.

>> Introducing a new product with unproven sales to the market increases your exposure to risk.

>> Negative feedback and reviews could sink your entire brand, hurting sales across all your private label products.

The cost of creating a private label and building and maintaining brand recognition discourages many sellers from taking this approach. However, if you can clear the initial hurdles, creating and selling your own private label products is very rewarding, and if you can establish a very good supplier base and control quality, you can build a very successful and profitable brand.

REMEMBER

You don't need to choose between arbitrage and private label. You can engage in both methods simultaneously.

Sellers with and without brand registry

Although Amazon provides various tools to help drive sales, including Fulfillment by Amazon (FBA) and sponsored ads, marketing copy is still fairly restrictive for most sellers. Amazon Brand Registry provides a way for brand owners to overcome many of these limitations to deliver more robust, visual, and interactive product descriptions that set brand owner listings apart from those of other sellers.

Table 1-2 presents a list of brand registry benefits, contrasting the advantages of brand registry owners to those without brand registry.

TABLE 1-2   **Brand Registry Benefits**

Brand Registry Benefit	With Brand Registry	Without Brand Registry
Accurate brand representation and increased sales	Increased control over product listings enables brand registry sellers to deliver more complete, accurate, and reliable product information, which often boosts sales.	Product listings can easily have partially or entirely wrong information updated by various sellers offering the same product, reducing trust among customers thus resulting in lower sales.
Access to search and report tools	Search tools such as global search, image search, and ASIN search simplify identification of potential infringement cases.	Without brand registry, you're likely to overlook threats to your brand.
Brand protection	Provides additional brand protection based on the information provided during the registration such as potential misuse of trademarked terms in other listings, images that contain your logo, unauthorized sellers, and counterfeit products.	Difficult to convince Amazon support team of potential abuse/misuse of trademarks, listings, and brands. Without brand protection, you need to gather a lot of material evidence to resolve trademark and similar issues.
Global support	Amazon provides dedicated 24-7 global support teams to resolve branding concerns on a priority basis.	No dedicated support teams. Sellers must go through regular customer support channels, which is often time consuming.
Brand building tools	Take advantage of additional marketing tools such as (A+ Content), Amazon Stores, Sponsored Brands, the Brand Dashboard, and Brand Analytics tools.	No access to those features without brand registry.

Tabulating the Costs

Selling on Amazon isn't cheap. In addition to the cost of the products you plan to sell are numerous expenses, including per-item closing fees (or monthly subscription fee), referral fees, inventory storage and shipping fees, and refund administration fees. To earn a reasonable profit from sales, you need to account for any and all fees when pricing your products. This section provides a full accounting of the costs.

WARNING

Amazon fees may change at any time. Check the Amazon Fee Schedule for the country in which you're selling to find the most recent fee details.

Product sourcing

When you're buying products from a supplier, consider both the cost of the product and any additional fees, which include packing, labeling, and freight charges and may include *duties* (taxes levied by a governing body, such as import duties).

For example, suppose you're ordering 500 units of a cellphone case, each of which costs $3.00. Additional costs may include a 4 percent import duty ($3.00 × 0.04 = $0.12), a freight charge of $100 ($100 ÷ 500 units = $0.20/unit), packing costs of $0.50 per unit, and labeling costs of $0.10 per unit. Your total cost per unit would look like this:

Supplier cost per unit	Duties	Freight	Packing	Labeling	Total cost/unit
$3.00	$0.12	$0.20	$0.50	$0.10	$3.92

Shipping and storage

Shipping and return costs vary considerably depending on the product size and weight and the carrier or service you use. If you're using Fulfillment by Amazon (FBA), you're charged for both shipping and storage. At the time of this writing, shipping costs ranged from $2.41 (for an item weighing 10 ounces or less) to more than $137 (for special oversized items).

FBA storage costs are charged by cubic foot and at the time of this writing were $0.69 per cubic foot (January – September) and $2.40 per cubic foot (October – December) for standard-sized items. Storage for oversized items cost $0.48 per cubic foot (January – September) and $1.20 per cubic foot (October – December).

When using FBA, you need to account for Amazon shipping and storage fees plus the cost of shipping product from your supplier (or yourself) to Amazon fulfillment centers.

For example, suppose the cost to ship 500 units from your supplier to FBA warehouses is $50 — that's $0.10 per item. The 500 units consume 10 cubic feet, so that's $24.00 for storage (October – December) or $24.00 ÷ 500 = $0.048/unit, which you can round up to $0.05/unit. Finally, you're charged $2.41 to ship the product from the FBA warehouse to your customer. Your per-item storage and shipping charges add to your total cost per unit:

Sourcing cost per unit	Ship to FBA Warehouse	Storage	Ship from FBA Warehouse	Total cost/unit
$3.92	$0.10	$0.05	$2.41	$6.48

Amazon Seller fees

Amazon Seller fees include the following:

>> **Per-item or subscription fee:** $0.99 per item or $39.99 per month

>> **Referral fees:** A percentage of the price the customer paid, which varies depending on the product category but is generally 15 percent or less

>> **Closing fee:** Applicable to items in certain product categories, such as books and DVDs

Assume a per item fee of $0.99, a sales price of $15, and a 15 percent referral fee (15% of $15.00 = $2.25). Your total cost per unit is now:

Cost per unit	Per item fee	Referral fee	Total cost/unit
$6.48	$0.99	$2.25	$9.72

Returns

Returns can be costly, especially if you sell items such as clothing that are commonly returned or exchanged. Depending on your shipping and returns policy, you could end up having to eat the costs of both shipping and returning the product along with an Amazon return processing fee (20 percent of the original order fees up to $5.00) and perhaps the cost of the product if it's defective or damaged.

Factor in a ballpark estimate of 5 percent of returned items. If you're planning to sell 500 units, plan to have 25 returned to you. In our example, if you pay the return shipping fee of $2.41, and 20 percent of the original order fees or 0.20 × ($0.99 + $2.25) = $0.65, you're looking at $2.41 + $0.65 = $3.06 loss per item or a total loss of 25 × $3.06 = $76.50. Divide $76.50 by 500, and you get a loss per item of about 15 cents. You may want to add this to the total cost per unit of $9.72 in the previous section prior to setting your sale price.

Other costs

When setting a price for your products, consider additional costs, including your operating costs (professional fees such as legal and accounting and bank charges) along with any money you plan to spend on marketing and advertising. To ensure that your Amazon selling venture is profitable, be sure to account for all costs. Otherwise, you may barely break even or perhaps lose money.

REMEMBER

As a retailer, you also need to collect sales tax on all sales and remit the collected taxes to the states in which your items are purchased. Sales tax isn't a cost to you; the buyer pays it.

Following Amazon's Rules

Amazon's success hinges on customer satisfaction and maintaining a positive reputation in the retail space. The company allows other sellers access to its marketplace on condition that they behave themselves and share the company's commitment to delivering superior customer service. In this section, we cover the rules that govern your participation in the Amazon marketplace.

REMEMBER

Amazon's changes its code of conduct and seller policies from time to time. For the most current information, click the Search icon (top right of Seller Central), type amazon code of conduct, press Enter, and click the Selling Policies and Seller Code of Conduct link.

Seller code of conduct

Amazon's seller code of conduct stipulates that sellers act fairly and honestly on Amazon to ensure a safe buying and selling experience. All sellers must comply with the following do's and don'ts:

- » Do provide accurate information to Amazon and your customers at all times.

- » Do act fairly and don't misuse Amazon's features or services.

- » Don't attempt to damage or abuse another Seller, their listings, or ratings.

- » Don't attempt to influence customers' ratings, feedback, and reviews.

- » Don't send unsolicited or inappropriate communications.

- » Don't contact customers except through Buyer-Seller Messaging.

- » Don't attempt to circumvent the Amazon sales process.

- » Don't operate more than one Selling on Amazon account without permission by Amazon.

Violating the Amazon's code of conduct or other seller policies may result in penalties such as having product listings removed, payments suspended or forfeited, or selling privileges revoked.

The following sections expand upon specific stipulations in the code of conduct.

Accurate information

As a seller, you're responsible for providing accurate, up-to-date information about your business and the products you sell. For example, you must list products in the correct category and post accurate photos and specifications. See Chapter 9 for more about creating product listings.

Acting fairly

Acting fairly means no cheating, such as:

- » Recruiting your friends to post positive reviews on your listings or negative reviews on your competitors' listings.

- » Hacking or hiring someone else to hack into Amazon to remove negative reviews.

- » Hijacking a listing from the original owner to use as your own.

- » Filing a brand or intellectual property infringement notice against a competitor to have competing listings removed.

Ratings, feedback, and reviews

Amazon prohibits any attempts to influence or inflate customer ratings, feedback, or reviews. You're permitted to contact customers to request feedback and reviews, but you're not allowed to request or coach a positive review. Examples of other prohibited behaviors in this area include the following:

>> Paying for or offering an incentive (such as a coupon or free product) in exchange for removing a negative review or posting a positive review

>> Requesting only positive reviews or asking a customer to remove or change a negative review

>> Reviewing your own or a competitor's products

Communications

Amazon requires that all communications to customers must be sent through Buyer-Seller Messaging and be necessary for fulfilling orders or serving customers. Don't contact customers with marketing or advertising content or send any unsolicited or inappropriate messages.

Customer information

Customer information such as names, addresses, and phone numbers is to be used only to fulfill orders and provide customer service. After processing a customer's order, delete the customer's information. Don't sell or share customer information with any third party.

REMEMBER

Customer information is the customer's property. If anyone approaches you to purchase your customer information, refuse to share that information.

Circumventing the sales process

Understandably, Amazon wants all sales to go through its marketplace, so it can collect fees and retain its customers. Any attempt to divert a sale to another website to avoid paying fees or to steal customers from Amazon is a violation of Amazon policies. Don't provide links or messages that prompt shoppers to visit any external website, order a product from a different store, or complete a transaction elsewhere.

Multiple Amazon Seller accounts

Amazon allows you to have only one seller account for each region in which you sell unless you have a legitimate business need to open a second account and all your accounts are in good standing. If any of your accounts aren't in good standing, Amazon may deactivate all your selling accounts until all accounts are in good standing. Here are a few examples of legitimate business needs that qualify you to open more than one seller account in a given region:

>> You own multiple brands, each of which is associated with a different business.

>> You manufacture products for two separate and distinct companies.

>> Amazon recruits you to participate in a program that requires separate accounts.

TIP

Use a different bank account and email address for each seller account in a given region. If you're selling across regions (for example, in North America and Europe), you may use the same bank account for the two seller accounts as long as your accounts are linked through Amazon Global Selling (see Chapter 19 for more info on selling globally).

Multiple Amazon Seller accounts

Chapter **2**

Selling on Amazon in a Nutshell

With any complex undertaking, you're often wise to take a bird's-eye-view of the entire process first. A general understanding of the entire process serves as a framework on which you can hang the more intricate details as you engage in specific tasks.

In this chapter, we provide the framework for understanding how to sell on Amazon by covering the entire process from start to finish. Here you discover how to identify products with high saleability and profit potential, find a low-cost source for those products, list them for sale on Amazon, and pack and ship them to customers. After presenting the overall selling-on-Amazon-process, we discuss two more important topics — advertising and customer service. In subsequent chapters, we take a deeper dive into these and other aspects of selling on Amazon.

First Things First: Finding Products to Sell

Selling on Amazon assumes you have something to sell. That's a foolish assumption, an assumption we didn't make when writing this book. To the contrary, we assume you *don't* have products to sell and that you're looking for some guidance on how to choose products with great sales and profit potential.

Choosing great products to sell is a key first step to becoming a successful Amazon Seller. If you acquire low-demand products or products with hair-thin profit margins, you risk getting stuck with costly inventory you can't sell or are forced to sell for a very disappointing profit or even a loss. On the other hand, high-demand products with generous profit margins make your job a whole lot easier and more rewarding.

Finding products to sell is a two-step process — deciding what to sell and finding suppliers that have the product and will sell it to you at the price you need to make profitable sales.

Deciding what to sell and not sell

We can't tell you what to sell and not sell on Amazon. That would be like trying to hit a moving target. What we can do is provide the guidance you need to find potentially profitable products on your own. First, you need to know what Amazon will and won't let you sell in its marketplace. Next, you need to know how to gauge demand for a product and estimate its profit margin.

REMEMBER

Here we cover the basics. Turn to Part 2 of this book for more detailed instruction and advice.

Brushing up on Amazon product limitations

Assuming you shop on Amazon (a foolish assumption we did make), you're aware that Amazon groups products into categories and subcategories, such as books, clothing, electronics, movies and TV, office products, and pet supplies. As a seller, you need to know that some of these categories are open, some are off-limits, and some are restricted:

>> **Open categories:** Amazon features product categories in which you can list items for sale with no prior approval, including clothing, shoes, and jewelry; electronics; home and kitchen; patio, lawn, and garden; sports and outdoors; and toys and games. However, even in some open categories, you may encounter restrictions, such as the following:

- **Restricted (gated) subcategories:** You need to obtain permission from Amazon before you can list products in certain subcategories.

- **Restricted brands:** You may be prohibited by the brand owner from listing its products.

- **Restricted products:** Certain products may be prohibited, usually due to health or safety concerns.

>> **Categories requiring approval:** To ensure product quality, safety, and authenticity for its customers, Amazon allows only reputable sellers to list products in certain categories, such as automotive, collectible coins, fine art, music, movies, and watches.

>> **Restricted products:** Amazon prohibits the listing of certain products deemed unsafe, unhealthy, illegal, or unacceptable for whatever reason, including products available only by prescription.

WARNING

Don't list any restricted products or products you think may be considered harmful or illegal. You're responsible for making responsible choices regarding which products to list, and the penalties for violating Amazon's policies are stiff; violations may result in account suspension, termination of selling privileges, destruction of inventory (held at Amazon distribution centers), and permanent withholding of payments.

Amazon does provide some guidance on which products you're permitted to sell. When you try to list a product, for example, you're prompted to select a category; restricted categories are displayed with a lock icon.

REMEMBER

Turn to Chapter 5 for additional details about what you're permitted and prohibited from selling on Amazon.

Conducting product research

Product research is an important step to ensure the salability and profitability of a product. You generally want products that meet the following criteria:

>> **High demand:** To spot the best sellers in each product category on Amazon, visit Amazon.com, and in the toolbar near the top of the page, click Best Sellers. Use the navigation bar on the left to choose the product category you're interested in.

>> **Weak competition:** Skim through the reviews for a product you're thinking of selling. If you see a lot of low product ratings and negative reviews, you may be able to beat the competition by creating a more accurate product listing, providing better customer support, or selling a similar but superior product.

>> **Decent profit margin:** Generally, look for products that sell for more than $25 and you can buy for 60 to 70 percent less than the sales price, which will give you a decent profit margin after subtracting your costs.

The Amazon Seller Mobile App is a great tool for conducting product research. For most products listed for sale on Amazon, you can see whether you're eligible to sell the product and the lowest price it's listed at, its sales rank, and your estimated profit after subtracting your costs, including Amazon selling fees, shipping fees, and the product's net seller proceeds (see Figure 2-1). (See Chapter 16 for more about the Amazon Seller Mobile App.)

>> **Light and easy to pack and ship:** Shipping and handling costs and complexity can leach the profit out of your product sales, so generally avoid products that are more than two pounds, fragile, or bulky. This will also save you money if you need to pay for storage.

>> **Not seasonal:** Look mostly for products that have steady sales throughout the year. Seasonal products, such as those that sell well only in the spring or summer or only near certain holidays are okay, but don't rely on them for a majority of your sales.

See Chapter 6 for additional guidance on researching products.

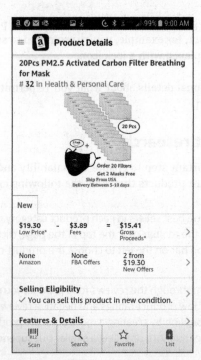

FIGURE 2-1:
Amazon Mobile
Seller App is a
great tool for
conducting
product research.

Exploring product sourcing options

Product sourcing is the process of finding items for a low enough price that you can sell for an acceptable profit. Numerous product sourcing options are available, including the following:

>> **Retail arbitrage:** You buy deeply discounted products, typically from large brick-and-mortar retailers, mark up the price, and list them for sale on Amazon. Retail arbitrage also applies to buying from online retailers, such as eBay sellers.

WARNING

Keep in mind that Amazon restricts some product categories and specific items, including many branded products. For example, you may not be permitted to purchase a pallet of brand name shoes from a major retailer at discount and list them for sale as "new" on Amazon.

>> **Auctions and liquidation sales:** Local and online auctions (and estate sales) allow you to bid on items and often buy them for significantly less than they would be sold for in traditional retail stores, although you may be required to list these items as "used."

>> **Drop-shipping:** With drop-shipping, you select items from a drop-shipper's catalog and list them on Amazon. When a customer orders the item, you pass the order to the drop-shipper who picks, packs, and ships the item to the customer according to your specifications, so it looks as though it came from you.

>> **Wholesalers:** Traditional processing involves purchasing a large quantity of products from a manufacturer, then selling them individually at a significant markup to consumers. You can find plenty of domestic and foreign suppliers that offer products at wholesale prices.

TIP

Product sourcing platforms such as Alibaba.com provide easy access to tens of thousands of manufacturers and other wholesalers. You can also connect with suppliers at popular tradeshows.

>> **Handmade products:** You can make your own products to sell on Amazon and list them for sale in the Handmade category. However, you must register with Amazon as an artisan, and your products must be hand-crafted, not mass-produced. (You can use hand tools and light machinery.)

REMEMBER

See Chapter 7 for additional information and guidance about these product sourcing options. In Chapter 8, we provide guidance on how to evaluate and negotiate with suppliers.

Listing Products for Sale on Amazon

When you have products to sell on Amazon, you can list them for sale. Amazon features several methods for listing products:

>> **List a product already for sale on Amazon.** This is the easiest way to list products one at a time. You simply search for the product by name, universal product code (UPC), Amazon Standard Identification Number (ASIN), or some other unique identifier, select the product, supply the requested details, including the price you're asking, and press the Sell This Product button.

>> **Add a product not listed on Amazon.** This method requires that you choose a product category most suitable for the product and create a product listing, complete with a product title and description, keywords (to help shoppers find the product), and product photos.

>> **Upload a file to list multiple products at once.** If you have a Professional Seller account, you can download and fill out a spreadsheet template with all the details required to list dozens or even hundreds of products at once. You then upload the file to Amazon.

Whichever method you choose, the first steps are always the same:

1. **Log in to your Amazon Seller account at** `sellercentral.amazon.com`.

2. **Open the Catalog menu and select Add Products.**

   Amazon presents a screen that enables you to search for products in Amazon's catalog, add a product not sold on Amazon, or upload a file to add multiple products (see Figure 2-2).

3. **Follow the on-screen directives to complete the process.**

   The steps vary depending on the method you chose to list products in Step 2.

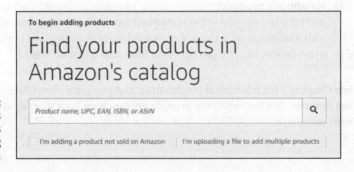

FIGURE 2-2:
Amazon offers
three methods
for listing
products.

See Chapter 9 for detailed guidance on how to list products for sale on Amazon along with tips on how to create product listings that boost your sales and profits.

Prepping and Shipping Products to Customers

As orders for your products pour in, you need to fulfill those orders. Order fulfillment involves picking, packing, and shipping. You pick all the items the customer ordered from you, pack them in a box or envelope, label the package, and drop it off at or have it picked up by a carrier, such as the U.S. postal service, UPS, or FedEx. And if that sounds too much like work, you can ship your products (or have your supplier ship them) to Amazon fulfillment centers, and let Amazon pick, pack, and ship your products for you.

In this section, we explain Amazon Prime, from a seller's perspective, and introduce your order fulfillment options. In Chapter 10, we cover these options in greater detail.

Introducing Amazon Prime

If you do much shopping on Amazon, you're probably familiar with Amazon Prime. For about $120 per year, Amazon Prime members (shoppers) get a bundle of benefits, including free two-day shipping, free same-day delivery in eligible zip codes, free Prime Video, exclusive savings in select stores and on certain products, and much more.

As an Amazon Seller, you can gain from Amazon Prime even if you're not a paying member. Any products you list that are eligible for Prime two-day shipping benefit in the following ways:

>> Your product listing earns the Prime badge, which gives shoppers more incentive to purchase the product from you instead of from a competing seller whose product isn't eligible for Prime.

>> Amazon rewards your product with a higher ranking in its search results and a better chance of winning the *buy box* — the box on the right side of a product's page where customers can add the product to their cart. Buy box placement accounts for more than 80 percent of all Amazon sales, so winning the buy box is a huge deal.

Your products aren't automatically eligible for Prime two-day shipping. For your products to be eligible for Prime, you must do one of the following:

>> Have your products enrolled in Fulfillment by Amazon (FBA) and maintain a sufficient number of items in inventory to meet shopper demand. (See the next section for more about FBA.)

>> Qualify for Seller Fulfilled Prime. (See the later section "Seller Fulfilled Prime.")

REMEMBER

You can choose to ship some orders yourself and have others shipped through FBA. Those shipped through FBA are eligible for Prime, and those you ship yourself won't be, unless you qualify for Seller Fulfilled Prime.

Fulfillment by Amazon (FBA) and Small and Light (SNL)

Fulfillment by Amazon and Small and Light are two order fulfillment options that enable third-party vendors like you to leverage the efficiency of Amazon fulfillment centers to their advantage. With both programs, you ship (or arrange with your supplier to ship) products to Amazon fulfillment centers ready to be scanned into Amazon's inventory system and be shipped to customers. When a customer places an order that includes one or more of your products, Amazon picks the product from the fulfillment center nearest the customer, packs it (by itself or with other products), and ships it to the customer.

FBA offers the following advantages:

>> Products enrolled in FBA instantly gain Amazon Prime status, assuming enough items are in stock to meet shopper demand.

>> Products enrolled in FBA have a better chance of winning the buy box.

>> Amazon does the picking, packing, and shipping, saving you the time and effort.

>> Amazon handles most after-sales customer service issues, including product support, returns, and refunds.

>> Total cost for FBA may be less than the cost of doing it yourself when you account for factors such as Amazon's ability to negotiate lower shipping costs with carriers.

Of course, Amazon charges sellers to cover the costs of storage, fulfillment, and customer support. Fees generally differ based on product weight and size, with different rates for clothing. However, FBA may cost less than if you were to pack and ship products yourself. By using FBA, you benefit to some degree from Amazon's ability to negotiate lower shipping fees with carriers, and you're not having to purchase packing supplies. In addition, using FBA saves you valuable time you can allocate to product research, creating excellent product listings, and performing other tasks to improve sales and grow your business.

Meanwhile, the Small and Light program is designed to lower your costs for packing and shipping products priced $7 or less, weighing 10 ounces or less, and 16-by-9-by-4 inches or smaller. Certain types of products aren't eligible, including restricted, adult, and hazmat products. For sellers, the Small and Light program offers the following benefits:

>> Free three- to five-day shipping to Prime customers

>> Lower fulfillment costs

>> Instant customer trust through Amazon's A-to-Z Guarantee program

Fulfillment by Merchant (FBM)

Unlike FBA, with Fulfillment by Merchant (FBM), you're doing all the heavy lifting — storing, picking, packing, and shipping products yourself. FBM offers a few advantages over FBA, including the following:

>> Ability to pack items yourself, which may be best for large, bulky products or fragile items

>> Greater control over inventory

>> Potentially lower costs

>> Ability to deliver more personalized customer service

The major drawbacks of FBM, as compared to FBA, are that you lose out on the many benefits of FBA described in the previous section.

TIP

When you're getting started with Amazon, packing and shipping a small number of products yourself may be the best approach. That way, you can take your time learning the basics of selling on Amazon without the added complexity of FBA and without the risk of buying large quantities of products. As your business grows and you become more comfortable and confident selling on Amazon, you can transition to FBA.

Seller Fulfilled Prime

Seller Fulfilled Prime (SFP) allows you to combine the benefits of FBA and FBM. With SFP, you ship products from your own warehouses directly to domestic Prime customers. (Amazon gives you access to the right transportation solutions to deliver products within the Prime two-day delivery window.) By committing to fill orders within two days at no additional charge for Prime customers, you ensure that your listings can display the Prime badge and have a better chance of winning the buy box.

As an Amazon Seller, you're not automatically eligible for SFP. You must register for the program and then successfully complete a trial period to prove that you're able to deliver products to Prime customers within the two-day delivery window. Assuming you're accepted into the program, you're required to buy shipping labels from an approved carrier, and you must pick, pack, and ship orders the same day you receive them.

REMEMBER

During the writing of this book, Amazon wasn't accepting new registrations for the SFP program, but interested sellers can add their names to a waitlist.

Drop-shipping

As we explain in the earlier section "Exploring product sourcing options," drop-shipping is a product-sourcing and order-fulfillment option that takes most of the heavy lifting off your plate. You list products on Amazon and pass any orders you receive to the drop-shipper who picks, packs, and ships the order to your customer. You never touch the product.

The benefits of drop-shipping are clear, but this option has several potential drawbacks, including the following:

>> You pay a premium for the convenience of having the drop-shipper do all the work.

>> You have no control over inventory. If the drop-shipper runs out of stock, so do you.

>> You can't promise two-day shipping, so your products won't be eligible for Prime.

>> Handling refunds and returns becomes more complicated with a third party involved.

>> Customer satisfaction relies heavily on the performance of your drop-shipper, which you can't control.

Multi-Channel Fulfillment

Amazon's Multi-Channel Fulfillment (MCF) enables you to leverage Amazon's worldwide fulfillment network to ship products to customers regardless of where they buy them online. For example, you can list products for sale on your own website, on an ecommerce platform such as Spotify, and on Amazon, and whenever (and from wherever) a customer places an order, Amazon picks, packs, and ships the product for you and handles customer support, refunds, returns, and so on.

MCF is very similar to FBA (but you don't need to be enrolled in FBA to take advantages of MCF). You ship (or arrange with your suppliers to ship) products to Amazon fulfillment centers, and Amazon picks, packs, and ships products for you. With MCF, you can provide the same speedy delivery to all your customers, wherever they choose to shop, and you manage all your inventory through Amazon. MCF provides an easy way to scale your business without increasing your fixed costs.

For details about MCF, click in the Search bar, near the top of Amazon Seller Central, type **multichannel**, press Enter, and click the link for finding out more about filling orders from other sales channels.

Boosting Sales with Advertising and Promotions

Amazon is an extremely competitive marketplace, where Amazon, brands, and retailers are all vying for customer attention and sales. Whether you're new to the marketplace or are a veteran trying to maximize your sales and profit margins, Amazon provides several tools for increasing your profile, getting your products in front of shoppers, and converting clicks into sales, including the following:

>> **Sponsored Products:** Sponsored Products are paid advertisements for individual product listings. Ads for your sponsored products appear on shoppers' search results pages and on product detail pages when shoppers search for keywords or products relevant to the ad. To control costs, you specify your budget and how much money to bid per click. You pay only when a shopper clicks your sponsored ad.

>> **Sponsored Brands:** Sponsored Brands are paid advertisements available only to sellers enrolled in Amazon Brand Registry. Like Sponsored Products, Sponsored Brands appear on shoppers' search results pages and on product

detail pages when shoppers search for keywords or products relevant to the ad. These ads feature a custom headline, brand logo, and collection of the brand's products.

>> **Sponsored Displays:** These ads run both on and off Amazon. You specify your audience, daily budget, and bid amount; choose the products to include in your ad, and create your ad campaign. These ads include a product image, pricing, badging, star rating, and Shop Now button that links to your product's detail page on Amazon.

>> **Amazon Store:** You can create your own multipage store on Amazon for free to expand your profile and promote customer loyalty. As you prove yourself a reputable seller on Amazon, shoppers may be more likely to visit your store and buy from you when they're in the market for the products you carry.

>> **Early Reviewer Program:** Product reviews can help boost your product search ranking and improve your chances of winning the buy box. This program allows you to offer customers who buy your products a $3 gift card for posting a review. You pay only when a customer posts a review. Amazon offers your reward to customers for up to a year or until your product has received five reviews.

>> **Prime Exclusive Discounts:** You can offer discount pricing on specific products to Amazon Prime members. Your discount will appear in the member's search results and on the product detail page with the original price struck out along with the discount price.

Your marketing and advertising campaigns need not be limited to Amazon. Consider ways you can promote sales off Amazon, such as the following:

>> Social media marketing via your accounts on Facebook, Instagram, YouTube, Pinterest, and so on

>> Blogging about a topic you know a great deal about that's related to the products you sell

>> Creating a website landing page for a product or collection of products and using it to drive traffic to your Amazon store where people can purchase related products

>> Launching an email marketing campaign to advertise directly to people on your mailing list

REMEMBER

See Chapters 11 and 12 for more about boosting sales with advertising and promotions.

Providing Stellar Customer Service

To be successful in the long term on Amazon, focus less on sales and profits and more on satisfying your customers. We're not advising that you sacrifice your own financial success to make Amazon shoppers happy. What we are advising is that you deliver sufficient value to create a shopping experience that makes people happy to pay what you're charging. Delivering quality customer service drives sales, enables you to increase your profit margins, and keeps you in Amazon's good graces.

To deliver quality customer service, you need to focus on several areas, including product quality, product listings, order fulfillment, communications, and returns and refunds. Here are a few tips for delivering quality customer service:

>> Give customers more than they expect in terms of product quality and customer service. If you're selling a low-end product to customers who aren't willing or able to pay for the high-end version, then don't present your low-end product as a high-end one.

>> Create product listings with the goal of helping the customer make a well-informed purchase decision, not with the goal of selling the customer on a product.

>> Respond to all customer questions, concerns, and complaints within 24 hours and preferably much sooner.

>> Always be courteous and respectful when communicating with customers, regardless of what they say or how they behave.

>> Do your absolute best to resolve issues directly with customers to avoid having the customer try to resolve the issue through Amazon or her credit card company. Having the customer file an A-to-Z Guarantee claim against you or contact her credit card company to request a chargeback isn't in your best interest.

>> Follow up on all customer product and seller feedback, whether it's positive or negative. Thank customers for positive product ratings and reviews and positive seller feedback. If you receive negative reviews or ratings, contact the customer to see what you can do to turn a negative shopping experience into a positive one.

REMEMBER

See Chapter 13 for additional guidance on providing superior customer service.

IN THIS CHAPTER

» Opening a new Amazon Seller Account

» Adding your business profile to your account

» Double-checking your account settings

» Tweaking your shipping and return settings

» Increasing security for your seller account

Chapter **3**

Setting Up Your Amazon Seller Account

B efore you can start selling on Amazon, you need to open an Amazon Seller account, create a business profile, and check and adjust a number of settings to reflect your preferences. In this chapter, we walk you through the registration process and provide guidance on how to configure your seller account to reflect the way you plan to do business on Amazon.

Registering to Become an Amazon Seller

An Amazon Seller account is your gateway to the Amazon marketplace. Although you can log in to Amazon Seller Central with the same username and password you use for shopping on Amazon, these two accounts are entirely separate.

To open an Amazon Seller account, first make sure you have all the information available that you'll be prompted to enter:

>> Your legal business name

>> The email address you want to use to receive notifications and other communications from Amazon

>> Your home or business address

>> Your home or business phone number

>> Credit card information (so Amazon can collect its fees)

>> Bank account routing number and account number (so Amazon can remit payments to you)

>> Tax identification number — Social Security number (SSN) or Employer Identification Number (EIN) (see the nearby sidebar)

>> A valid passport or driver's license (you'll need to provide the ID number *and* submit a scan or digital photo of the document)

>> A scan or digital photo of an additional document for identification, such as a bank or credit card statement with your name and address on it

To start the registration process, take one of the following steps:

>> Go to sell.amazon.com and click Start Selling.

>> Go to sellercentral.amazon.com and Register Now (near the top of the page).

>> Go to www.amazon.com, scroll down to the Make Money with Us section, and click Sell on Amazon.

Regardless of where you start, you're directed to the same signup page. Follow the on-screen prompts to enter the information requested and upload the documentation required. After you provide all the information and documentation required, you will receive a confirmation email message indicating that your account is active.

To be sure your account is active, go to sellercentral.amazon.com, hover over Settings (in the upper-right corner of the page), and choose Account Info. If you see a message near the top of the page stating, "You currently have limited access to Amazon selling services," scroll down the page and hover over any red text to find out the nature of the issue and access instructions on how to resolve it. Follow the on-screen instructions to resolve any issues.

EIN OR SSN?

Obtaining and using an EIN instead of an SSN is always a good idea to prevent identity theft, but you really don't need an EIN unless you plan to do one of the following:

- Hire employees

- Offer a Keogh or Solo 401(k) retirement plan

- Buy or inherit an existing business that you operate as a sole proprietorship

- Incorporate or form a partnership or limited liability company (LLC)

Applying for an EIN is easy. Just visit www.irs.gov/businesses/small-businesses-self-employed/apply-for-an-employer-identification-number-ein-online and follow the instructions.

TIP

If you intended to sign up for an Individual plan and were signed up for a Professional plan by mistake, downgrade to the Individual Plan and email a refund request to Amazon Seller support. To downgrade your plan, take the following steps:

1. Hover over Settings (upper-right corner of the Amazon Seller page) and choose Account Info.

2. Scroll down to the section Your Services (lower left) and choose Manage.

3. Next to Sell on Amazon if you see "Professional," choose Downgrade.

4. Follow the on-screen instructions to downgrade to the Individual plan.

After you downgrade your plan, you may continue to see (for up to 120 days) that you're signed up for the Professional plan, but as long as you receive an email notification from Amazon indicating that your Professional plan has been cancelled, you won't be enrolled in or charged for that plan.

Next, you must contact Amazon to request a refund for the $39.99 you were charged initially for being enrolled into the Professional plan:

1. Select Help.

2. Scroll down to Need More Help? at the bottom of the page and select Get Support.

3. Select Selling on Amazon to see additional options.

4. Choose Your Account and then Other Account Issues.

5. **In the Describe Your Issue box, type an explanation of what happened, followed by your request for a refund.**

6. **Press Continue and follow the on-screen instructions to complete your communication.**

   Someone from Amazon's support staff will follow up with you, via email or phone, to resolve the issue and process your refund.

Completing Your Amazon Seller Business Profile

To become fully integrated into the Amazon marketplace and be able to run your ecommerce business without any hiccups, you must provide Amazon certain details and documentation about your business, including any relevant government filings.

To access Business Information links, which you can use to supply the necessary information and documentation, log on to Seller Central, hover over Settings (upper right of the opening Seller Central page), and choose Account Info. The Seller Account Information page appears, which includes a Business Information section. Use the links in this section to pull up pages for checking/editing the items explained in the following sections.

Business Address

When you choose Business Address, the Business Address page appears, displaying any business address and phone number you entered when opening your Amazon Seller account. This address may be the same as your home address, if you're running the business out of your home, or it may be a different address, if you run your business from a different location. Most importantly, this is the address to which all returned items will be sent (except Fulfilled by Amazon items, which will be returned to an Amazon fulfillment center).

REMEMBER

You can enter a different return address in your return settings, as we explain in the later section "Entering Shipping and Return Settings." The address you enter in your return settings will override your business address as the default return address. You can override the return address when you authorize individual returns.

The Business Address page provides two options for changing your business address:

>> **Select an Address:** Choose this option to select from a list of addresses Amazon already has on record for you. (Amazon may have numerous shipping addresses from the account you use to shop on Amazon.)

>> **Add a New Address:** Choose this option to display a form that enables you to enter a new location, fill out the form, and click Submit.

WARNING

Though, technically, you can have different entries for business address, official registered address, and legal address, using the same address across Amazon can lead to faster approvals. Having different addresses or changing addresses frequently may attract additional scrutiny from the Amazon team.

Official Registered Address

Your official registered address is the address used to legally register your business with government agencies, such as your state's Secretary of State office, business bureau, or business agency.

To check or change your official registered address, choose Official Registered Address and then choose one of the addresses in the list or click Add New Address and enter the address you want to use. Click Save to submit the change.

Language for Feed Processing Report

By default, error codes in any downloaded reports from Amazon are in U.S. English, but you may have the option to switch to a different language that matches one of the marketplaces in which you're selling.

To check out your options, choose Language for Feed Processing Reports. If you're greeted with the message "Forbidden. You do not have the rights to perform this action." then Amazon will assign the most suitable language for you. If you see other languages, choose the language you want Amazon to use for downloaded reports and press Save.

Legal Entity

The legal entity you choose for your business determines how your business is taxed. You may have entered some or all the required information when you first opened your account or you may need to do so after opening your account.

To check your legal entity or change it, choose Legal Entity. The Legal Entity page appears, indicating whether your tax information is complete and providing a way to enter any missing information or update your tax information. If your tax information is complete, you're good to go. To check or change existing tax information, press Update Tax Information and proceed through the Tax Information Interview. To complete the interview, you'll need the following information:

>> **Tax classification:** Individual (for example, sole proprietorship) or business (for example, C-corporation)

>> **Citizenship:** Whether you're considered a U.S. citizen or a citizen of another country for tax purposes

>> **Tax identification:**

- Your name as shown on your income tax return and (optionally) your business or trade name

- The address used on your income tax return

- Your Social Security Number or Taxpayer Identification Number

Merchant Token

Your merchant token is a unique number assigned to each third-party seller that enables Amazon to identify each of its sellers. It allows you to access Amazon's Marketplace Web Service to use a variety of third-party software and applications designed to simplify and enhance your work as an Amazon Seller.

You can't change your merchant token, but you can view it. On the Seller Account Information page, in the Business Information section, select Merchant Token. The Merchant Token page appears, displaying your merchant token.

WARNING

Every seller's merchant token is unique. Don't try to share yours with other sellers or use a token from one seller account on another.

Display Name

Your display name is what customers see when they view one of your product listings or an order that includes one of your products. On the Seller Account Information page, in the Business Information section, select Display Name to change your display name, storefront link (if applicable), email address, and phone number for the various marketplaces you serve (for example, the United States, Canada, and Mexico). The Seller Information page appears where you can choose to edit the details for each marketplace.

Checking and Adjusting Your Account Settings

Soon after signing up to become an Amazon Seller and every so often thereafter, you should check your account settings to be sure all your information is accurate and up to date and the actual settings reflect your preferences.

To access your account settings, hover over Settings (in the upper–right corner of Seller Central), and click the desired option:

>> **Account Info:** Displays the Seller Account Information page, which includes the following information and settings:

- Your seller profile, which you can choose to edit

- Your listings status (countries where you can sell products)

- Your services (whether you're signed up for a Professional or Individual plan and whether you're registered for Fulfillment by Amazon [FBA])

- Payment information, including deposit methods and invoiced order payment settings

- Business information, including your business address and display name

- Shipping and returns information, including your shipping and return address and default shipping methods

- Tax information, which is information used to determine your tax liabilities and ensure your information is reported properly to the taxing authorities

>> **Notification Preferences:** Enables you to specify how you would like to receive a variety of notifications and reports — via text (short message service [SMS]) or email.

>> **Login Settings:** Enables you to edit your login information, including your name, email, and password, and enable or disable two-step verification. (With *two-step verification*, you log in and receive a code via text message on your cellphone that you must enter to complete your login.)

REMEMBER

We strongly recommend that you enable two-step verification to secure your account. (See the later section "Securing Your Amazon Seller Account" for details.)

>> **Return settings:** Here you can change the marketplace-specific return settings such mailing labels, return instructions, returnless refund, and return address settings. See the next section, "Entering Shipping and Return Settings," for details.

- » **Gift options:** Choose this option to modify gift messaging and wrapping preferences.

- » **Shipping Settings:** Displays your default shipping address and default shipping preferences for standard, expedited, two-day, one-day, international, and international-expedited shipping. See the next section for details.

- » **User Permissions:** If you're registered as a Professional Seller, you can use this option to add or remove users from your account.

- » **Your Info and Policies:** This option enables you to add custom content and policies about your business to pages such as About Seller, Shipping, Privacy Policy, Frequently Asked Questions, and so on. You can also upload an image to use as your seller logo.

- » **Fulfillment by Amazon (FBA):** This page provides a long list of options to customize FBA, such as specifying who preps and labels the package for shipping, where your inventory is stored, whether unsellable customer returns are to be refurbished, and many more. See Chapter 10 for more about FBA.

Entering Shipping and Return Settings

Before you start listing products for sale on Amazon, be sure to check your shipping and return settings to ensure they match what you want to offer to your customers, as we explain in the following sections.

Shipping settings

Your shipping settings establish the default shipping service levels for orders you ship to buyers (Fulfillment by Merchant, not Fulfillment by Amazon). Amazon requires standard shipping for all sellers but allows you to offer other shipping level options such as expedited and two-day.

To check and (optionally) change your shipping levels from Seller Central, go to Settings, Shipping Settings. The Shipping Settings page appears, as Figure 3-1 shows.

Check the default shipping address at the top. If you'll be shipping from a different location, press the Edit button, enter the location's name and address, and press Save.

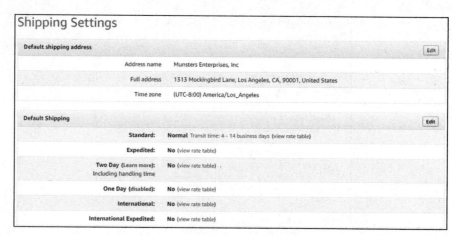

Shipping Settings

Default shipping address			Edit
	Address name	Munsters Enterprises, Inc	
	Full address	1313 Mockingbird Lane, Los Angeles, CA, 90001, United States	
	Time zone	(UTC-8:00) America/Los_Angeles	

Default Shipping		Edit
Standard:	**Normal** Transit time: 4 - 14 business days (view rate table)	
Expedited:	**No** (view rate table)	
Two Day (Learn more): Including handling time	**No** (view rate table) .	
One Day (disabled):	**No** (view rate table)	
International:	**No** (view rate table)	
International Expedited:	**No** (view rate table)	

FIGURE 3-1:
The Shipping
Settings page.

Under Default Shipping are the available shipping service levels. Initially, the only level you're set up to offer to shoppers is Standard. Next to this option is "Normal," indicating a standard transit time of 4 to 14 days. All the other service levels have "No" next to them, indicating that you don't offer these shipping service levels.

To the right of each shipping service level is "view rate table," which you can select to find out how much Amazon charges buyers for various items at that particular shipping service level and how much will be credited to your account.

REMEMBER

Note that your shipping cost may be more or less than what Amazon charges the buyer and credits to your account, so you may gain or lose on shipping.

To offer additional shipping service levels or change the transit time for different levels, press the Edit button, enter your preferences, and press the Submit button.

TIP

You can override your default shipping settings for individual products by entering your shipping preferences when you list products for sale. See Chapter 9 for guidance on how to create product listings.

Return settings

Your return settings enable you to specify, for each market (country), where you want buyers to send product returns, the conditions under which you want to allow return-less refunds, whether you want to receive return request emails, how requests are authorized, and how Return Merchandise Authorization (RMA) numbers are generated. To access your return settings from Seller Central, go to Settings, Return Settings. The Returns Settings page appears, as Figure 3-2 shows.

Check the settings on all three tabs of the Returns Settings page to be sure they reflect your preferences:

>> **General Settings:** On this tab, you have three options:

- **Email Format:** You can choose to receive return request email messages from buyers with links to Authorize, Close, or Reply to the request.

- **Default Automated Return Rules:** You may want to authorize each request when you're getting started to stay on the safe side. Later, to save yourself valuable time, consider selecting I Want Amazon to Automatically Authorize All Requests That Meet Amazon Policy. The third option, to have Amazon automatically authorize all requests is risky; you could end up having Amazon authorize illegitimate return requests — for example, buyers consuming nearly an entire container of supplements and returning it.

- **Return Merchandise Authorization (RMA) Number Settings:** You can have Amazon generate a unique RMA for you or supply it yourself. Unless you have a good reason to use your own RMA numbers to track returns, save time by letting Amazon generate RMA numbers for you.

>> **Returnless Refund:** The Returnless Refund tab contains an Add New Rule button you can click to display a form that enables you to add a rule that sets the conditions for a *returnless refund* (the customer keeps the product and is refunded her money). Enter a name for the rule, a price range, choose one or more product categories the rule applies to, choose one or more return

reasons, and specify a return window (number of days from the estimated order delivery date). Click Save to save the rule. The rule is added to your Returnless Refund tab with buttons next to it to Edit or Delete it.

>> **Return Address Settings:** Unless you specify otherwise, items you ship to customers are returned to the business address you entered when you enrolled as an Amazon Seller. You can press the Set the Address button on this tab to enter a return address that overrides the business address.

TIP

To the right of the three tabs is the Return Attribute Overrides button that enables you to download a template you can use to enter return attributes that override the default return settings for specified products. You'll find a button for down-loading the template and instructions in the template for filling it out.

Securing Your Amazon Seller Account

As the world's largest ecommerce marketplace, Amazon draws the attention of bad actors, who target sellers to gain unauthorized access to their accounts. If someone gains access to your account, she may be able to:

>> Lock you out of your own account.

>> Divert deposits from your Amazon account to her bank.

>> Sell fake or counterfeit merchandise under your business name.

>> Gain access to other related accounts, such as a PayPal or email account (if the same or similar credentials are used to log in to other accounts).

>> Obtain valuable insights into your business, such as ad performance and which products are most profitable, to gain competitive advantage.

>> Ruin your reputation among shoppers, which could lead to account suspen-sion or lawsuits.

To protect your Amazon Seller account from unauthorized access, take the follow-ing precautions:

>> **Enable two-step verification.** With two-step verification, every time you try to log in to your seller account, Amazon sends a security code to your mobile phone that you must enter to confirm your identity. Check to make sure two-step verification is enabled. In Seller Central, go to Settings, Login Settings, and next to Two-Step Verification (2SV) Settings, press the Edit button. If two-step verification is disabled, Amazon prompts you enroll. Press the Get Started button and follow the on-screen instructions.

>> **Use a unique username and password for every account.** If you use the same username or password on multiple sites, a breach on one site places other sites at risk.

>> **Use strong passwords.** Make your passwords long and use a random combination of letters, numbers, and special characters. Don't use publicly available information in your passwords, such as your phone number or birthdate.

TIP

Write down your login credentials for every service you use and store them somewhere only you can find them.

>> **Change passwords when necessary.** For example, change your passwords when a service you use discloses a security breach, your account has been broken into, you become aware that spyware has been installed on your computer, or you logged on to a service over an unsecured public network.

>> **Keep the email address and mobile number you use to sign on to your account or verify your identity updated on Amazon.** To check this info from Seller Central, go to Settings, Login Settings.

>> **Set up your notification settings to be notified of important actions taken on your account.** To access your notification settings from Seller Central, go to Settings, Notification Preferences.

>> **If you're a Professional Seller with multiple users on your account, remove users whenever they no longer need access to the account.** For example, if a user on your account leaves your business, remove the user. To set and edit user permissions from Seller Central, go to Settings, User Permissions.

>> **Don't let your web browser store you login credentials.** If your browser stores your login credentials, anyone who has access to the device on which that browser is installed, including someone who steals the device, can log into your accounts.

>> **Be careful using public Wi-Fi.** If you must log in to sensitive sites over public Wi-Fi, do so through a virtual private network (VPN), which provides a secure, encrypted connection between your computer and any site it connects to.

>> **Use a reputable password manager.** With a password manager, such as LastPass, you store all your login credentials in a secure vault that you can access with a single username and password. You can then create long, complex, random passwords that you don't have to remember.

Most common means to break into an account is a *phishing attack*, which typically involves sending the account holder an email message with a link to a site that looks like Amazon but is set up to capture the username and password the seller enters. To avoid succumbing to a phishing attack, take the following precautions:

>> Be suspicious of any email that contains an attachment or a link, especially if the email message is warning you of a serious issue that needs your immediate attention. Fear makes people do stupid things, and phishers know it.

>> Don't click any email attachments or links unless you know and trust the sender.

>> Install reputable Internet security software, such as ESET, that filters out spam and email likely to contain spyware and other malicious software.

>> Hover over a link before clicking it. The link's address will appear in a pop-up or at the bottom of the email message window, showing where the link will really take you, so you can make a well-informed decision of whether to click it.

>> Watch out for website names or links that may appear to be from Amazon but have a slightly different spelling, such as Amason or Amzon.

>> Don't provide login or account information over the phone. Amazon never calls customers to verify information. So, if you receive any such phone calls, be alert and don't disclose the sensitive information being requested.

>> If you receive a suspicious email message or phone call, report it to Amazon via www.amazon.com/gp/help/contact-us/report-phishing.html.

Chapter **4**

Becoming Familiar with Seller Central

E very ecommerce website has a backend available exclusively to sellers for listing products, managing inventory, communicating with buyers, and performing other administrative tasks. Amazon refers to its backend as *Seller Central* — a sophisticated interface that integrates all business functions required to successfully manage any size retail business with relative ease.

Before you start listing products, familiarize yourself with Seller Central, so you know your way around.

Finding Your Way around Seller Central

At first glance, Amazon Seller Central is deceptively simple (see Figure 4-1). Across the top is a header that contains the Amazon Seller Central logo; a notifications flag; the Marketplace Switcher; the search bar; options for accessing messages, help, and settings; and a menu bar for everything else.

Menu bar   Search bar

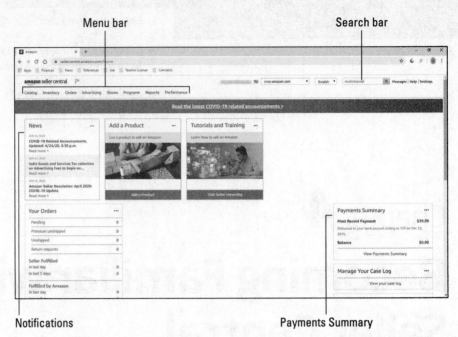

FIGURE 4-1:
Amazon
Seller Central
home page.

Notifications   Payments Summary

In this section, we explain how to use these navigational tools to access **key fea-tures** and functions within Seller Central. Consider this section **Seller Central** orientation day.

Switching marketplaces

In the upper right of the opening Amazon Seller Central screen is a double-headed arrow button (or a drop-down menu). Hover over the button or drop-down menu, and a toolbar tip indicates that it's the Marketplace Switcher. If you sell in more than one market (for example, the United States and Canada), you can use the Marketplace Switcher to check your account information for each marketplace. The flag shown in the Marketplace Switcher indicates the selected Marketplace.

REMEMBER

If you sell on Amazon in one or more marketplaces, be sure to change **market-places** before accessing any of your account information via Seller Central; otherwise, you may be looking at the wrong information.

Navigating the menu bar

Just below the Amazon Seller Central logo (upper left) is the primary menu bar, which serves as the jumping-off point for every seller activity — from **adding** products to your catalog to managing inventory and orders to accessing reports and monitoring your performance.

This section takes you on a nickel tour of these menus, so you know your options.

REMEMBER

Menu options may differ depending on your account type — Individual or Professional. For example, Professional Sellers have more options on their Advertising menu than do Individual sellers.

Catalog

Head to the Catalog menu when you're ready to list products for sale. Hover over Catalog and choose the desired option:

>> **Add Products:** To list a product that's already in Amazon's catalog or create a new listing for a product that's not yet in Amazon's catalog.

>> **Complete Your Drafts:** If you started to list a product and had to stop because you were missing information Amazon requested, your listing is saved as a draft. Select this option to access drafts and complete any product listings that were in progress.

>> **View Selling Applications:** If you need Amazon approval to sell certain products, choose this option to apply for approval and to check the status of your applications.

TIP

Clicking certain menus, such as Catalog and Inventory, instead of an option on the menu starts an on-screen tour of the resulting page, highlighting key features.

Inventory

The Inventory menu provides several options for managing and planning your inventory, adding products, and managing FBA shipping options:

>> **Manage Inventory:** Selecting this option opens the Manage Inventory page, displaying all your Fulfilled by Amazon (FBA) and Fulfilled by Merchant (FBM) product listings. To the right of each listing is an Edit button you can click to access commands to close the listing or delete the product and listing.

>> **Manage FBA Inventory:** If you're using FBA to fulfill orders, you can monitor and manage all products in your FBA inventory here. The Manage FBA Inventory page displays detailed information regarding your available and inbound inventory. You can also choose to replenish inventory when supplies are low.

>> **Inventory Planning:** Choosing this option displays a dashboard that enables you to monitor and plan your inventory. Near the top of the dashboard are three tabs — Inventory Age, Fix Stranded Inventory, and Manage FBA Returns. On the far right is an Inventory Settings link that enables you specify values

for Cost of Purchase, Recovery Rate, and Supplier Lead Time, so Amazon can recommend actions to optimize your inventory performance. (See Chapter 15 for details.)

>> **Add a Product:** This option takes you to the same place as the Add Products option on the Catalog menu, where you can list a product that's already in Amazon's catalog or create a new listing for a product that's not in Amazon's catalog.

>> **Add Products via Upload:** If you're signed up as a Professional Seller, this option appears on your Inventory menu, enabling you to list multiple products at once by downloading, completing, and uploading category-specific templates. (See Chapter 9 for details.) You can also download processing reports to check for any errors in posting product listings in bulk.

>> **Inventory Reports:** Select this option to display a page where you can download a variety of inventory reports, from active listings reports to FBA inventory reports and listing quality reports.

>> **Sell Globally:** This option takes you to a page where you can begin to explore opportunities in selling globally. Here, you can choose to list certain eligible products across the Americas, Europe, Asia-Pacific, Middle East, and North Africa regions where Amazon operates.

>> **Manage FBA Shipments:** This option takes you to the Shipping Queue page, where you can monitor your FBA shipments, manage your shipping plans, and view the Received Inventory Report.

>> **Upload & Manage Videos:** Registered brand owners can use this option to upload and manage all their product videos from one central location.

Pricing

Some sellers have a Pricing menu that simplifies the process of monitoring and changing prices. This menu features four options:

>> **View Pricing Dashboard:** The Pricing Dashboard provides metrics to help inform your pricing decisions. It provides options to view the dashboard, manage pricing, automate pricing, and more.

>> **Manage Pricing:** Choose this option to view current prices for all your products and quickly adjust prices.

>> **Fix Price Alerts:** If you set any price alerts for products, such as potentially high price or low price, you can access and adjust them by selecting this option.

>> **Automatic Pricing:** Automatic pricing enables you to specify rules for adjusting your products' prices automatically to avoid spending excessive time manually adjusting prices in response to ever-changing market conditions.

WARNING

Be very careful with automatic pricing. You could end up selling a large volume of product at a loss if you set the wrong repricing rules.

Orders

Options on the Orders menu enable you to monitor and manage orders, returns, and SAFE-T claims and download order reports:

>> **Manage Orders:** Choose this option to view all pending, unshipped, cancelled, and shipped orders and take relevant actions on those orders, if desired.

>> **Order Reports:** Click this option to access a page where you can download various order reports organized by date.

>> **Upload Order Related Files:** Professional Sellers can make changes such as shipment confirmation, adjustments, or cancellations to orders in bulk by downloading specific templates, filling them out, and uploading them.

>> **Manage Returns:** If any of your customers have returned products, you can find information about those returns by clicking this option. You can also search for returns by Order ID, Return Merchandise Authorization (RMA) number, Tracking ID, or Amazon Standard Identification Number (ASIN).

>> **Manage SAFE-T Claims:** Choose this option to appeal Amazon's decision to issue a refund to a customer. Amazon may reverse the refund decision if it determines you weren't at fault.

Advertising

The Advertising menu provides access to all the tools you need to manage the advertising and promotions options available to you as an Individual or Professional Seller:

>> **Early Reviewer Program:** Choose this option if you want to enroll products in Amazon's Early Reviewer Program. You can get up to five reviews for a new product by offering customers a small reward (a $3 gift card) for posting a review.

>> **Prime Exclusive Discounts:** If you're an FBA Seller, you can use this option to offer discounts to Amazon Prime customers for selected products. The product offer will display the discounted price with the regular price crossed out and a

message about how much the customer will save; for example, "You Save: $10 (10%) as a Prime Member."

>> **Campaign Manager:** Choosing this option displays a page where you can create and manage Amazon pay-per-click advertisements and check each ad's performance. See Chapter 12 for details about advertising on Amazon.

>> **A+ Content Manager:** If you're a brand owner, you can choose this option to access an area where you can create and manage *A+ Content* — robust advertising content that contains product descriptions, rich images, charts, narrative copy, and other content and formatting beyond what's typically available in standard product listings.

>> **Deals:** Choose this option if you want to offer special seasonal deals; for example, Black Friday, Cyber Monday, Labor Day, and so on.

>> **Coupons:** To offer coupons to shoppers, click this option and create your coupon, specifying details, such as which products the coupon applies to, whether the customer receives a dollar or percentage discount, the start and expiration dates, and so on.

>> **Manage Promotions:** Choose this option to create and manage all promotions.

Stores

The Stores menu has only one option — Manage Stores. When you first select this option, you're taken to the Stores page where Amazon enables you to create your own multi-page store on Amazon for free to promote your brands and products.

REMEMBER

Only registered brands are allowed to create and manage their own Amazon store. If you're a brand owner, click the Amazon Brand Registry link and follow the on-screen instructions to register your brand. You can then return to the Stores page to create your store. (See Chapter 14 for more about creating and managing your own store on Amazon.)

Programs

The Programs menu contains a list of Amazon Seller Central programs you can enroll in. Hover over Programs to view your options. Options vary among sellers; for example, most sellers have a choice of fulfillment programs, but only some sellers may qualify for Amazon's Lending program (an invitation-only program designed to help qualified sellers to apply for short term loans to meet the working capital requirements). See Chapter 15 for more about Amazon's Lending program.

You can click Fulfillment Programs to check out what's available, enroll in any available fulfillment programs, and manage any fulfillment programs you're enrolled in.

Reports

The Reports menu contains several options for accessing non–inventory reports:

» **Payments:** The payments report details all payments Amazon has remitted to you.

» **Business Reports:** If you've sold anything, you'll see this option; you can choose to view the Amazon Sales Report dashboard and view and download various business reports based on the criteria you specify, including the start and end dates and the type of data to include in the report. (See the later section "Viewing your payments summary" for details.)

» **Fulfillment:** This option displays a page that provides access to all reports related to Amazon Fulfillment regarding inventory, sales, shipping, and so on.

» **Return Reports:** If your customers have returned any products, choose this option to view seller fulfilled return reports. If you use FBA to fulfill orders, you can click View FBA Reports to access reports about returns processed by FBA.

» **Tax Document Library:** At the end of each quarter (when estimated tax payments are due) and at the end of the year, be sure to visit the Tax Document Library to access tax information related to your Amazon sales. (See Chapter 16 for more about sales tax.)

Performance

When you're wondering how well you're performing as a seller, you need go no further than the Performance menu for answers. Here, you find several options for displaying different performance metrics:

» **Account Health:** Account Health is divided into two sections:

- **Customer Service Performance:** Where you can check your order defect rate, which is a composite of negative feedback, A-to-Z Guarantee claims, and chargeback claims

- **Product Policy Compliance:** Where you can check on any policies you've violated or complaints you've received

» **Feedback:** Choosing this option displays the Feedback Manager, where you can check your percentage of positive, negative, and neutral feedback for different periods — 30 days, 90 days, 365 days, and Lifetime.

» **A-to-Z Guarantee claims:** When you handle both sales and fulfillment, customers can file an *A-to-Z Guarantee claim* against you with Amazon if they feel that you've treated them unfairly, and you can file an appeal. Click this option to check the number of A-to-Z Guarantee claims that have been filed against you (if any) and to check their status.

>> **Chargeback Claims:** A *chargeback* occurs when a buyer contacts her bank or credit card company to dispute a charge. Click this option to find out whether your account has any chargebacks, to check their status, and to find out whether you're required to take any action.

>> **Performance Notifications:** Click this option to access any and all account related alerts that may impact your seller performance or account health.

WARNING

Don't ignore any performance notifications instructing you to take action. Failure to address issues on a timely basis may result in account suspension.

>> **Voice of the Customer:** For additional feedback on how your products and product listings have impacted the customer experience (CX) and to fix any issues, click this option. CX Health listings are broken down into several categories, ranking your listings from Very Poor to Excellent. CX health doesn't impact your overall account health. (Voice of the Customer was still in Beta during the time of this writing, so it may have changed by the time you read this.)

>> **Seller University:** Choose Seller University to access a multimedia library of instruction and guidance on how to succeed as an Amazon Seller. See the later section "Exploring Amazon's Seller University" for details.

App Store

Visit the Amazon App Store to find Amazon and third-party apps to automate business operations and to manage and grow your business. Select an app category and browse that category for solutions. (See the later section "Checking out Amazon's app store: The Solution Provider Network (SPN)" for details.)

Using the search bar

Near the upper-right corner of Seller Central is the search bar — the easiest, quickest tool for finding specific instruction and information in Seller Central. Type any key word or phrase in the search bar to describe what you're looking for, and press Enter. A search panel appears with all the relevant links to the content that matches your keyword search followed by links to additional resources. Just click the link to the item that interests you. (Note that on smaller screens, a magnifying glass icon appears in place of the search bar; click the magnifying glass icon to display the search bar.)

At the bottom of the panel are links to navigate to discussion forums, Amazon's help section, and your *case log* — any tech support issues you may be discussing with Amazon support staff. See the later section "Managing your case log" for details.

Viewing your payments summary

As you rack up sales on Amazon, Amazon handles your accounting for you, recording your total sales, deducting fees, and then paying you your share of the profits. To keep track of payments from Amazon, open the Reports menu and click Payments. The Payments page appears providing access to four payment summary tabs: Statement View, Transaction View, All Statements, and Date Range Reports. The following sections describe what's on each of these tabs.

Statement View

Statements View displays a weekly summary of your Amazon account broken down into seven sections:

>> **Beginning balance:** The amount owed to you or the amount you owed Amazon at the end of the previous period.

>> **Paid to Amazon:** The charge made to your credit card or bank account to cover a previous balance owed to Amazon.

>> **Orders:** Order totals since the end of the previous period.

>> **Refunds:** Refund totals since the end of the previous period.

>> **Closing balance:** The amount owed to you or the amount you owe Amazon at the end of this period.

>> **Transfer amount scheduled to initiate on [date]:** This indicates the date on which the closing balance will be transferred to or from your account.

>> **Balance available for transfer now:** If you have a balance available to be transferred at this time, you can click the Request Transfer button to request that the amount be transferred now instead of waiting until the next scheduled transfer date.

REMEMBER

Open the "Your Statement for" list just above the statement, and select the desired period. You can also click Previous or Next below the list to switch statement periods.

Transaction View

Transaction View displays a list of transactions in any given statement period. This page also contains a "Find a Transaction" box you can use to search for a transaction by its order number; a Filter View by list that lets you focus on specific types of transactions, such as order payments, refunds, or service fees; and options to specify the desired statement period.

All Statements

The All Statements page displays all your account statements between the specified From and To dates. By default, statements available for the most recent two months are displayed. To view a statement for a specific period, simply click its link in the Settlement Period column.

You can view statements either as a summary form in Seller Central or by downloading a plain text file. Click the desired file type in the Actions column to the right of the desired statement.

Date Range Reports

To generate your own custom payment report, click the Date Range Reports tab, specify the desired date range and the information to be included in the report, and click Generate Report.

Taking advantage of Amazon business reports

As soon as you rack up some sales on Amazon, you can access Amazon's business reports to monitor your sales performance, traffic, and conversion rates to obtain insight and guidance on how to improve sales.

To access business reports, hover over Reports (in the menu near the top of Seller Central) and click Business Reports. (If you don't see Business Reports, this feature is disabled in your account.) Assuming you do see and select Business Reports, a navigation bar appears on the left divided into three sections:

- » Sales Dashboard
- » Business Reports
- » Amazon Selling Coach

Sales Dashboard

The Sales Dashboard is an interactive tool that enables you to filter data by date, product category, and fulfillment channel by specifying one or more filters near the top of the dashboard. You can choose to display data in graph or table view by clicking the desired option (just above and to the right of the graph or table). You can also hover over different points in time on the graph or table to compare data from different dates, as selected below the graph or table.

Business Reports

The Business Reports section (in the navigation bar on the left) presents a list of available reports grouped by report type:

>> **By Date:**

- **Sales and Traffic report:** Shows number of units ordered, average sales per order, average sales per order item, average selling fee, number of user sessions, and so on.

- **Detail Page Sales and Traffic report:** Contains all the data included in the Sales and Traffic report along with page views and additional details.

TIP

Sales and traffic reports by date give very valuable insights into the shopper's relative activity in respect to your product pages during specific periods such as holidays, Cyber Monday, or shopping seasons.

- **Seller Performance report:** Contains all the essential data on seller performance metrics, including refund rate, feedbacks received, negative feedbacks received, claims amount, received negative feedback rate, A-to-Z Guarantee claims granted, claims amount, and so on. Details on this report help you track your overall account performance.

>> **By ASIN:**

- **Detail Page Sales Report:** This report contains sales and traffic data along with Child ASIN, Parent ASIN, product title, and SKU.

- **Detail Page Sales and Traffic by Parent Item:** Contains the same data as in the preceding report but grouped by parent ASIN.

- **Detail Page Sales and Traffic by Child Item:** Contains the same data as preceding report but grouped by Child ASIN and without the SKU data.

TIP

Sales and traffic reports by ASIN give valuable insights into the shopper's relative activity with respect to your product pages during events such as new product launches and discounts you're offering on specific products.

>> **Other:**

- **Sales and Orders by Month:** This report contains monthly sales and orders data. This reports gives the quick overview of sales over a long period of time up to two years and provides the sense of the direction to the business is heading.

REMEMBER

You can choose to display the data in each of these reports by different date ranges of up to 7 Days, 1 Month, 3 Months, 6 Months, 1 Year, and 2 Years from the custom date range selection except reports by ASIN, which can be displayed only by custom date range.

Accessing the Buyer-Seller Messaging Service

All communication between buyers and sellers occurs through Amazon's Buyer-Seller Messaging Service. To access your messages, click Messages (in the upper-right corner of the opening Seller Central page).

Communicating with buyers through the Messaging Service offers several advantages for both buyers and sellers:

>> Amazon encrypts both buyer and seller email addresses to protect everyone's identity and prevent any abusive or otherwise inappropriate communications outside the Amazon marketplace.

>> Amazon maintains a record of all communications between buyers and sellers, so if a dispute arises, Amazon can help to resolve it, and neither party can bend the truth about what was stated or not stated between them.

>> Communications through one central hub facilitates faster resolution of any issues.

>> Improved buyer-seller communication reduces returns and improves buyer satisfaction.

WARNING

Adhere strictly to Amazon guidelines that govern buyer-seller communications. First and foremost, contact buyers only for valid reasons, such as completing an order or addressing a customer's question or concern. Don't include any of the following content in your message:

>> Links to any external websites

>> Links to Amazon products or your storefront

>> Marketing or promotional messages or promotional messages

>> Any promotions or referrals to third-party products or promotional products

>> Requests for positive reviews or to have a negative review removed

See Chapter 1 for additional guidance regarding Amazon rules and guidelines.

REMEMBER

Buyer-seller messaging is enabled by default for Fulfillment by Merchant (FMB) orders. You can enable it for FBA orders, as well, but it's limited only to product enquiries intended to improve customer satisfaction. You can respond only to messages about products marked as "gift." Redirect other FBA customer service queries to Amazon Customer Service.

Getting Help and Information

When you have a specific question or need the most up-to-date information, your best option to is to consult Seller Central's help system. To access the help system, click Help (in the upper-right corner of nearly every Seller Central page).

Initially, the help system displays a Recommended for You section with links to topics that Seller Central has deemed to be most relevant to you. If you see a box for the topic or task you're looking for, click it for more information. If you don't see what you're looking for, scroll down the page and choose one of the following options:

>> **Search help:** Type a few keywords or a question to describe what you need help with and press Enter or click the button with the question mark on it.

>> **Seller Forums:** Click Launch Seller Forums to explore a wide range of topics being discussed by fellow Amazon sellers. See the later section "Engaging in the seller forums" for details on how to navigate the seller forums.

>> **Need more help?** Click Get Support to browse the help system for guidance related to managing your account settings, adding products, Fulfillment by Amazon (FBA), updating product listings, and managing orders and sales. Click a topic to view a list of subtopics and then select the desired subtopic. If you don't see a topic that's relevant to what you need, click Can't Find What You Need? for links to Seller University, the seller forums, and a Contact Us page.

>> **Seller University:** Click Launch Seller University to access a collection of videos on a wide range of topics. On the left is a navigation bar prompting you to choose a course. Click the desired course name to view a list of lessons in that course, click the desired lesson, and then click the video that appears on the right to start playing it. (See the later section "Exploring Amazon's Seller University" for details.)

In the following sections, we explain in greater detail how to use certain features of the help system and provide guidance on how to access additional help and information on Seller Central.

Engaging in the seller forums

Seller forums are one of the best ways to connect with other sellers to ask questions, talk shop, raise concerns, and request help when you can't find the answers or solutions you're looking for among Seller Central help topics.

To access the seller forums, click Help (in the upper-right corner of nearly every Seller Central page), scroll down the page, and click Launch Seller Forums. The Seller Forums page appears. Here are a few ways to find a topic of interest:

>> Scroll down the list of all Seller Forum categories on the left of the Seller Forums page and click the desired category. Categories include the following:

- Selling on Amazon

- US Announcements

- Fulfilled by Amazon

- Amazon Marketplace Web Services (AWS)

- Amazon Pay

- Global Selling

- Health & Safety

>> Click the All Categories box (near the top left of the page) and select the most relevant category. You can then click the All box next to it and select a subcategory to narrow your focus. Discussion topics are listed from newest to oldest. You can sort the list by number of replies or views or by most to least active by clicking the applicable column heading.

>> Click in the search bar, in the upper-right corner of the page, type a few keywords to describe what you're looking for, and press Enter. (Remember, on smaller screens, you may see a magnifying glass icon in place of the search bar; click the icon to view the search bar.)

>> If, after skimming through the topics, you don't see your question or issue addressed, click + New Topic in the upper-right corner of the Seller Forums page and use the resulting form to post your question or concern.

Contacting Amazon support for help

If you can't find the help you need in Seller Central's help system or the nature of your issue requires action from Amazon's support staff, contact Amazon for help:

1. **Click Help (in the upper-right corner of nearly every Seller Central page).**

2. **Scroll down the help page and under Need More Help? click Get Support.**

3. **Under Get Support, click Can't Find What You Need? and click Contact Us.**

4. **Choose the most relevant topic and subtopic (if required) and follow the on-screen instructions to obtain the help you need.**

   (Not all issues listed provide an opportunity to contact Amazon support, but several do.)

Managing your case log

Whenever you contact Amazon support for help resolving an issue, your communication is converted into a case for follow-up. Amazon will then contact you to request further information, if needed, or to inform you when the case has been resolved.

Cases are also posted to your case log, where you can access them at any time. To view your case log, take the following steps:

1. **Click Help (in the upper-right corner of nearly every Seller Central page).**

2. **Scroll down the help page and under Need More Help? click Get Support.**

3. **Under Get Support, click Can't Find What You Need? and click Contact Us.**

4. **Under What Can We Help You with? click View Case Log.**

   Your case log appears, showing a list of cases, the case ID for each, its status, the primary email address used for the communication, and a short description of each case.

   Just above your case log are options to filter your cases to view All, Your Cases and Requests, or those cases Needing Attention.

You can click the View button next to a case to view the conversation. When viewing a case, you can go through the history of the entire case communication and send a reply if the case is still opened. You can also mark a case as "Urgent" if it's important and needs to be resolved quickly.

REMEMBER

Answered cases can't be reopened after two days with no activity.

Consulting Amazon Selling Coach

Amazon is a stakeholder in your selling success. The more you sell, the more money Amazon collects in seller fees, so Amazon wants you to be successful. To optimize your sales success, Amazon features it Amazon Selling Coach — a tool that provides personalized recommendations to improve your performance.

REMEMBER

Recommendations are based on your activity on Amazon, so Amazon Selling Coach doesn't appear as an option until you've received some orders and engaged in other seller activities.

To access Amazon Selling Coach recommendations, open the Reports menu and click Amazon Selling Coach.

Most Selling Coach recommendations are grouped into five categories:

>> **Inventory:** Indicates when you have less than optimal stock based on recent inventory and sales data, so you can avoid the risk of running out of stock.

>> **Products:** Helps you discover additional products to sell based on product availability and customer interest or based on products you're already selling in one country that may sell well in another country.

>> **Pricing:** Notifies you of opportunities to adjust your prices on specific products to improve sales. Selling Coach also notifies you when someone is selling the same product you're selling but at a lower price.

>> **Fulfillment:** Highlights products in your inventory that may benefit from additional fulfillment options such as FBA.

>> **Advertising:** Notifies you of any products you're selling that are eligible for paid advertising on Amazon, such as Sponsored Products, so you can improve your visibility.

Each report has the option to vote on the recommendations. A yes vote on any recommendation helps to personalize future recommendations, whereas a no vote tells Selling Coach to no longer deliver that or similar recommendations.

Skimming Amazon headline news

To remain abreast of important announcements and the latest developments in the Amazon marketplace, tune into Amazon's headline news. To access News, click the Amazon Seller Central logo (in the upper-left corner of every Seller Central page) and scroll down the page to the News widget. Here, you'll see the latest headlines, each of which includes a link you can click to read the full story. At the bottom of the widget is a link called "See All Recent News. . .," which you can click to access the News page, where you can view additional stories. At the right of the News page is a navigation bar that enables you to filter stories by category, month published, bookmarked stories, or stories suggested for you based on your activity on Seller Central.

Checking out Amazon's app store: The Service Provider Network (SPN)

Amazon Seller Central features a directory of third-party providers that can ease the process of selling on Amazon. To access Amazon's Service Provider Network (SPN), visit `sellercentral.amazon.com/apps/store`. Via SPN, you can access apps and other support for help with the following:

>> **Account management** to obtain support for your daily Seller Central operations and guidance on how to grow your Amazon Seller business.

>> **Accounting** to help with tasks such as reconciling Amazon payments at the order level, analyzing product profitability, and integrating Amazon Seller Central with an account system such as QuickBooks.

>> **Advertising** to gain insight into increasing sales through advertising on Amazon.

>> **Cataloging** to simplify the process of listing new products and maximize sales by optimizing the use of product attributes that adhere to Amazon guidelines.

>> **Compliance** to obtain help for ensuring that products you intend to sell meet the rules, regulations, and laws of the targeted marketplace. Compliance services test, certify, inspect, audit, label, and ensure quality of products for Amazon marketplaces around the world.

>> **Enhanced brand content (EBC)** service providers assist in building rich content pages, enhanced product descriptions, quality images and video, and other content for branded pages, which are available only to sellers included in Amazon's brand registry.

>> **Fulfillment by Amazon (FBA) prep** providers label, poly-bag, quality-check, store, bundle, and so forth in preparation to send products to FBA distribution centers.

>> **Imaging** providers snap high-quality, custom images to include with product listings, which can often help to increase sales.

>> **International shipping and returns** service providers can help get your products into markets in other countries and handle any customer returns.

>> **Storage** providers offer an alternative to FBA, so you can stock products in other countries for faster delivery to customers.

>> **Tax** services help with tax registration, filings, and payments based on Amazon sales and returns.

>> **Training** services bring you up to speed on how to sell on Amazon, use FBA, choose and list products, and grow your Amazon Seller business.

>> **Translation** services can help you expand your sales to markets in other countries where you don't speak the language.

Exploring Amazon's Seller University

Click Help, scroll down the page, and click Launch Seller University to access a multimedia library of instruction and guidance on how to succeed as an Amazon Seller. Here you'll find reference guides and education videos covering everything from Amazon Seller policies to listing guidelines to advice on filling orders and growing your business. Whenever you have some spare time, we strongly encourage you to visit Seller University to build your knowledge and expertise.

2

Procuring Products to Sell on Amazon

Find out what you can and can't offer for sale on Amazon to ensure you're not violating any Amazon policies.

Discover how to find and choose products that you can be reasonably sure will sell for a profit that makes your time and effort worthwhile.

Explore your product sourcing options, which include retailers, wholesalers, drop-shippers, overseas suppliers, tradeshows, and manufacturing.

Choose reputable and reliable product suppliers, negotiate prices and terms that work for you, and team up with them to further your success.

Chapter **5**

Knowing What You Can and Can't Sell on Amazon

P rior to choosing products to sell on Amazon, familiarize yourself with the product types you can sell, what you're prohibited from selling, and what you can sell by under certain conditions. Any products you offer for sale on Amazon must comply with all laws and regulations in the country where you're selling and with all Amazon policies.

In this chapter, we bring you up to speed on Amazon's two main product categories (open categories and those that require approval), call your attention to restricted products, and explain Amazon's food and safety rules.

WARNING

Amazon strictly prohibits the sale of any illegal, unsafe, or other restricted products, including those available only by prescription.

Recognizing Products You Can Sell: Amazon's Product Categories

Amazon organizes all products into dozens of categories and subcategories, some open to all sellers and others restricted to only those sellers who request and are granted permission. In this section, we explore the differences among Amazon's product categories, so you have a clearer idea of the types of products you're allowed and prohibited from selling on Amazon.

Open categories

Amazon offers more than 20 open categories in which you're allowed to list products with no prior approval from Amazon. These categories include Amazon device accessories, beauty, camera & photo, cellphones, clothing and accessories, electronics, home & garden, and several more.

REMEMBER

Even in open categories you may encounter subcategories, brands, or products you're prohibited from listing. These restrictions are divided into the following three groups:

>> **Restricted (gated) subcategories:** An open category, such as Beauty, may include subcategories in which permission is required to list products.

>> **Restricted brands:** Some brands are picky about who lists and sells their products. You may need a brand owner's authorization before you can list the brand's products.

>> **Restricted products:** Restrictions may be placed on certain products, usually due to their chemical composition or safety concerns.

REMEMBER

Before you decide to offer a product on Amazon, do your research and obtain any authorizations required to list the product. To find out about any listing limitations, take the following steps:

1. **Search for the item you're thinking of selling.**

2. **In the search results, next to the item, look for a Listing Limitations Apply link.**

   If no such link appears, you're free to list and sell the product.

3. **If you see the Listing Limitations Apply link, click the link to view details about the listing limitations.**

   If you still want to list the product for sale, click the Request Approval button.

4. **Follow the on-screen directives to complete the application process.**

TIP

If the product you want to sell isn't already being sold on Amazon, try to create a product listing. If you see the Listing Limitations Apply link, you can assume that the category, brand, or product is restricted. Click the link for details.

Categories that require approval

Over the years, Amazon's reputation has taken a beating from complaints about counterfeit products and faulty or substandard products sold by third parties. To mitigate these risks, Amazon has identified certain categories that are more problematic than others and placed restrictions on who can sell products in these categories, which include the following:

>> Automotive and power sports

>> Collectible coins

>> Fine art

>> Fine jewelry

>> Grocery and gourmet food

>> Industrial and scientific products

>> Music and videos, DVDs, and Blu-ray

>> Professional services

>> Sports collectibles

>> Toys and games (during the holiday selling season)

>> Watches

REMEMBER

To list products in restricted categories, you must provide more details about your business and the products you're planning to sell, so Amazon can ensure that only genuine sellers of authentic products are listing them.

To sell in a restricted category, you typically must meet the following requirements:

>> Be an Amazon Professional Seller (Individual sellers aren't permitted to apply for approval to sell products in restricted categories)

>> Submit the required application form

>> Maintain good seller performance in certain categories

>> Have any required brand lease/distribution agreements in place

>> Present business details supporting your authenticity

>> Have invoices that support product authenticity

REMEMBER

Prior to listing anything for sale on Amazon, read and understand Amazon's current code of conduct and policies and strive to comply with all restrictions and requirements. Remaining in good standing with Amazon is always a wise policy. (See Chapter 1 for more about following Amazon's rules.)

Steering Clear of Restricted Products

Amazon restricts the listing and sale of certain products. Commonly restricted products fall into the following categories:

>> Alcohol

>> Animals and animal-related products

>> Art: Fine art

>> Art: Home decor

>> Automotive and powersports

>> Composite wood products

>> Cosmetics and skin/hair care

>> Currency, coins, cash equivalents, and gift cards

>> Dietary supplements

>> Drugs and drug paraphernalia

>> Electronics

>> Explosives, weapons, and related items

>> Export controls

>> Food and beverage

>> Gambling and lottery

>> Hazardous and dangerous items

>> Human parts and burial artifacts

>> Jewelry and precious gems

>> Laser products

>> Lighting

>> Lock picking and theft devices

>> Medical devices and accessories

- » Offensive and controversial materials

- » Pesticides and pesticide devices

- » Plant and seed products

- » Postage meters and stamps

- » Recalled products

- » Sex and sensuality

- » Subscriptions and periodicals

- » Surveillance equipment

- » Tobacco and tobacco-related products

- » Warranties, service plans, contracts, and guarantees

- » Other restricted products

REMEMBER

The list of restricted goods isn't exhaustive. Amazon updates the list regularly through consultations with various stakeholders, including regulators, carriers, and third-party experts. Also, certain products may be restricted only in specific countries or parts of a country; be sure to offer such products with the applicable shipping settings, which you can find in Seller Central by choosing Settings, then Shipping Settings.

Additionally, Amazon requires sellers to get pre-approval to sell products in certain categories such as clothing, grocery, dietary supplements, and certain brands (to protect against counterfeit products). Products that require pre-approval are considered *gated*. To gain pre-approval, obtain an invoice from the brand or supplier showing the purchase of at least the minimum quantity Amazon requires for permission to sell that product and use the product's Listing Limitations Apply option to request approval. Sales of some products are restricted to only Amazon Business Account (BA) holders; see Chapter 10 for details.

If you're unsure whether a product is restricted or gated, try listing the product through the Amazon Seller App or Seller Central. If the Listing Limitations Apply option appears next to the product you're trying to list, select the option and follow the procedure specified to apply for approval. If you're unsure whether you're permitted to list a certain product, contact Amazon, as we explain in Chapter 4.

WARNING

As a seller, you're responsible for making informed decisions of which products to list and not list on Amazon. Amazon has sophisticated mechanisms in place that flag questionable products based on the product title, ingredients, or evolving database of commonly restricted products. Listing a restricted or gated product prior to obtaining approval could derail a successful business overnight for violations. If you're uncertain about Amazon policies, contact Amazon or seek outside legal counsel prior to listing any questionable product.

REVERSING COURSE

Amazon has been known to change course on restricted products. For example, in late October, early November of 2019, Amazon announced to its third-party retailers that they could no longer list Nintendo products for sale without first receiving expressed approval.

In the announcement, Amazon didn't mention whether Amazon, Nintendo, or the two companies together were responsible for the sudden restriction or explain the reason for it. Nor did Amazon include a list of restricted products or their ASINs.

Within hours of the announcement, Amazon received many complaints and decided to reverse course, stating "Yesterday's email was sent in error," and all impacted listings were reinstated within hours.

Because the restricted or gated product status is subject to change, you're always wise to check the status of a specific product prior to deciding whether to list it on Amazon.

TIP

For additional information and guidance regarding category, product, and listing restrictions, log in to Seller Central and choose Help, Program Policies, Category and Product Restrictions. Here, you'll find numerous links grouped by product compliance requirements; safety and labeling requirements; content and listing requirements; and category, product, and listing restrictions.

Brushing Up on Food Safety Rules

Because people directly consume food products, Amazon regulates their sale closely to ensure that its customers receive safe, fresh, high-quality products.

Every product being offered for sale in the grocery or gourmet food category must meet the following requirements for quality, branding, and consumer safety:

>> Is properly prepared, packaged, sealed, and labeled.

>> Has all required approvals from relevant government agencies.

>> Complies with all applicable federal and state laws.

>> Is new (can't be used or open).

>> Has a permanent expiry date printed clearly on the packaging, unless otherwise exempt for any reason. The expiry date can't be altered or removed.

>> Has an expiration date on the multi-pack packaging that matches the earliest expiration date of the individual products contained in the multi-pack.

>> Is labeled in English according to the guidelines of FDA Food Labeling and Nutrition, FDA Pet Food, and USDA Label Approval web pages, assuming the product comes under the purview of U.S. federal or state laws.

>> Is packaged using the suitable materials to prevent contamination, damages, spoiling, and melting during shipping.

>> Ships to Amazon distribution centers with enough shelf life remaining. If you're using the category specific templates to upload the products, as we explain in Chapter 9, set the value of the is_expiration_dated_product field to "true."

>> Is listed using the manufacturer's UPC code.

These sections examine organic and chilled or frozen food in greater detail.

Organic products

To be listed as organic on Amazon, each product must comply with organic regulations set by the USDA or an equivalent international organization recognized by USDA. Every organic product must comply with the following rules:

>> Be produced in compliance with USDA organic requirements.

>> Comply with USDA organic labeling guidelines.

REMEMBER

USDA organic specifies the standards to be followed in order to be categorized as "organic" and wear the USDA organic seal. Though these guidelines are provided for information purposes, refer to the following official USDA web pages for updated standards and specifications:

>> www.ams.usda.gov/rules-regulations/organic

>> www.ams.usda.gov/about-ams/programs-offices/national-organic-program

>> www.ams.usda.gov/grades-standards/organic-labeling-standards

>> www.ams.usda.gov/sites/default/files/media/Importing%20 Organic%20Products%20Factsheet.pdf

>> www.ams.usda.gov/sites/default/files/media/Labeling%20 Organic%20Products.pdf

>> organic.ams.usda.gov/integrity

>> www.ams.usda.gov/services/organic-certification/certifying-agents

TIP

For additional guidelines regarding organic products, log in to Seller Central and choose Help, Program Policies, Category and Product Restrictions, Food Safety and Compliance, Organic Products.

Chilled and frozen products

Every seller offering refrigerated food, frozen food, or temperature-controlled foods must meet the following requirements:

>> Seller must be registered as an Amazon Professional Seller.

>> Seller must provide all documentation required by Amazon.

>> All refrigerated, frozen, and raw agricultural products must be packaged and sealed with suitable materials for safe shipping.

>> All temperature-controlled foods must meet temperature requirements for quality and safety.

>> Raw agricultural products that don't have valid expiration dates must have acceptable shelf life remaining specified on the product.

>> Sellers offering temperature-sensitive products are expected to validate the chill chain by demonstrating theoretically how the temperatures are maintained in worst-case scenarios. Similarly, a verification program is recommended to confirm the performance of products in a real business world. Sellers are expected to maintain the validation and verification data with all recorded activities to be produced to Amazon and other relevant regulatory departments upon request.

>> Sellers who are planning to sell food products should have proper awareness of all the nuts and bolts of the processes in order to avoid any unexpected disruptions to the Amazon business.

To access more information on food safety and organic requirements, use the Seller Central Search bar to access relevant help pages and contact the Amazon Seller support team for further assistance.

TIP

For additional guidelines regarding chilled and frozen foods, log in to Seller Central and choose Help, Program Policies, Category and Product Restrictions, Food Safety and Compliance, Chilled and Frozen Foods.

Chapter **6**

Finding Products with Profit Potential

A s a retailer, you want to move a lot of product, but you also want every sale to generate a sufficient return to compensate you fairly for the time, effort, and expertise you invest in your venture. By identifying and buying products with respectable sales volume and profit potential, you boost your return on investment (ROI), alleviate some of the pressure to sell large quantities, and reduce the risk of getting stuck with a product you can't sell for a profit.

In this chapter, we shift the focus from selling on Amazon to buying products to sell on Amazon. In many ways, buying and selling on Amazon is like scoring profits on real estate properties, where experts often advise investors to "make your money when you buy," meaning if you buy the right property, you're almost guaranteed to earn a handsome profit when you sell it.

REMEMBER

If you're planning to sell your own branded products on Amazon, go to Chapter 17 to find out how to trademark your brand first. If you launch a brand on Amazon before securing trademark/intellectual property protection, you could run into trademark conflicts that are more difficult to resolve than if you had trademarked your brand before listing products for sale.

Recognizing the Characteristics of Products with High Profit Potential

When you're getting started as an Amazon Seller, look for the low-hanging fruit — products that have certain qualities characteristic of products with high sales and profit potential. While conducting product research (as we explain in the later section "Conducting Your Own Product Research") will reveal such products, you can often identify them more quickly by looking for products with these specific qualities.

Uniqueness

Selecting unique products that set you apart from the competition gives you greater flexibility to charge what you want without the pressures of competitive pricing. According to the law of supply and demand, the more generic the product, the stiffer the competition, and the lower the price and profit margin.

Here are a few ways to find/create products that stand out from the competition:

- » Make your own handcrafted products, such as jewelry, clothing, soaps, toys, games, and so on.

- » Invent and patent your own product idea(s), hire a manufacturer to produce them, and then sell them on Amazon. (See Chapter 7 for details.)

- » Start listing trending products before the competition notices the product is trending.

- » Find products that use difficult-to-source raw materials that you can access more easily than the competition. If you can control the supply chain for a specific product, your competitors won't be able to offer the same product.

REMEMBER

Any opportunity to offer a unique product is a good place to start your Amazon journey.

Price range and profit margin

The sweet spot for profitable products exists where the product price is above $25 retail with a 40-percent net profit margin or cost to produce of 25 to 30 percent of the retail price to produce it.

WARNING

Generally, steer clear of products that sell for $20 or less, because Amazon selling fees are likely to gobble up a good portion of your profits. When you sell products for at least $25, you increase your profit margin, which is revenue/cost. For example, if you buy a product for $3.25 and sell it for $10, Amazon selling fees, FBA fulfillment fees, and the costs related to shipping products to an FBA distribution center are likely to exceed what you paid for the product, leaving you a tiny profit, if any.

Sales volume

Although you want to earn a decent profit on each item, selling only a few of an item isn't going to make you the affluent retailer of your dreams. You want something with a high profit margin *and* strong sales volume. Unless you're trying to get ahead of a trend or have invented an amazing product that addresses a serious customer need or fulfills consumers' longing desires, look for products that meet the following criteria:

>> Strong market demand

>> Items that people commonly consume, wear out, or replace

REMEMBER

Market conditions change over time. For example, computers and cellphones are still strong sellers, but as the quality and functionality of these items have increased over time, consumers are finding that they need to upgrade or replace their electronic devices less frequently, leading to slower sales and increasing competition. The moral of this story is to keep an eye on changing demand and be ready to adjust your product-selection strategy.

You can find plenty of product research and analysis tools (free and not) on the Internet to estimate total sales for main product keywords or product lines. Use those tools to identify products that have steady market demand higher than average sales volume. (See the later section "Using product research tools" for details.)

TIP

One free and easy way to tell whether a particular product sells well is to pull it up in Amazon and add 999 of them to your cart. If the seller has fewer than 999 of those items, the number in stock appears. You can check this number daily to monitor the number of items sold daily and gauge its sales potential. (Of course, the number of items may increase if a shopper returns a product or the seller adds inventory. Also, this tactic doesn't work if the seller limits the quantity of items a shopper can add to his cart.)

Shipping cost/complexity

Shipping costs and complexity are a one-two punch that can knock the stuffing out of your profits. When considering whether to sell a particular product, look for the following traits:

>> Easy to pack. Avoid products with complex packaging requirements, such as fragile items or those that require refrigeration or temperature control.

>> Two pounds or lighter to ship (and return).

>> Easy to ship.

>> Sturdy enough to handle shipping, returns, and customer handling.

REMEMBER

Shipping costs consume a good chunk of any online retailer's profits, especially when a customer returns a product, hitting you with a double dose of shipping fees.

Reviews

Customer ratings and reviews serve as a window through which you can view and understand the competition and how customers are responding to the product and seller. Just find a product you're thinking of selling and check out the customer ratings and reviews. Look for the following criteria:

>> **Relatively low number of ratings/reviews posted.** When competitors already have hundreds of positive customer ratings/reviews, you'll have a tough time increasing your listing's search ranking for that product.

>> **Relatively high number of low ratings and negative reviews.** Low ratings/reviews can be a sign of a problem or opportunity. If reviews indicate dissatisfaction with a product, you may not want to sell it, or you may want to find a similar, higher quality version to sell. If the reviews indicate a dissatisfaction with the seller, you may be looking at a golden opportunity to beat the seller by offering better customer service.

Steering Clear of Troublesome Products

Some products are more trouble than they're worth. They can lead you into a legal quagmire, suck your time and energy with complaints and requests for technical support, wipe out your profits with shipping and return fees, or set you up to compete with big-box retailers who are almost guaranteed to undercut whatever low price you can afford to offer. Some products even have the potential to disrupt your business unexpectedly if Amazon suspends your account while investigating a claim against you.

In this section, we point out some red flags that may cause you to think twice before listing certain products for sale.

Trademarked products

When choosing a product, check for a registered trademark for any part of the brand or logo. If a product is trademarked, you're prohibited from selling it on Amazon unless you have written permission to do so from the trademark owner. If you list a trademarked product without a proper agreement, Amazon considers it to be a counterfeit item.

In the United States, you can research trademarks via the United States Patent and Trademark Office (USPTO) website at www.uspto.gov. In the Find It Fast box choose Trademarks, and then choose the desired trademark search and follow the on-screen instructions to complete the process. Here, you can find information about the trademark owner along with additional tools for researching, filing for, and managing trademark registrations.

Another, simpler, option is to search online for the trademark to pull up a list of links to patents, trademarks, and branded websites that match your search term.

WARNING

Amazon is very serious about trademark infringement and expects its sellers to comply strictly with federal, state, and local laws, along with respective Amazon policies. If a trademark owner files a trademark infringement complaint against you with Amazon, it can result in Amazon suspending or canceling your account.

Mechanically complex products

When starting on Amazon, avoid mechanically complex products with moving parts or complex designs, those that require complicated assembly or installation, those likely to require more than minor technical support, and those that can be easily damaged or even made dysfunctional by minor mistakes during assembly or installation. Products like these are highly susceptible to high return rates, low ratings and reviews, and time-consuming communications and tech support you don't get paid for. They chip away at your profit margins and can even undermine your account performance, decreasing the ranking of your products in search results.

Several underlying issues contribute to the fact that listing mechanically complex products isn't a good practice for first-time sellers, including the following:

>> Amazon strongly encourages free, no-hassle returns for just about any reason, even if the buyer made a bad purchase decision, changed her mind, or became frustrated after a few minutes of trying to assemble or use a product.

>> You typically have to charge more for mechanically complex products to account for the extra time you'll need to invest in customer service, which can make your product listings less attractive to shoppers.

>> Demonstrating product functionality in an environment like Amazon where buyer's attention span is less than a half minute on average is often challenging, if not impossible. Prospective buyers are likely to lose interest in a listing that requires them to spend more time grasping the intricacies of the product or its assembly or use.

TIP

Mechanically complex products can present an opportunity, as well. If you can figure out a way to eliminate or reduce the complexity, you may be able to succeed where others have failed.

Products that are difficult and costly to store and ship

Storage and shipping represent significant costs and complexities, so carefully consider listing any products that are large, heavy, or irregular in shape or size. Recognize the factors that contribute to storage and shipping difficulties and costs, including the following:

>> Carriers calculate the larger of the actual weight or volume, so you pay extra whether a product is heavier or the package is larger.

>> Items shipped in larger containers are more likely to be delivered by ground, thus taking longer to reach the customer. Even though customers can pay more for expedited shipping, the additional cost drives down sales because customers may prefer to buy it at a nearby brick-and-mortar store to get it faster and for less.

>> Certain products, including some beauty products, are perishable and more likely to spoil if not refrigerated during transit. Insulating packaging and cold packs can add significantly to the cost of packing and shipping, and customers are more likely to return products if they notice any damage to either the packing or the product.

Products sold in large retail stores

You may want to steer clear of products available at large retail stores simply because you probably can't compete with their price and customer service. Big-box retailers have several advantages over mom-and-pop operations, including the following:

>> **Lower prices:** Large retail stores usually have multiple branches all over the country and even the world and procure any products in bulk quantities at better than wholesale prices through exclusive deals.

>> **Product displays:** Customers can often see and touch products such as laptops, TVs, vacuum cleaners, cookware, and tools before buying them.

>> **No wait for delivery:** Products are more widely available to the customers nearby their house without having to wait days for delivery.

>> **Fast, easy returns:** The customer service counter provides a quick and easy way for customers to get refunds and process exchanges.

Conducting Your Own Product Research

You can certainly pick winning products (and avoid many losers) by following the general guidance we present in the previous sections, but if you're looking for a more formal, scientific approach, you can dive deeper with product research. With a passion to find winning products, a willingness to refine your search, and one or two product research tools, you're well-equipped to find products that will take off pretty quickly. In this section, we explain how.

Using product research tools

Type **product research amazon** into your favorite search engine to find links to numerous software tools for conducting product research both on and off Amazon, including the following:

>> **AMZBase (www.amzbase.com):** A great tool for speeding up your product research. Simply hover over a product image to view the product's Amazon Standard Identification Number (ASIN) and title description; click to view historical prices, source any related content, check listing info on other retailing sites, and more.

» **AMZScout** (`https://amzscout.net`): Presents a spreadsheet interface that calls your attention to potentially high-volume, highly profitable products, identify growing trends, verify niche ideas, research other sellers, estimate fees and profits, and predict future competition.

» **FBA Wizard** (`https://fbawizard.com`): If you're into retail arbitrage (buying products from other retailers to resell, as we explain in Chapter 7) consider FBA Wizard, which is designed specifically to help find profitable products to resell on Amazon. (During the writing of this book, FBA Wizard was available by invitation only, requiring that you supply a valid email address to register for notification of availability.)

» **Helium10** (`www.helium10.com`): This product is perhaps the most robust product research tool on the market and is available by subscription only (with a free trial). Features include Black Box Product Research into a database of more than 450 million products; Xray, a Chrome browser extension that provides a window into products listed on Amazon search results and product pages; Scribbles, a keyword optimizer for listings; Cerebro, a reverse ASIN search engine for researching competitors; and more.

» **JungleScout** (`www.junglescout.com`): Another very robust product research product, JungleScout features a product database, product tracker, supplier database, keyword scout, sales analytics, and inventory manager. The product database in particular is designed to help you find winning products by drilling down to identify products with high demand. With product tracker, you can keep up on any Amazon product's daily sales, inventory data, and revenue.

» **Keepa** (`https://keepa.com`): This product is a collection of browser extensions that provide access to a variety of product information, including price history charts of more than 100 million Amazon products, price drop and availability reports, international Amazon prices, and daily deals. Very limited access is free, but you'll need to pay a monthly subscription price to increase your data quota.

» **Seller App** (`www.sellerapp.com`): A full-featured application for managing your Amazon business. Features are broken down into three categories — marketing, sales, and operations, with marketing including product research, product ideas, and keyword research. The product ideas feature is especially useful to identify potentially profitable products. You can choose from proven best sellers, trending products, new product releases, or even most wish-listed products.

» **Sonar** (`http://sonar-tool.com`): This tool is driven heavily by keywords, showing you what Amazon shoppers are actually searching for and then helping you optimize keyword selection for your listings accordingly. You can ping keywords for free on the Sonar website, but to dig any deeper requires a subscription.

>> **Unicorn Smasher** (`www.unicornsmasher.com`): This tool is dedicated to helping sellers identify products that show potential for high volume, profitable sales without getting bogged down in the numbers. Although it provides comprehensive data and a full dashboard packed with detailed sales info, it also boils down the numbers into sales estimates and an opportunity score to simplify product selection.

Sizing up the competition

One of the best ways to stay ahead of your competitors is to get into their heads to see what they're doing and figure out their sales strategies. But first, you have to figure out who your top competitors are. The good news is that Amazon Sellers are equipped with various features and a goldmine of information to help identify their top competitors. Here are a few tips to help identify your top competitors and start gathering the information and insight you need to figure out what they're up to. These tips are crucial to sail through the competitive Amazon marketplace and find your success.

>> Identify the top three primary keywords for your products and get the list of products that appear in the first and second pages of the search results for the selected keywords. The top sellers of those products are real competitors; they're selling well, liked by customers, and are on top.

>> Navigate to your product detail pages and head to the "Amazon Best Sellers Rank" right below the product description. Select the categories and subcategories to explore the various Amazon Best Sellers pages for each category and subcategory in which you sell products. (Each Amazon Best Sellers page contains a list of 100 of the top selling products in the selected category or subcategory.) This is the real time data updated every hour and is considered the most reliable source of product sales and trends. Sellers can boost their sales significantly if they can use this data to their advantage.

>> Amazon product detail pages are crowded with tons of clues about what your competitors are offering to beat your product. Amazon places several important product carousels in various parts of the product detail page to target the shoppers who are interested in specific products. Scroll down each relevant product detail page, and note the following:

- Sponsored products related to this item

- Items frequently bought together

- Other items customers commonly buy after viewing this item

- Items related to those you've viewed

These are the products being placed by Amazon and other competitors strategically through the use of proven algorithms targeting the shoppers who are interested in these (and, hence, your) products.

After identifying your real competitors, assess them to develop a deeper understanding of the challenges they pose to your business. One of the best ways to stay ahead of your competitors is to get into their heads to see what they're doing and figure out their sales strategies. Track the following details:

>> **Products listed by your top competitors, recently added to their catalogs, and selling well:** Closely monitoring what's selling and what's not selling for your competitors provides very good clues as to what products you should be selling.

>> **Competitor product ratings and reviews:** Steer clear of any products your competitors are already dominating with lots of positive ratings and reviews. Gravitate toward products with no or few positive reviews or those with numerous one- to three-star reviews. Low ratings/reviews may signal an opportunity — indicating that buyers have problem with the offering and you may be able to outsmart your competitors by offering a higher quality product or superior customer service.

>> **Competitors' sponsored products:** Sponsored products reveal where your competitors are putting their money and hoping to gain traction, usually on products they expect to start selling well.

Exploring Alibaba and other Chinese online wholesale marketplaces

China is the world's manufacturing hub, without a doubt! Millions of different products are being produced in China and are exported across China and around the world. Researching products in China can provide a window into the future of what's likely to be trending in the United States or other markets down the road. Here are several Chinese sources from which to gather valuable product information:

>> **Alibaba** (www.alibaba.com) is poster child of Chinese ecommerce industry — the largest B2B marketplace on the planet, where you can connect with suppliers to source products for resale on Amazon (see Chapter 7 for details). Browse the website to find hundreds of suppliers offering just about any imaginable product. Choose the product category of interest and select Best Selling Products to view a list of hot sellers. Compare quotes from available suppliers to find the best price/quality balance for your business.

TIP

» **AliExpress** (`www.aliexpress.com`) is a great place for small sellers to source smaller quantities at best prices. Head directly to "New User Section" where hot deals are listed for new users — deals starting from $0.01. This section will help you to get the best deals on thousands of products.

Check out AliExpress's new Dropshipping Center. (With *drop-shipping*, you never touch the product. Customers place their order with you, and the drop-shipper packs and labels the product and ships it directly to the customer. It's the ideal no-hassle way to sell retail.) To go to the Aliexpress drop-shipping center, you can either google it or visit home.aliexpress.com/dropshippercenter/dashboard.htm.

To explore the Dropshipping Center, you need to create an AliExpress account. Upon logging into your account, you're presented with a three-tab dashboard, two of which are great for conducting product research. The Hot DS Items tab lists more than 250 pages of hot-selling products, while the Product Analysis tab helps to track sales trends to gain insight into the sales and profit potential of different products.

» **DHGate** (`www.dhgate.com/`) bills itself as "The Gateway to China's Finest." It's a wholesale marketplace that connects suppliers with retailers, enabling retailers to purchase in bulk from high-quality factories "at significantly lower prices than retail." It serves approximately 2.2 million sellers globally and boasts more than 22 million product listings.

» **Global Sources** (`www.globalsources.com`) connects wholesale suppliers with "more than 1.5 million international retailers, including 94 of the world's top 100 retailers." Here you can find suppliers in numerous product categories, including auto parts and accessories, consumer electronics, electronic components, fashion accessories and footwear, gifts, tools, home products, machinery, mobile electronics, and more. Scroll down to view the top 20 products listed by category.

» **Made-in-China** (`www.made-in-china.com`) is a free product sourcing platform with more than 10,000 verified suppliers in more than 20 industries. It's not the greatest site for researching products to find products with respectable sales potential, but when you find a product you want to sell, you can scroll down and submit a request for a quote.

» **DIY Trade** (`www.diytrade.com`) is a B2B online trading platform that provides access to more than five million products. Suppliers post their products, and as a retailer you can subscribe to product alerts to get early notification of new products. The DIY Trade website also runs a list of popular keywords across the top and a list of product categories along the left that can aid in product research.

REMEMBER

Conducting serious research on these platforms will help you identify some of the best products to sell while boosting your overall product knowledge and your ability to pick products with high sales and profit potential.

Validating or Rejecting Product Ideas

When conducting product research, you're likely to get overwhelmed with dozens of products ideas which all seem great bets but may fizzle when they hit the market. After coming up with a long list of product candidates, whittling down that list to the top 10 or top 20 can help to hedge your investment. In this section, we lead you through the process of vetting products based on their merits and true potential.

Weighing the pros and cons of carrying the latest, greatest products

A cool new tool or gadget that hasn't yet shown up on the general consumer's radar can be very enticing to an eager Amazon Seller, but avoid the temptation until you've had a chance to weigh the pros and cons.

Here are the pros:

» You can charge premium pricing for innovative products because they have limited to no competition.

» Selling bleeding-edge products helps you build a reputation among sellers as someone in-the-know, which can increase loyalty to your personal brand and can help drive future sales.

Meanwhile, here are the cons:

» You may need to invest more time, energy, and expertise educating prospective consumers on the features, functionality, and benefits of new products. In the process, you may end up losing customers with shorter attention spans.

» Innovative products tend to sell for higher prices as designers and manufacturers try to recoup research, development, and manufacturing costs incurred to introduce the new product to the market. New products won't appeal to late adopters and budget-conscious consumers.

>> You may end up spending considerable time and suffering anguish from trying to keep up with customer questions and complaints if the product is complex or buggy and the manufacturer offers limited or no product support.

TIP

Don't rule out an entire product because one version of it doesn't meet the desired criteria. Weigh the pros and cons based on your area, target customers, their spending patterns, and alternative products of the same type.

Considering seasonal products

Seasonal products can lead to boom or bust — a short-term boost in sales and profits during the season in which they're popular followed by a bust over the rest of the year, during which time, you're footing the bill for storage of products you may never be able to sell.

REMEMBER

Amazon typically ships around one billion products during the Christmas holiday season. Although Amazon is tight-lipped about total sales figures, that represents a lot of money however you choose to look at it.

Although selling seasonal products can be rewarding over a limited period of time, it carries some significant risks you need to consider, such as the following:

>> Seasonal sales are inconsistent and often unpredictable from year to year, making inventory planning that much more challenging.

>> Seasonal trends are often driven by temporary trends such as the popularity of Angry Bird toys, increasing the challenge of predicting demand.

>> Betting on a single season is a risky venture. To be successful on Amazon, you need a year-round selling strategy.

TIP

As you plan your Amazon retail business, be sure to offer core products that sell well all year. Then add seasonal products. Don't build your plan for success solely on having a successful holiday sales season.

Giving new brands a try (or not)

In some product categories such as athletic shoes and watches, brands carry a lot of weight. When a new brand tries to wedge its way in between strong existing brands, consider carefully whether to offer that brand. On one hand, the new brand faces stiff headwinds in becoming established, but if the product is superior, being an early adopter of that brand can pay handsome dividends.

Here are a few key factors to consider before taking on a new brand in a product category dominated by strong brands:

>> **Trust:** With established brands such as Nike, Adidas, and Rolex, people already trust the quality and durability of the products and know that these companies stand by their products with excellent warranties. Such isn't the case with products from relatively unknown brands; customers may have concerns about longevity, functionality, materials quality, and after-sales service.

>> **Familiarity:** Over time, customers find brands that are generally better at meeting their needs and preferences. For example, they may prefer the fit and feel of Brooks athletic shoes over those of Nike or vice versa. Breaking through this barrier with a new brand can be tough.

>> **Cost:** On a positive note, you may be able to find great deals on new brands if the manufacturer is eager to drop the price in exchange for an opportunity to increase its market share. The results: increased sales, higher profit margins, or both.

>> **Opportunity:** If the new brand is superior to established brands in one or more ways, it may eventually win a commanding position in a certain product category. By picking up the new brand early, you have a chance to help customers discover it and thus establish yourself as the go-to retailer of that brand.

Consider all the aspects of offering a relatively new brand before you get onboard.

Focusing on Price and Sales Volume

In some ways, product selection boils down to price and sales volume. For every product you're thinking of listing, ask yourself, "Will I be able to sell enough of these items at a high enough price to earn a worthwhile profit?" If you can answer "yes" to that question, you should probably list the product.

In this section, we present a few techniques to help you develop clearer insight into evaluating price and sales volume and making informed product and pricing decisions. By following this guidance, you'll be better equipped to pick products that are the right fit for your business and price your products more strategically.

Checking out different pricing strategies

Seasoned retailers use a host of different product pricing strategies to increase sales volume, revenue, and profits. Here are a few pricing strategies you may want to consider:

» **Cost-plus pricing:** A simple pricing model in which you calculate your cost and then add a markup that reflects the profit you want to earn from each sale, either as a percentage or dollar amount. This strategy alone won't help much on Amazon where pricing is highly competitive.

» **Competitive pricing:** Set your price based on what the competition charges. You may want to set a lower price to undercut the competition or a higher price to reflect a superior product or the customer service a buyer can expect.

» **Value-based pricing:** Set your price based on the price of a comparable product and then add to that price for all the features/benefits that make your product or customer service more valuable. Just be sure that the additional price exceeds your investment in adding value.

» **Price skimming:** For new products or brands, consider setting a high price at the beginning to cash in on high demand and low supply of the product and then lower the price as the market matures.

» **Penetration pricing:** When you're trying to break into a new market, consider setting prices low to establish yourself and then raising your prices later.

» **Loss-leader pricing:** This tactic involves selling one item at a loss in the hopes of getting customers to buy other products that you sell profitably. For example, grocery stores often offer milk, meats, or eggs at ridiculously low prices to get people into the store where they'll buy plenty of other regularly priced items.

» **Destroyer pricing:** If a competitor is trying to move in on your territory, and you're in a strong enough position to fight, you can temporarily sell products for less than your competitor can afford to for the purpose of discouraging that seller.

Keeping an eye on the competition

Competitive pricing plays a major role on Amazon because Amazon actively encourages it. After all, a big part of the reason people shop on Amazon is for its low prices, and Amazon wants to please its customers. By keeping tabs on your competitors' pricing data for products that are the same or similar to yours, you stand to reap the following benefits:

>> Gain insight into competitor price trends and strategies.

>> Spot opportunities to increase your profit margin without hurting sales volume.

>> Devise your own pricing strategy backed by competitor data.

>> Use your pricing data to negotiate lower prices with your suppliers.

>> Develop an intuitive sense of product value. When you can quickly ballpark the market value of an array of similar products, you can quickly buy and sell in certain product categories at a profit.

TIP

Several third-party tools, including some of those we discuss in the earlier section "Using product research tools," show the price fluctuations of any product over a period of time. Tracking price movements over time provides a gold mine of information into your competitors' pricing strategy and tactics.

However, merely staring at the data isn't sufficient if you don't look at it in a way that reveals valuable insights. As you examine the data, ask yourself the following questions:

>> Who are the top sellers offering same or similar products to yours? Keep a list of your competitors, so you know whom to watch.

>> How often they do change the prices? The frequency of price changes tells you clues about how they're playing their pricing strategies around important holiday and off seasons.

>> By what percentage do your competitors increase or decrease their prices? The percentage increase indicates how they are keeping up with their margins while increasing sales volumes.

>> How do the top sellers react when competitors change their prices? These reactions reveal their strategy to beat the competition and how they're winning despite the competition.

>> Based on the price fluctuations, where do you predict the price is heading in the near future and why? This exercise can help you to take precautionary measures to ward off future risks threats presented by the competition.

Consider a few scenarios in which a seller can use such data to boost sales and profits:

>> Imagine you and your competitor have been offering a similar product at the same price of $60 during Cyber Monday. Immediately after Cyber Monday, your competitor raises his price to $90. If you've been tracking the price

change, you could immediately raise your price to $80, increasing your profit margin while beating your competitor in sales volume. Had you not been tracking, you would still beat your competitor in terms of sales volume but would have left some revenue on the table.

» When tracking your competitor's historic pricing variations and inventory levels, you notice your competitor raises prices whenever her inventory levels are low — usually a few months out of the year, even though sales remain steady. This could indicate your competitor has a supply chain problem. You could take advantage of this situation by increasing your inventory levels at the same time while reducing your price slightly, thereby increasing your sales volume and perhaps even capturing some market share.

» In another scenario, based on sales and traffic reports, you've noticed that a few of your ASINs have three times more traffic in July compared to March. More likely, the conversions follow the pattern. You could increase sales by fully optimizing those ASINs while increasing your inventory during historical periods of increased traffic.

» By identifying the best sellers in a category/subcategory offering similar products as yours, you could create sponsored advertisements by targeting the selected top performing ASINs of your competitor, which otherwise would are very difficult to compete against organically.

Estimating sales volume

Estimating the sales potential of any product is important when deciding whether to invest your time and money in it. Although businesses always struggle to predict sales, an informed guess is better than a blind guess and can help you lessen your exposure to risk.

TIP

The easiest way to estimate sales on Amazon is to use a product analysis tool that offers such a feature. JungleScout provides a free online sales estimator you can use to project sales for best-selling products in certain popular categories. To use JungleScout's Amazon Sales Estimator, take the following steps:

1. **Go to** www.junglescout.com/estimator.

2. **Choose an Amazon Best Seller's Rank number.**

   We realize that this may not be a ranking for a specific product you're thinking of selling, but the estimator will give you a general idea of what to expect based on product category and Best Seller rank in that category.

3. **Choose your Amazon Marketplace (for example, United States, Canada, Mexico).**

4. **Choose one of the available categories such as appliances, baby, electronics, or home & kitchen.**

5. **Press the Calculate Sales! button.**

   The Amazon Sales Estimator displays the total number of the specified items likely to be sold per month.

6. **Based on the total number of those items sold on Amazon, guesstimate the percentage of the total you can win and the total revenue you can expect to earn in a month of sales.**

   This step is more art than science.

You can continue with this exercise to multiply values from Step 6 by 3 or 12 to project future quarterly or annual sales and revenue. For a more comprehensive estimate of total sales and profits, consider repeating the exercise for everything in your product line and developing a three-year projection — something the big-box stores commonly do to remain competitive.

You can also gauge sales volume by researching other sources, such as trade magazines, quarterly reports, and small-business talk shows during which this topic is often discussed. Try to identify businesses similar to yours — about the same size, selling similar products — and evaluate your sales based on theirs. You may even want to contact retailers who operate outside your market and are willing to talk shop without much concern over your competing with them.

Setting realistic profit projections

Although sales volume is all about revenues, profits are influenced by a host of factors, including wholesale and retail pricing; storage, picking, packing, and shipping costs; returns; and more. As a result, you can end up losing money on a product even when sales volume is rising. To reduce your risk, remain vigilant about controlling the cost factors that impact profits. In this section, we lead you through the process of setting realistic profit projections, which are key to monitoring costs and running a sustainable business.

Step 1: Estimate your gross sales revenue for next 12 months

As we discuss in the previous section "Estimating sales volume," calculate your monthly sales for all products you carry and multiply by 12 to project your annual gross sales revenue for the year.

When calculating sales volume and revenues for the year, factor in supply and demand fluctuations; for example, brisk sales during the holiday seasons and slower sales during the normal times, or if you sell summer items, peak sales in the spring that slow over the summer and may be nonexistent during the fall and winter. The possibility of new product launches by competitors could also impact your sales volume and revenues.

Step 2: Calculate/estimate variable costs

Variable costs are those that are likely to change over time due to impacts from other factors, such as a distributor charging higher storage costs or a marketplace increasing its selling fees. Unexpected and significant changes in variable costs are often the root cause of business failures.

Though variable costs at Amazon are minimal, consider other possible variable costs outside Amazon that could negatively impact your profitability, such as the following:

>> Raw material prices

>> Employee/employment costs

>> Machinery, equipment, tools

>> Maintenance, upgrades, and repairs

>> Supply chain disruptions

>> Damaged goods at any point of time, such as due to severe weather or mishandling

>> Unexpected product returns or recalls, due to design or manufacturing defects or other quality aspects

Estimate all variable costs to arrive at total monthly or annual variable costs.

Step 3: Calculate gross profit

Subtract your total variable cost estimate from your gross revenue estimate for the same period to determine gross profit. Keep in mind, however, that you still have some work to do to identify your net profit, which we discuss in the following section.

Step 4: Calculate net profit

Net profit is the amount of money you get to keep after paying all expenses. To estimate your net profit, subtract from your gross profit your fixed costs over the same period. Items that contribute to fixed costs include the following:

» Employee salaries

» Rents/lease

» Utilities

» Accounting and bookkeeping

Consider calculating net profit for the month, quarter, and one year out to stay on top of these numbers. (Many large retailers project out as far as three to five years.) If you find that your net profit is falling, reevaluate your product line, the cost of sourcing products, and your fixed and variable costs to gain clarity on what's causing the decline in profits, and then address those issues.

» **Outsourcing the heavy-lifting to drop-shippers**

» **Buying at wholesale prices and charging a markup**

» **Getting products for less from foreign suppliers**

» **Hand-crafting and selling products of your very own**

Chapter **7**

Exploring Your Product Sourcing Options

Before you can sell stuff on Amazon, you need something to sell, and you need to get it for significantly less money than you can sell it for. In fancy language, acquiring products to sell at a markup constitutes *product sourcing*. Fortunately, the world has plenty of stuff to go around and plenty of product sources, including manufacturers, wholesalers, other retailers, drop-shippers (more about this in the section "Weighing the Pros and Cons of Drop-Shipping"), auctions, antique stores, factory outlets, yourself (handmade items), and more.

This chapter introduces you to common product sourcing methods, some of which you may not have considered, and presents some of the potential advantages and disadvantages of each method. We also provide guidance on how to find suppliers and take full advantage of your product sourcing options.

Mastering Retail Arbitrage

Retail arbitrage involves buying products at local retail stores, marking up the price, and selling them for a profit. For example, you head to local department store that has a bin of DVDs on clearance. You dig through the bin and find ten copies of a movie that's popular on Amazon, and you buy them for $3 each. You list them on Amazon for $19. After subtracting the cost of the item, shipping fees, and Amazon's selling fees, which come to a total of about $9, you earn a profit of $10 per disc or $100 total.

Retail arbitrage is one of the best ways for beginners to start selling on Amazon, because it provides a low-cost, low-risk entry point. In this section, we encourage you to consider the potential benefits and drawbacks of retail arbitrage, provide guidance on how to engage in retail arbitrage with brick-and-mortar and ecommerce retailers, and explain the importance of obtaining purchase orders or receipts for all products you buy.

REMEMBER

For any product you plan to resell on Amazon, be sure to have a receipt or purchase order proving you bought the product from another party. Amazon may request a purchase order to help resolve any buyer-seller disputes about the product or questions about its source.

TIP

To succeed in retail arbitrage, be prepared to diversify your product portfolio with many categories rather than sticking to a single product category. A diversified portfolio helps you manage the risks more effectively and balances your profit margins across product categories.

Buying from brick-and-mortar retailers

Large brick-and-mortar retailers (often referred to as *big-box stores*) are the obvious first choice for those seeking to engage in retail arbitrage. These stores are locally accessible and often have a large number of a variety of products on sale or clearance. Some of the larger and more popular brick-and-mortar retailers are

- » Big Lots
- » Costco
- » CVS
- » Dollar General
- » GameStop
- » Home Depot

- » Lowes
- » Marshalls
- » Meijer
- » Menards
- » Office Depot
- » Ross
- » Sears Holdings
- » Staples
- » Target
- » TJ Maxx
- » Walgreens
- » Walmart

TIP

Visit any big-box store and comb through the aisles looking for deeply discounted products, such as discontinued items. Some stores relegate these items to clearance shelves or racks, which makes your job easier. You can then purchase the items at a deep discount and sell them for close-to-regular price, especially if those items are popular but scarce in other parts of the country.

If you find a product that looks like a great deal, use the Amazon Seller Mobile App on your smartphone to scan the item's barcode. (See Chapter 16 for details on how to download, install, and navigate the Amazon Seller Mobile App.) The Mobile App displays any product that matches the bar code and is being sold on Amazon (see Figure 7-1).

If you see the matching product, tap the arrow to the right of it to display additional information about the item, including the following very useful details (see Figure 7-2):

- » Sales rank in its product category
- » Product rating
- » The lowest price the item is currently listed at
- » Estimated Amazon selling fees
- » Gross proceeds (estimated profit; tap the arrow to the right of Gross Proceeds for additional details)
- » Seller eligibility, which indicates whether you're permitted to list the product for sale

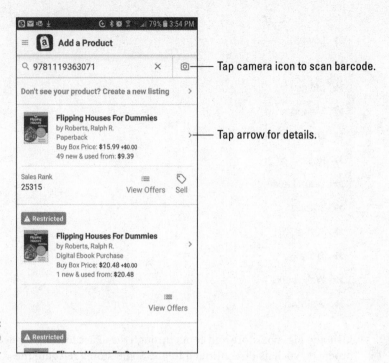

Tap camera icon to scan barcode.

Tap arrow for details.

FIGURE 7-1:
The Amazon
Seller Mobile App.

Sales rank   Product rating

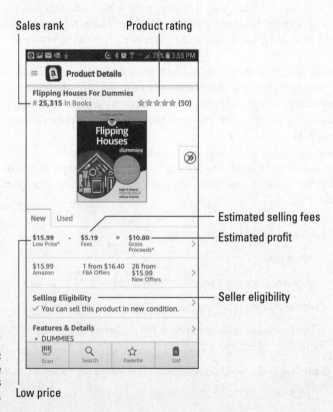

Estimated selling fees

Estimated profit

Seller eligibility

FIGURE 7-2:
Gauge the
product's
profitability.

Low price

WHY WOULD SHOPPERS BUY FROM YOU?

You may wonder why shoppers would buy from you when they could get the same product probably for less at a local big-box store. Here are a few reasons:

- **Deals and bargains vary by location.** A store in your neighborhood may have a surplus of slow-moving items in its inventory, so it offers the item at clearance prices. At the same time, at the other end of the country, demand for the product is so high that stores generally charge 20 percent more than the manufacturer's suggested retail price. As an Amazon Seller, you can offer the same product at the same price to everyone regardless of location.

- **Shoppers may prefer convenience.** Many Amazon customers are willing to pay the same or even a little more to have products delivered to their homes.

- **Some products may not be available everywhere.** Some stores don't carry certain products, or demand for the product is so high that the stores can't keep it in stock.

This information helps you determine the sales and profit potential of the product. See Chapter 6 for guidance on evaluating a product's salability and profit potential.

If the product doesn't have a current listing on Amazon, you'll be the only seller listing this product, in which case you have zero competition. Having no competition doesn't guarantee sales, but if you think you can sell the product for a price that will earn you a decent profit, you may be able to corner the market for a time.

Buying from online retailers

Online arbitrage involves buying products in one online marketplace at a low price and selling them in another marketplace for a profit. The most common forms of online arbitrage are Amazon-to-eBay, eBay-to-Amazon, and Amazon-to-other-marketplaces.

The process is similar to that of buying products from brick-and-mortar stores and selling them on Amazon. The only difference is that you can't simply scan a bar code to get most of the information needed to gauge a product's profitability. Instead, you need to do some research on your own, as we explain in Chapter 6, to estimate the potential salability and profitability of a product.

WARNING

Prior to engaging in online arbitrage, check the policies that govern the source and target markets to ensure that the method you have in mind is permitted. Here are a couple examples of policies that restrict online arbitrage:

» Amazon prohibits its Prime members from purchasing products on Amazon for the purpose of reselling them anywhere. However, if you're buying products on Amazon as a regular (not Prime) shopper, you're permitted to resell the items you buy.

» eBay prohibits its sellers from taking orders on eBay and then buying the product in another marketplace and having that seller ship the product directly to the customer.

REMEMBER

Be prepared to encounter challenges with online arbitrage that aren't likely to arise when you're using more traditional product sourcing methods, such as the following:

» **Refund delays:** When a customer requests a refund, processing it may take four to six weeks due to variations in payment cycles across marketplaces. Delays may lead to dissatisfied customers, who leave negative customer feedback about you. One way to work around this problem is to issue the customer a refund immediately and wait for reimbursement (for example, from the eBay seller who sold you the item and shipped it to your customer).

» **Uncertain inventory levels:** When you source products through retailers in other marketplaces, keeping your inventory levels updated on the target marketplace is difficult and often results in cancellations/refunds. You can avoid cancelling an order by getting the product from a different seller at a higher price, but that option will negatively impact your profits and may even result in a loss.

» **Inconsistent packaging:** If you're having eBay sellers ship products to your Amazon customers, your customers may receive products packed in eBay boxes, which can be confusing for your customers and embarrassing to you and result in a breach of Amazon's policies.

» **Evolving marketplace policies:** To improve the customer satisfaction on their platforms, Amazon and eBay (the main platforms for online arbitrage) regularly revise their policies. If you fail to keep abreast of and comply with current policies on either platform, you could have one or both of your accounts suspended.

Recognizing the importance of having a purchase order (PO) or receipt

A *purchase order (PO)* is an official document prepared and sent by a buyer to a seller indicating the types, quantities, and agreed prices for products or services. Whenever you're buying products to resell on Amazon, be sure to obtain a purchase order or receipt and save it as proof of purchase. Having proof of purchase is essential for the following purposes:

>> **Category approvals:** New sellers may not be permitted to sell products in certain categories until providing proof that the products have been sourced through approved channels. A PO or receipt provides that proof.

>> **Legal protection:** If a dispute arises over where a product was manufactured or whether the product is authentic, Amazon requests a copy of the PO or receipt to help verify the claims made in your product listing.

Beyond arbitrage, POs are essential for the following:

>> **Inventory tracking and price protection:** Amazon wants to know that its third-party sellers can fill orders and provide some price stability to customers, which also impacts your success. Having a PO, complete with pricing information and quantities, serves as proof that you have a relationship with a supplier that can ensure adequate stock at affordable prices.

>> **Inventory management:** POs provide insight into product demand based on dates and frequencies of orders, enabling you to make more accurate sales projections and prevent overstocking and understocking.

>> **Accurate transaction history:** POs provide you with a transaction history that's useful whenever you audit your inventory. With your POs and inventory reports in hand, you can identify the source of any discrepancies in your inventory records. See Chapter 16 for more about the inventory reports you can generate from within Seller Central.

Sourcing Products at Auctions and Liquidation Sales

Auctions and liquidation sales can provide great opportunities for you to snag great deals on products, assuming you know what you're doing. You should be able to find a number of local auctions, estate sales, and liquidation sales in your town or city or in nearby locations. Just search online for the terms "auction," "estate sale," or "liquidation sale" followed by your location (for example, city and state) or followed by "near me," if you're using a GPS-enabled device.

In addition to local auctions, your search is likely to turn up several websites where auctions and sales are conducted online. Of course, you can go directly to popular online auction or liquidation sales sites, such as eBay (`www.eBay.com`) and Liquidation (`www.Liquidation.com`).

Whether you're bidding in person or online, heed the following advice to improve your odds of getting potentially profitable products at a good price:

TIP

>> **Do your homework.** Know which products are in high demand on Amazon, the price they generally sell for, and whether you can list the product for sale on Amazon (eligibility).

Before you bid on or buy a product, know how you're going to sell it and for how much; in other words, know your exit strategy. People who earn lots of money buying and selling stuff always know how much something is worth *before* they buy it.

>> **Verify that the product complies with all Amazon policies.** Amazon has strict policies on product expiration, authenticity, product safety, and warranties. Any product refunds resulting from policy violations can prove to be a double whammy, because you're required to issue a refund to the buyer as well as pay Amazon's penalties for policy violations.

>> **Inspect the goods.** Whenever possible, get a look at the product(s) before bidding. Check product condition and look for any hidden damage that could prove to be costly. If you're bidding on a pallet of items, be sure the pallet has the products you want without undesirable products mixed in; check product tags to be sure.

>> **Don't exceed your maximum bid.** Prior to bidding, establish the maximum you can pay to earn the desired profit when you sell, and don't exceed that amount. If you're a competitive person, you may be driven to "win" the bidding war, but that could mean losing your shirt.

>> **If a required opening bid seems too high, wait.** Sometimes, the required opening bid may be lowered later.

>> **Pay with a credit card if possible.** Credit card payments have an extra layer of protection. If you encounter an issue with the seller or marketplace and are unable to resolve it, your credit card company may be able to resolve the issue or process a chargeback to credit your account.

TIP

Here are some additional tips for gaining the upper hand in online auctions:

>> **Deal only with reputable sellers.** Review seller profiles, ratings, and feedback.

>> **Look for auctions that end in the wee hours of the morning.** Bidding after midnight and before five or six o'clock in the morning reduces the competition.

>> **Bid in the final moments of an auction.** Bidding usually heats up near the end of an auction, so don't waste your time bidding in the early stages.

>> **Bid in odd amounts (such as a few cents) around your target price.** This technique may help you outbid others who bid in round (even) numbers.

Weighing the Pros and Cons of Drop-Shipping

Drop-shipping is a product sourcing option in which the seller takes a customer's order and passes it to the drop-shipper for order fulfillment. The drop-shipper picks, packs, and ships the product to the buyer in packaging that makes the product appear as though it came directly from the seller. It's the ultimate in no-hassle product sourcing.

Before hopping aboard the drop-ship bandwagon, carefully weigh the potential advantages and disadvantages. Here are some of the key benefits of drop-shipping:

>> **Quick and easy startup:** All you need to do is find a reliable drop-ship supplier that carries a broad selection of products.

>> **Low initial investment:** You don't have to buy inventory in bulk. Whenever you sell a product, you buy the product from the drop-ship supplier at a discount and keep the profit.

>> **Low risk:** Because you don't carry inventory, you avoid the risks of buying and storying inventory you can't sell and having products lost or damaged in storage.

>> **Broader selection of products:** Because you don't have to invest in inventory, you can afford to offer a broad selection of products.

>> **No warehouse required:** You don't need to store products in your living room or garage. The drop-shipper has its own warehouse facilities and ships the products for you.

At this point, drop-shipping may sound too good to be true, but you may change your mind after considering the potential drawbacks, including the following:

>> **High costs:** You pay for the convenience in the form of one or more of the following fees: per-item markup, shipping and handling fee, account setup fee, and monthly or annual membership fee.

>> **Little or no control over product sourcing:** Drop-shippers contract with various suppliers, some of which may not comply with Amazon policies or quality standards, which can result in disgruntled customers and policy violations charged against your account.

>> **No control over inventory:** If a drop-shipper runs out of stock of an item you sell, you're out of luck if you can't find a supplier who carries the product.

>> **No control over shipping or returns:** If the drop-shipper drops the ball on shipping the item or ships to the wrong address, you're held responsible. In addition, when a customer returns a product, you're likely to be charged a restocking fee, which complicates your relationship with the drop-shipper and your accounting.

>> **Customer dissatisfaction:** With little to no control over product quality, inventory, or shipping, you're likely to disappoint many customers and suffer the consequences — negative seller feedback, which could lead to having your seller account suspended.

Buying from Manufacturers, Distributors, and Wholesalers

Sourcing products directly from reputable suppliers is one of the best ways to build a thriving ecommerce business and ensure its long-term success. In addition to giving you more control over product quality, inventory, and shipping, teaming up with established suppliers can bring experienced partners on board to propel your success.

When you're in the market for a supplier, you can narrow your search by first deciding the type of supplier you're interested in partnering with — manufacturer, distributor, or wholesaler. In the following sections, we explain how they differ.

Deciding whether a manufacturer is best

A *manufacturer* is an individual or company that makes products for sale. Large manufacturers typically mass-produce merchandise in factories. The big benefit of sourcing directly from a manufacturer is cost; because manufacturers are at the bottom of the value chain, they sell products for less, enabling you to offer lower prices or boost your profit margins. However, manufacturers may not be the ideal choice for small retailers for the following reasons:

>> Manufacturers may have exclusive deals with brands or distributors; they may not even sell merchandise directly to retailers like you.

>> Most manufacturers stipulate a minimum order quantity (MOQ), which can be risky; you could get stuck with a large quantity of items you can't sell.

REMEMBER

Working with a manufacturer is usually best if you have a design for a product you need mass produced.

Several online sources are available for locating a manufacturer, including the following:

>> **Maker's Row** (https://makersrow.com/) connects entrepreneurs with U.S. manufacturers.

>> **Global Sourcing Specialists** (www.productgss.com) helps inventors bring their ideas to fruition from design to production.

>> **MFG.com** (www.mfg.com/) enables you to search for manufacturers, obtain competitive bids, and find the right manufacturer for your product.

WARNING

Prior to sharing your idea with a manufacturer, hire a lawyer to write up a contract that protects your intellectual property rights and includes a detailed non-compete clause and nondisclosure agreement (NDA). Have the manufacturer sign the agreement before sharing any detailed information or product designs.

Knowing when to opt for a distributor

If you track down the manufacturer that makes the product you want to sell and find out that it contracts exclusively with a select group of distributors, ask for the list of authorized distributors. You can then contact distributors on the list to determine whether they're willing to sell the product to you. By working directly with authorized distributors, you avoid the risk of listing and selling counterfeit products obtained from unauthorized dealers.

REMEMBER

A manufacturer may make a product exclusively for a brand, in which case the brand owner is likely to have a list of authorized distributors or may sell products only to authorized retailers.

Deciding when a wholesaler is best

If you're just getting your feet wet as an Amazon Seller, you probably want to source your products from one or more wholesalers. A *wholesaler* is an individual or company that buys merchandise in large quantities and sells smaller quantities to retailers at a slight markup.

REMEMBER

Wholesale prices are largely a factor of volume. Expect higher prices when you're just getting started and ordering lower quantities. As you grow your business and gain the confidence to order in larger quantities, you'll be able to negotiate lower prices.

Steering clear of posers

WARNING

Be wary of individuals who pose as wholesalers but actually serve as intermediaries between wholesalers and retailers like you. They take your order, pass it to the wholesaler, and then sell the products to you at a higher price, squeezing your margins.

Look for the following signs of fake wholesalers:

>> No contact information on the individual's or company's website.

>> No street address or a fake address.

>> You're not asked for any business documentation or sales tax info.

>> The prices seem too good to be true.

Finding reliable wholesalers

Finding reliable wholesalers can be challenging. Here are a few suggestions to steer you in the right direction:

>> Start your search on business-to-business (B2B) sites such as Alibaba.com and TradeWheel.com, where wholesalers are vetted to some degree. (See the later section "Sourcing Products from Alibaba.")

>> Research the wholesaler online and pay special attention to customer ratings and reviews.

>> Ask for and check business references to find out what other retailers have to say about working with the wholesaler.

>> If you know any other online sellers, ask them about the wholesalers they use, or visit online seller or business forums and look for discussions about wholesalers or suppliers.

SELLING BRANDED OR UNBRANDED PRODUCTS?

When sourcing products, another decision you need to make is whether to sell branded or unbranded (generic) products or both. When making the decision, consider the following factors:

- Generic products cost less, giving you a potential opportunity to increase sales volume and/or improve your profit margin.

- Branded products tend to be higher quality because the manufacturer invests more in materials, manufacturing, and quality control to protect the brand's reputation.

- Customers may care more about price than quality/brand or vice versa depending on the product type.

- Selling branded products can backfire if you knowingly or unknowingly source knock-offs and list them as authentic.

- Shoppers who knowingly buy generic products are less likely to complain as long as the product is decent and serves their purpose.

- Building a sustainable business and earning loyal customers by selling generic products is difficult if not impossible.

- Generic products generally are more suitable for sellers who offer seasonal products during the holidays when shoppers are looking for less expensive items to present as gifts.

When you find a wholesaler who seems to be a good match, be sure to get answers to the following questions:

>> Do you have any MOQs or minimum spend (on the purchase of multiple products)?

>> How often and in what way do you communicate information on product updates, product discontinuations, and other key issues with your retail clients?

>> Am I required to sign a contract? (If the answer is yes, obtain a copy of the contract for you and your attorney to review.)

>> What is your order fulfillment period and what are the logistics involved? If you're registered for Fulfillment by Amazon (FBA), ask whether the wholesaler can ship products directly to Amazon fulfillment centers and what you need to do on your end to facilitate that process.

>> What is the total price and what factors into that price, such as production costs, shipping and handling fees, and any other fees not yet mentioned?

Also, before contracting with a wholesaler, order samples of products you're interested in selling. Getting your hands on actual products is a great quality assurance precaution. Most suppliers charge for product samples. As long as the price is reasonable, you're wise to order product samples, so you can check product quality before ordering a large quantity.

Sourcing Products from Alibaba

Alibaba is a Chinese ecommerce behemoth serving both consumers and businesses. It has revolutionized product sourcing, enabling hundreds of thousands of businesses across the globe to access millions of products at prices previously available only to big-box retailers. To optimize your success as an Amazon Seller, we strongly encourage you to become familiar with Alibaba, where you'll often find the best deals.

Start by conducting some basic product research, as Chapter 6 explains, to answer the following questions:

>> What kind of products do you want to sell — clothing, tools, toys, household products?

>> Which products have the greatest sales and profit potential?

» What price are consumers willing to pay for each product?

» How much will it cost you to sell each product? Consider the product's cost, Amazon selling fees, and any FBA fees.

When you have a pretty good idea of a product you want to sell, visit Alibaba.com, open the drop-down list to the left of the Search box, and choose Suppliers (see Figure 7-3). Click in the Search box, type a brief description of the product, and press the Search button. (The Search box also has a camera icon you can tap to search for a product by uploading an image of it.)

FIGURE 7-3:
Search for
suppliers on
Alibaba.

Alibaba displays a long list of suppliers that sell products like the one you searched for. Use the filters above the list of suppliers and those on the left side of the page to narrow your search. You can narrow your search by product category, supplier type and location, company size (by revenue or number of employees), and more.

As shown in Figure 7-3, for each supplier in the list, Alibaba displays its name, how long it has been in business, and other details to help you make an informed choice of supplier. Details about each supplier include the following:

» **Badges:** A supplier may have one or more of the following badges to indicate its credentials:

● **Trade Assurance** indicates the supplier supports Alibaba's Trade Assurance service, which protects your order from payment to delivery.

- **Gold Supplier** indicates the supplier supports Trade Assurance and has passed one or more onsite checks to verify the business type and commercial or industrial capabilities. The Gold Supplier badge gives the supplier more credibility, but it doesn't guarantee product quality or authenticity.

- **Verified Supplier** indicates the supplier has been assessed and certified by independent third-party entities via online or offline methods. Again, this badge gives suppliers more credibility but doesn't guarantee product quality or authenticity.

» **Transaction Level:** The more diamonds a supplier has the greater the number of transactions it has on the Alibaba platform.

» **Response Rate:** This metric indicates the percentage of buyers who have received a response within 24 hours of contacting the supplier.

» **Transactions:** This metric indicates the number of transactions and their total dollar value over the past six months.

If you need additional information from a supplier, press the Contact Supplier button for the chosen supplier and use the resulting form to compose and send your question.

To obtain quotes from a number of suppliers, submit a request for quote (RFQ). Return to Alibaba's homepage, open the Services menu, select Submit RFQ, and use the resulting form to enter the details of your RFQ, including the product name and category, quantity, and terms. Within hours and over the course of the coming days, you'll receive quotes from suppliers. You can manage your RFQs by going to My Alibaba and choosing Manage RFQ.

As you evaluate prospective suppliers, follow these best practices:

» Arrange a phone call or videoconference with the supplier before placing an order, so you can get a feel for how trustworthy the supplier is.

» Ask questions to obtain all the details you need to make a well-informed choice. Legitimate suppliers won't hesitate to provide the requested details.

» Visit the supplier's warehouse, if possible. If an in-person visit isn't possible, request a video tour of the facility.

Big suppliers may have warehouses in multiple countries to avoid the hassles and headaches of dealing with customs and taxes. Ask the supplier if it has a warehouse in your country that would be more convenient for you to visit.

» Search the warehouse and business location online to verify their existence.

WARNING

Beware of fraudsters, even on Alibaba:

>> Compare the supplier's name and address on its website and any correspondence you receive from the supplier with the name and address on Alibaba.

>> Verify the supplier's email address and website. Reputable suppliers often have email addresses associate with the domain instead of "google.com" or "yahoo.com."

>> Think twice before moving forward on any offer that seems to be too good to be true; it probably is.

>> Avoid suppliers who ask for early payment, because fraudsters often want to grab the money and disappear. Legitimate suppliers won't ask for payment prior to signing an agreement.

Also, before contracting with a supplier, order product samples. Getting your hands on actual products is a great quality assurance precaution.

After deciding on a supplier, you're ready to start negotiations and work out the logistics, such as agreeing to payment terms and methods, customs and import process, and any arrangements to ship products to Amazon fulfillment centers. See Chapter 8 for details.

Finding Suppliers at Tradeshows

A great way to find reputable suppliers is to attend ecommerce tradeshows, where suppliers gather to sell their products and services to online retailers like you. Don't underestimate the importance of tradeshows in this era of online suppliers and directories like Alibaba. For various reasons, online retailers who attend tradeshows tend to be more successful than those who don't.

Tradeshows deliver many of the same benefits as online supplier directories like Alibaba with the additional benefit of enabling you to meet suppliers in person. Unfortunately, tradeshows run for a limited number of days and some attract hundreds of thousands of visitors, so you can waste considerable time just finding your way around. To get the most out of a tradeshow, prepare in advance. Here are a few tips:

>> **Register early.** Most tradeshows let you preregister online, so you don't have to wait in a long line to register on opening day.

>> **Filter the exhibitors list.** Download and print the list of participating suppliers and major exhibitors and highlight those that interest you most.

>> **Survey the tradeshow map.** Highlight the exhibition halls and booths that interest you most and plot an efficient route so you don't waste time wandering aimlessly through hallways and rooms.

>> **Introduce yourself to suppliers before the tradeshow.** Get past the preliminaries so you can engage in more productive talks in person and have more time to scope out other suppliers.

>> **Be prepared.** Bring the following:

TIP

- A thick stack of business cards.

  Create an alternate email address for tradeshows, so that your primary email account isn't inundated with unsolicited promotional messages. Carry some business cards with the alternate email address on them.

- A smartphone, notebook, or tablet computer with a note-taking app to capture ideas, tips, and crucial details of any meetings.

- Chargers for your electronic devices.

- Power and outlet converters if the destination country's power service differs from that of your home country.

- A virtual private network (VPN) service, which enables secure connections over public Wi-Fi and enables you to connect to sites that may be blocked in the destination country. (Practice with the VPN before your trip to make sure it's working smoothly and you understand how to use it.)

To avoid wasting your time and the time of prospective suppliers, ask questions specifically worded to weed out suppliers who can't meet your needs, such as the following:

>> Can you supply me with <specific product>?

>> Are you a manufacturer, distributor, or wholesaler?

>> Do you export to retailers in <my country>?

>> Are you able to ship directly to Amazon fulfillment centers?

>> Are you equipped to make custom or private label products?

>> What is your MOQ, if any?

>> What is your estimated price with all fees included?

REMEMBER

Your time is limited, so don't waste it engaging in unfruitful discussions with suppliers who can't meet your needs. If the answer to any of the questions eliminates the supplier as a candidate, move on to the next supplier on your list.

Here are a few additional tips for successfully navigating a tradeshow without making any major mistakes:

» Don't make snap purchase decisions, especially if you feel pressured to do so. You're on a reconnaissance mission to collect information. Leave the decisions for later.

» Don't start the negotiation process. Get ballpark quotes, MOQs, and contact information and move on.

» Photograph products, booths, or people to help you recall later what you learned at the tradeshow and whom you need to follow up with.

» After the tradeshow but while they're still fresh in your mind, review your notes, photographs, and contact information and organize them for following up with suppliers.

» Follow up with any suppliers you're interested in partnering with.

Making and Selling Your Own Products: Amazon Handmade and Custom

Amazon features a couple product categories that allow you to source your own products — either by crafting them by hand or enabling shoppers to customize their own products. In this section, we bring you up to speed on these two product-sourcing methods.

Selling your own hand-crafted products

If you're one of the lucky few whose passionate creativity merges with an entrepreneurial zeal, Amazon provides the perfect platform for you to deliver hand-crafted love to customers. As Amazon states so succinctly:

We empower Artisans with the tools necessary to showcase their products to Customers around the world. Together we are growing craft communities and successful businesses.

To build a thriving community of artisans, encourage their creativity, and provide them the financial means to support their crafts, Amazon's handmade category offers the following benefits:

» **Artisan only:** Amazon carefully screens applicants to ensure that only artisans are allowed to list products in the handmade category, thus eliminating competition from commercial products.

» **Flat fee:** Artisans pay a flat 15 percent fee on every sale, no monthly fees or referral fees.

» **Artisan profile:** Artisans can create their own profiles each with a unique URL to help shoppers find them on Amazon.

» **A sizeable community of shoppers hungry for handcrafted products:** Shoppers are ready to pay a premium for the quality, handmade products, paving way for earning higher profit margins.

» **No Universal Product Code (UPC) required:** This removes one of the hassles of selling products on Amazon.

» **Customer customizations allowed:** You can add fields to your product listing that enable shoppers to request product customizations, such as having their name added to a product.

» **Fulfillment by Amazon (FBA):** You can ship products to Amazon fulfillment centers to have orders packed and shipped by Amazon. Doing so enables you to display the Amazon Prime Badge on your listings, which is likely to boost sales.

» **Sell across North America:** You can sell products in Canada, the United States, and Mexico all from a single account.

REMEMBER

Products must meet strict specifications to qualify as *handmade*. Every handmade product must be created, altered, and assembled almost entirely by hand (hand tools and light machinery are permitted). Mass-produced items don't qualify. For more about the handmade eligibility criteria, open the Search bar at the top of Seller Central, search for Amazon Handmade Terms, and select Amazon Handmade Terms.

To get a glimpse of the types of products sold under this category, log in to the Amazon shopping site, open the main menu (upper-left corner of the page), choose Handmade, and then All Handmade. For more details about the program and a link to register as an artisan, visit https://services.amazon.com/handmade/handmade.html.

Selling customized products on Amazon

Amazon's custom category enables you to offer products that are customized or personalized to the customer's specifications. This is a great category for listing personalized gifts for special occasions, such as Valentine's Day, Mother's Day, and Father's Day.

As of this writing, you can offer shoppers the following customization options:

>> **Text customization:** Shoppers can add text to an item and select from color and font options you specify. Text customization is great for engraving, embroidery, printing, painting, and more.

>> **Image customization:** Shoppers can upload an image or logo and have it applied to the product, such as a coffee mug, T-shirt, smartphone case, or pillow. They can also add text to display in the foreground.

>> **Product configurations:** You can add to your product listing a drop-down list of options that customers can select to build their own product.

For more details about the custom category and instructions on how to register to have the Custom feature set applied to your Professional Seller account, visit `https://services.amazon.com/custom.html`. (Note that only Professional Sellers are permitted to list products in this category.)

Chapter **8**

Evaluating and Negotiating with Suppliers

On Amazon and in other ecommerce marketplaces, you're only as successful as your suppliers are affordable and reliable. You can't deliver quality products at competitive prices to your customers on the promised delivery dates unless your suppliers deliver low-cost, high-quality products to you according to the agreed-upon schedule.

To optimize your success as an ecommerce retailer, you need to choose suppliers who share your commitment to customer satisfaction, then work closely together to meet or exceed your customers' expectations. In this chapter, we explain how to do just that.

REMEMBER

Finding and negotiating with top-notch suppliers is one of the keys to building a successful Amazon business. Your success hinges on your suppliers' ability to manufacture or procure quality merchandise at affordable prices and replenish inventory on a timely basis. A Fulfillment-by-Amazon-friendly supplier is an added benefit.

Deciding Whether to Use Domestic or Foreign Suppliers or Both

The global economy provides you with a broad selection of suppliers that extends far beyond the borders of the country(ies) in which you sell products, giving you access to a wider variety of quality products at competitive prices. However, importing products from suppliers in other countries isn't always best for business. When deciding between domestic suppliers or their across-the-border counterparts, consider a variety of factors, including shipping costs and times, customs inspections, language barriers, and more.

In this section, we highlight the potential benefits and drawbacks of working with suppliers in other countries versus those in your own country, so you have a general idea of whether to focus your efforts on working with domestic or foreign suppliers. Many sellers choose to work with a combination of the two, evaluating each supplier based on its own merits.

Recognizing the pros and cons of working with domestic suppliers

The major benefit of working with domestic suppliers is that you have a lot in common with them:

» **Location:** Proximity to you and your customers offers several advantages, including the following:

- **Better quality control:** You have more freedom to check out local manufacturing operations and inspect products.

- **Improved inventory control:** You may be able to reduce your inventory-carrying costs by ordering in smaller batches and holding less product in inventory.

- **Increased responsiveness:** Local supplies are likely to respond more quickly and effectively to any problems that arise.

- **Improved supply chain efficiency and lower shipping costs:** You avoid customs, import taxes, port charges, and duties, and avoid having to ship products great distances.

- **Fresher products:** If you sell time- or temperature-sensitive products, sourcing from nearby suppliers can help ensure products are fresh.

» **Jurisdiction:** By operating in the same country, you're generally familiar with the rules and regulations suppliers must follow. You're at less risk of unknowingly teaming up with a business that operates illegally or unethically. More importantly, if you have a supplier in a foreign country manufacturing a product you invented, you may have less protection over your intellectual property rights; in other words, the supplier may be freer to steal your invention or idea.

>> **Language:** Because you and your domestic supplier probably speak the same language, you're less likely to have disagreements or miscommunications that can negatively impact your business.

>> **Currency:** By using a common currency, you avoid the complexities of having to convert prices from one currency to another.

>> **Customers:** Sourcing products domestically enables you to market the products as being manufactured domestically, which may provide an advantage over sellers who source products from foreign manufacturers.

The potential drawbacks of working with domestic suppliers include the following:

>> **Higher prices:** Suppliers in other countries may be able to offer similar quality products at a lower price for various reasons, such a being able to operate in a jurisdiction with less stringent workplace regulations.

>> **Limited product variety:** Domestic suppliers may not have access to the products you want to sell.

>> **Limited production capacity:** Foreign suppliers may have greater production capacity and hence be better equipped to fill large orders.

Weighing the pros and cons of working with foreign suppliers

Foreign suppliers may offer benefits over their domestic counterparts, including the following:

>> **Lower prices for comparable quality:** Suppliers that operate in countries with fewer regulations and lower pay can manufacture similar products for significantly less money and pass the savings along to retailers and their customers.

>> **Broader product selection:** Foreign suppliers often have access to products that aren't available from domestic suppliers.

>> **Greater production capacity:** Some countries have much larger manufacturing plants than others, enabling them to fill large orders faster and offer deeper discounts on purchases of large quantities.

Although foreign suppliers may offer a greater variety of products at lower prices, consider their potential drawbacks:

>> **Language and cultural barriers:** Communicating with foreign suppliers may pose a challenge.

>> **Distance:** Performing due diligence with suppliers in distant countries is a challenge. You may need to rely on third-party service providers to vet foreign suppliers for you. In addition, distance increases the difficulty and costs of overseeing manufacturing processes and quality assurance.

>> **Negative public relations (PR):** Depending on the supplier and the country in which it operates, having a business relationship with a foreign supplier or using foreign suppliers when domestic suppliers are struggling and unemployment is high could generate negative PR.

>> **Different currencies:** When suppliers use a different currency than you're accustomed to, calculating and comparing prices among different suppliers becomes more challenging.

>> **No guarantee of intellectual property (IP) rights:** Given the weak IP laws in certain countries, protecting your valuable product ideas and designs can be very difficult and costly. After hiring a foreign supplier, you may start to see lower priced counterfeit products on the market that look suspiciously like the one you invented.

TIP

International suppliers are easy to find on B2B ecommerce sites such as Alibaba.com, which features more than six million products from more than 35,000 suppliers in various countries. See Chapter 7 for details on how to find suppliers.

Selecting Suppliers with the Right Stuff

Whether you decide to use domestic or foreign suppliers (or a mix of the two), you need to vet each supplier under consideration to ensure that your suppliers can deliver the products and the level of customer service to needed to meet or exceed your customers' expectations. In this section, we highlight key criteria to consider when evaluating suppliers.

REMEMBER

To avoid future misunderstandings, conflicts, and business disruptions, invest some time and effort in evaluating your supplier options. Avoid the common temptation to choose a supplier based solely on price.

Gauging experience and expertise

Supplier experience and expertise in a certain product or product line may be the most important consideration. Look for manufacturers of a single product or product line — athletic shoes, sewing machines, mattress pads, oil diffusers, whatever. Suppliers that offer a broad selection of products are more likely to be traders or vendors, not manufacturers. Contact the supplier and ask the following questions:

>> **What products do you manufacture at your own facilities?** Look for suppliers that manufacture the products they offer. Otherwise, you're likely to get lesser quality products with additional markups.

>> **Into which markets/countries do you export most of your products?** This question enables you to gauge the supplier's experience doing business in your country without disclosing which country you're in. If the supplier ships products to your country, and you're concerned about certain compliance issues, ask follow-up questions to ensure that the supplier is familiar with those issues.

>> **What quality control issues do your customers most commonly complain about?** This question gives the supplier an opportunity to be transparent about quality control issues at its facilities and how it addresses those issues. If a supplier seems evasive in answering this question, it may be hiding something.

TIP

Ask for customer references. Though most suppliers refuse to share customer information, if you can get references, speaking with the customers can provide you with excellent insight into the supplier's performance and any quality control issues.

>> **What quality assurance standards and procedures do you have in place?** The purpose of this question is for you to get a sense of the supplier's ability to detect and correct production issues as early as possible in the production line. This ability is crucial for minimizing product defects and keeping production costs low.

Ensuring clear communication

Whether you're working with domestic or foreign suppliers, clear communication is essential for coordinating your efforts and addressing any issues that arise. Poor communication can lead to delays and mistakes with orders — for example, receiving the wrong product or having a product delivered to the wrong location. Look for suppliers who meet the following criteria:

>> **Communicates in your preferred language:** The supplier's ability to communicate with you in a language you understand, both in spoken and written language, is essential.

>> **Is readily available:** You should be able to get in touch with a supplier during regular business hours. If you leave a message, the supplier should get back with you within 24 hours (preferably much sooner), via email, text message, or phone call.

>> **Is transparent:** Try to work with suppliers who are honest and open and admit their mistakes. If a supplier gets defensive, blames others for mistakes, or makes excuses, consider choosing a different supplier.

>> **Is understanding/empathetic:** Look for suppliers who understand the challenges you face in filling orders and serving your customers, so you don't have to explain why certain issues are so important to you. The best suppliers anticipate your needs and concerns and address them before you feel the need to bring them up.

Sizing up a supplier's reputation

A supplier's past performance and reputation are generally good indicators of future performance and whether the supplier will be a reliable partner for a long time to come. In this section, we describe qualities to consider for evaluating a supplier's reputation.

WARNING

Don't rely solely on what you find on a supplier's website (or whether it even has a website) to choose or rule out a candidate. Small, independent suppliers may not have a website, whereas a con artist can easily build a website to make a fake company appear legitimate. Contact the supplier yourself and check its references from other retailers and sources (such as supplier directories).

Longevity

Contact the supplier and ask how long the company has been in business and specifically how long it has been manufacturing the products you're interested in sourcing. A supplier that's been in the business for several years is more likely than a recent startup to remain in the business for years to come.

TIP

Participation in major tradeshows is a great indication of a supplier's longevity and positive reputation. Suppliers that participate in these tradeshows are generally well established.

Ethical considerations

Over the past few years, some major brands have been embarrassed and even punished by customers for the unethical practices of their suppliers, such as using child labor or having employees working in unhealthy or unsafe conditions. In some cases, customers have called for boycotts to pressure brands to take corrective action. In addition to boycotts, the negative publicity often grabs the attention of regulatory agencies that have the power to shut down the suppliers, which can lead to disruptions in the supply chain.

Whenever possible, prior to choosing a supplier, tour its manufacturing facilities and talk to employees. Look for any evidence of unethical or unfair business practices, such as the following:

>> Child labor

>> Unhealthy or unsafe working conditions

>> Forced overtime

>> Sexual harassment

>> Discrimination based on race, ethnicity, gender, age, and so on

Regulatory compliance

Short of committing to ethical business practices, every supplier should comply with the laws of the land in both its home country and any countries in which it does business. Any failure of one of your suppliers to comply with regulatory requirements, especially in transactions that directly involve you, could lead to disruptions in your supply chain or even get you into legal trouble.

To assess a supplier's commitment to regulatory compliance, obtain the following information/documentation from the supplier:

>> Tax identification

>> Business registration information

>> Production facility certifications for any sensitive products such as medical products, food items, skincare or children products — documents such as FCC Declaration of Conformity, Restriction of Hazardous Substances (RoHS), Good Manufacturing Practice (GMP), General Certificate of Conformity (GCC), Children's Product Certificate, and Model Toxics in Packaging Legislation

>> Any other documentation the business may be required by law to have to do business in its country or your country or to deal in a certain product you sell

THE RISE OF THE VALUES-BASED CONSUMER

Consumers are becoming increasingly sensitive to the values that businesses embrace and practice, so consider a supplier's values when making your choice. Values that typically rank high among consumers include the following:

- Environmentally friendly business practices
- Community giving
- Social responsibility
- Diversity, equity, and inclusion (DEI)

You may be judged by the company you keep, so perform your due diligence when choosing suppliers to work with and brands to sell. You don't want other establishments' problems and shortcomings to reflect negatively on you.

Assessing a supplier's responsiveness

Responsiveness is the quality of reacting quickly and positively, which is an important quality in a supplier. You want a supplier that's responsive not only when you're ready to place an order, but also when you encounter delayed deliveries, product defects, compliance issues, and other problems. Responsive suppliers:

>> Are easy to contact via phone, text, or email

>> Respond withing minutes or hours, not days or weeks

>> Listen and ask questions to fully understand a situation

>> Solve problems and collaborate to achieve the best outcome for you and your customers

TIP

The best suppliers are open to third-party quality checks and even help third-party inspectors with the product documentation and relevant processes during the audits. If you request a third-party quality-control check, and the supplier refuses or is reluctant to grant your request, that's a red flag indicating the supplier is probably hiding something.

Comparing prices

When evaluating suppliers, a key consideration is price. Lower prices enable you to compete more effectively with other Amazon Sellers while improving your profit margins.

TIP

When comparing prices, look beyond the price of the items you want to source to consider all costs involved, including production costs, shipping costs, and Fulfillment by Amazon (FBA) fees. The following sections explain the costs you need to consider.

Product and production costs

When comparing the prices of a certain product from different suppliers, try to understand the reasons behind the price differences. Suppliers that offer lower prices may be able to do so due to one or more of the following factors:

>> Negotiating lower prices for raw materials

>> Using lower quality materials that cost less

>> Paying workers lower wages

>> Operating in jurisdictions with fewer regulations

>> Using more efficient manufacturing processes or equipment

>> Offering discounts are larger production runs

By knowing the underlying factors that enable a supplier to offer the same product for a lower price, you can make a well-informed decision of whether paying a lower price is worth whatever you may be required to give up.

Shipping and related fees

When comparing prices from different suppliers, consider all the costs of moving the items from the supplier to you or to Amazon fulfillment centers. These costs include shipping, handling, and any customs fees. Find out the total cost of shipping and related fees and who's responsible for paying them — you or the supplier.

Some suppliers may be able to offer lower shipping and related fees than others due to the following factors:

>> **Location:** For example, domestic suppliers don't pay customs fees and can generally ship items faster and for less by ground because they operate in the

same country. Some foreign suppliers may be able to save on shipping costs because they're closer to a major shipping port.

>> **Labor costs:** Some suppliers may have lower labor costs than others, enabling them to charge less in processing or handling fees.

>> **Shipping volume:** Suppliers that ship a large volume of products often negotiate for better shipping rates and can pass these savings along to you.

FBA fees

A great way to slash your overall costs and save yourself valuable time is to have your suppliers prepare and ship products directly to Amazon fulfillment centers instead of to you. Many suppliers, domestic and foreign, offer this service. Of course, they charge for it, but they can probably do it for less than it would cost you to do it yourself.

Ask your prospective suppliers if they're able to ship directly to Amazon fulfillment centers and if they're familiar with and have the processes in place to comply with Amazon packaging guidelines.

WARNING

Choose only reputable, reliable suppliers who have an excellent track record with FBA. When suppliers ship directly to Amazon fulfillment centers, you lose your ability to check shipments from the supplier for defects in products and packaging. You're placing your trust in the supplier.

Negotiating Prices and Terms

Prior to signing any formal agreement or contract with a supplier, negotiate the pricing and terms. Although suppliers may present their prices and terms as a take-it-or-leave-it offer, they're usually open to negotiation. They don't want to leave money on the table and would prefer negotiation over losing an additional source of business.

In this section, we provide guidance on how to negotiate with suppliers to improve the price and terms they initially offer.

Prepping for negotiation

Prior to contacting a supplier to open the negotiating process, do your homework:

>> Write a list of price and terms you want to discuss, including price, quality expectations, shipping and delivery costs, and FBA fees. If you're negotiating with a manufacturer to produce a unique product you developed, you'll also want to include intellectual property rights, non-disclosure, and non-compete agreements in your discussions and contract.

>> Prioritize the items on the list from most to least important, so you have some criteria to guide your trade-off decisions. You should have some idea going into negotiations which terms you're willing and unwilling to negotiate and to what degree.

>> Write a list of your strengths, such as high-volume orders, the likelihood of repeat orders, your plans for expansion, and so on. Think in terms of what you bring to the table to sweeten the deal for the supplier.

REMEMBER

Don't make price the sole or top criteria for negotiation. What you get for your money (the total value of the deal) is more important. As you write a list of terms to negotiate and prioritize the items on your list, be sure to consider the following terms:

>> **Product value:** The quality of the product you're getting for the price quoted.

>> **Shipping and delivery terms:** The supplier's ability to deliver the products to the target destination on time, in good shape, and affordably.

>> **Deposit and payment terms:** Flexible deposit and payment terms can enable you to gain access to inventory you might not otherwise be able to afford.

WARNING

Never agree to pay 100 percent up front. If you're hiring a company to manufacture a branded product you own the rights to, you typically pay a 30 to 50 percent deposit with the remainder due after the products have been manufactured and passed inspection.

>> **Manufacturer's warranty:** To protect you from having to cover the cost of returns due to defective or poor quality products from the manufacturer.

Brushing up on effective negotiating tactics

Negotiation is more art than science, but certain tactics have proven to be effective in getting suppliers to give more than they initially offer. Here are a few negotiating tactics that are useful whether you're a novice or seasoned negotiator:

>> Don't accept the first offer. Always make a counteroffer.

>> If a supplier offers an unbelievably low price, dig deeper to find out why. If a deal seems too good to be true, it probably is. Maybe the supplier is compromising on product quality or using substandard materials. Perhaps the supplier is cutting costs by not offering a warranty.

>> If a price seems high, present concrete reasons the price should be lower, such as demand for the product is dropping, the cost of materials has dropped recently, or other suppliers are offering the same product for less.

>> Be willing to give on terms that are less important for you and more important for the supplier in exchange for terms that are more important for you and less important for the supplier.

>> If a product has features or functionality your customers don't need or use, ask the supplier if the product can be manufactured for less by removing those features or functionality.

>> Ask whether the supplier offers discounts for high-volume or repeat orders.

WARNING

Don't squeeze the supplier too much to the extent that the negotiator backs out or makes hidden compromises, such as secretly reducing product quality. Demanding cutthroat prices can also result in a supplier feeling unhappy about the relationship and providing second-rate customer service as a result or cause the supplier to start looking for better customers to replace you.

Obtaining a purchase order contract

After negotiations, have your attorney prepare a purchase order contract detailing the agreed upon price and terms, which both parties must sign. Be sure your purchase order contract contains the following:

>> Product specifications

>> Inspection/testing requirements (for example, arrangements for third-party product inspections during and after a product run)

>> Confidentiality/intellectual property agreements (if applicable), including language to protect branding, logos, and other trademarked items

>> Detailed pricing structure, including discounts for orders of different quantities

>> Deposit and payment terms, including deposit amount (if any), when payment in full is required, and method of payment

Telegraphic transfer (T/T), which is a direct wire transfer from one bank to another, is typical. Consider arranging payments through an escrow company, which holds the funds until the supplier meets its responsibilities under the contract — for example, completing the production run and successfully passing inspection of the products.

>> Packaging and labeling requirements, if any, including any FBA requirements

>> Shipping and delivery terms, including costs, which party is responsible for covering the costs, where products are to be shipped, and estimated time from order to delivery

>> Manufacturer warranty, if applicable

>> Any agreements related to after-sales services and product support such as requirements to service or repair products or provide replacement parts or software updates

>> Any penalties or compensation due to each party in the event that the other party fails to comply with the terms of the agreement

>> Language to establish the jurisdiction in which the terms of the agreement are to be enforced

Get any exclusive agreements in writing, clearly stating the end use of the products and any and all after-sales services and support provided by the supplier. Amazon will require these agreements to help field any customer complaints or claims that challenge your intellectual property rights.

We strongly encourage you to hire a qualified business lawyer to write up your agreement or review the agreement presented by the supplier before you sign anything. That way, if a disagreement arises between you and the supplier, you have an attorney available who's been involved since the start.

3
Getting Down to the Business of Selling

Discover what you need to accomplish to own the buy box — to have your products placed where shoppers will see them.

Create product listings that improve your product placement and convince shoppers to choose your product over your competitors' offerings.

Discover a variety of methods for boosting sales, including Sponsored Product ads on Amazon, external marketing options (Facebook, Instagram, YouTube, and so on), email marketing, and promotional deals.

Increase your sales volume and profit margins through marketing and advertising.

Find out how to deliver the level of customer service that earns you and your products high customer rankings, stellar reviews, and premier product placement.

Build and manage your own Amazon Store to give your loyal customers a convenient place to shop and start building your own brand recognition.

Maintain inventory in a way that reduces your overhead while ensuring timely product delivery to customers, so your product placement doesn't suffer from having insufficient quantities in stock.

Chapter **9**

Listing Products for Sale on Amazon

To be successful on Amazon, you need to do everything right — product selection, pricing, shipping, product listings, returns, customer service, and more. Perhaps the biggest make-or-break item on that list is the product listing. No doubt about it, competition is stiff. For many products, you can even expect to be competing against Amazon! To outcompete your competitors, you must compose product listings that earn a top ranking and catch shoppers' interests, and your listings need to earn premium placement. In this chapter, we explain how to make that happen.

Here you discover how to win (and own) the all-important buy box, procure product photos that sell, compose superior product listings, and boost your product ranking with savvy keyword selection. With this chapter in hand and a commitment to impeccable customer service, you have just about everything you need to be a top seller on Amazon.

Knowing What's Required to Own the Buy Box

The Amazon buy box (also referred to as the featured offer) is the rectangle at the top right of each product detail page that contains the buttons Add to Cart and Buy Now. When you list a product for sale on Amazon, you're usually competing with other sellers that carry the same product, including Amazon, to occupy (win) the buy box. Why is every seller on Amazon obsessed with winning the buy box? Several reasons, including the following:

» More than 90 percent of all Amazon sales are through the buy box.

» Buy box placement earns you credibility and trust. Amazon customers associate buy box placement with legitimate, trusted sellers who are compliant with all Amazon policies. Buy box winners are considered to deliver the highest quality products and top-notch customer service.

» On the mobile version of product details page, other sellers aren't listed, so if you don't win the buy box, you have very little chance of selling that product. With mobile shopping on the rise, winning the buy box is increasingly important.

» Losing the buy box is a huge handicap because it results in lost sales, velocity, organic growth, and ranking. Most importantly, all your sponsored ads associated with the product stop running the moment the buy box is lost. So virtually, all your sales channels are impacted in one way or the other if you lose the buy box.

» If you're running sponsored brand ads (for example, for brand promotion) and you lose the buy box, your sponsored brand ad begins to redirect shoppers to product pages where the seller who occupies the buy box is likely to make the sale. In other words, your sponsored ads are helping to sell the product for a competitor!

REMEMBER

The buy box can make or break a business on Amazon.

Now that you're clear about what the buy box is, why winning it is so important, and why losing it can be so devastating, you're ready to find out more about buy box eligibility and how to earn consistent buy box placement.

Ensuring buy box eligibility

Because Amazon has been committed, since its inception, to being "Earth's most customer-centric company," not all sellers are eligible to win the buy box. To be eligible to earn the buy box, you must meet the following criteria as a seller:

>> **Must be a Professional Seller.** Only Professional Sellers are eligible for buy box placement. Individual sellers aren't.

>> **Listing must be buy box eligible.** To check buy box eligibility, open the Inventory menu and select Manage Inventory, click the Preferences button, click Buy Box Eligible (under Column Display), and then scroll to the bottom and click the Save Changes button. Now when you open the Inventory menu and choose Manage Inventory, your product list will have a column displaying whether each product is eligible for the buy box.

>> **Product must be new.** Used products aren't eligible for the buy box.

>> **Product must be available.** Out-of-stock items aren't eligible.

Meeting the quality metrics for winning the buy box

Buy box eligibility alone doesn't guarantee that you win the buy box. Amazon uses a super-secret algorithm that determines which seller wins the buy box. The algorithm weighs a variety of price, product, and customer service metrics to make its determination. (See the later section "Harnessing the power of the A9 algorithm" for details.) In this section, we suggest several techniques for improving your chances of winning the buy box.

Amazon holds the key to the criteria and algorithm that decide the buy box winner, and these are subject to change at any time, making it difficult to game the system. Best practice for consistently winning the buy box is to maintain the highest standards in regard to product quality, pricing, customer service, and business ethics.

Check your listing quality

To check the quality of your product listings for any issues that may be causing Amazon to suppress your listings or prevent them from appearing in the buy box, take the following steps:

1. **Log on to Seller Central, open the Inventory menu, and select Manage Inventory.**

   The Manage Inventory page includes links to all product listings, including any suppressed listings (due to quality issues) and listing enhancements.

2. **Skim the Status column, looking for any yellow triangles or similar notation indicating a problematic listing.**

3. **Address any issues indicated in the Status column preventing the listing from qualifying for buy box consideration.**

To quickly check for suppressed product listings, open the Inventory menu, select Inventory Reports, Listing Quality, and Suppressed Listings Report. This report contains a comprehensive list of product listings that require your attention.

Offer products through Fulfilled by Amazon (FBA)

Amazon is committed to customer satisfaction, especially among its Prime customers, so Amazon wants to be sure its sellers have products in stock before awarding a seller the buy box.

If you're a new seller and are packing and shipping orders yourself, Amazon has no way of knowing for certain whether you have sufficient inventory to fulfill orders. However, if you list a product through FBA, Amazon closely monitors your inventory and, if the product is in stock, will list it as a prime product, which is one key to winning the buy box.

To significantly improve your chances of winning the buy box, fulfill orders through FBA instead of shipping them yourself. (See Chapter 10 for more about FBA.)

Practice transparent and competitive pricing

Price is a key factor in awarding the buy box. When you price a product, make sure your price meets the following criteria:

>> **Transparent:** Include everything in your price, such as the shipping fee.

>> **Competitive:** Selling at the lowest price (shipping included) improves your chances of winning the buy box. Unfortunately, due to automated pricing, Amazon Sellers are continuously lowering their prices to win the buy box, which drives down profit margins for everyone.

Don't get caught up in a price war to the extent of incurring a loss just to win the buy box, unless doing so makes sense as part of your larger business strategy. Offering the lowest price is no guarantee you'll win the buy box. Price your products competitively and wisely considering all the cost factors versus sales volumes. (See Chapter 6 for more about pricing strategies.)

Ship and deliver products fast

Sellers that ship and deliver products faster have higher chances of winning the buy box, so be sure you have the infrastructure and logistics in place to ship products soon after receiving an order and that the delivery service you use is up to the task.

Using FBA instead of trying to pack and ship products yourself can significantly improve your delivery times and help you avoid customer complaints over shipments that haven't arrived on time.

Meet or exceed Amazon's performance and compliance standards

Amazon has established stringent performance and compliance standards for all sellers. To win the buy box, you need to maintain nearly perfect scores in areas related to customer service, shipping, and product compliance, as presented in Table 9-1. Consistently maintaining these near perfect scores is essential to winning the buy box, although it won't guarantee a win.

TABLE 9-1   **Scores Needed to Win the Buy Box**

Criteria	Score Required
Customer service performance	
Order defect rate	Less than 1 percent
Return dissatisfaction rate	Less than 10 percent
Shipping performance	
Late shipment rate	Less than 4 percent
Pre-fulfillment cancellation rate	Less than 2.5 percent
Valid /tracking rate	Higher than 95 percent
On-time delivery rate	Higher than 97 percent
Product policy compliance	
Suspected intellectual property violations	Target 0 violations
Received intellectual property complaints	Target 0 violations
Product authenticity complaints	Target 0 violations
Product condition complaints	Target 0 violations
Product safety complaints	Target 0 violations
Listing policy violations	Target 0 violations
Restricted products policy violations	0 violations
Customer product reviews policy violations	0 violations

TIP Selling products through FBA instead of packing and shipping products yourself guarantees high ratings in the critical areas of shipping and handling and customer service.

Thinking outside the buy box

If you lose the buy box, all is not lost. Although it plays a major role in boosting sales volume, you can still make sales as long as you meet Amazon's quality standards in respect to listings, content, and customer feedback and reviews. Following are other areas on Amazon where you can still make sales even if you lose the buy box:

>> **The other sellers on Amazon box:** When viewed on a desktop or laptop computer, the product details page contains a box labeled "Other Sellers on Amazon" (below the buy box). Here, Amazon allows shoppers to buy from other sellers on Amazon who offer a competitive price and maintain a solid seller rating.

>> **Offer listings:** Also on the product details page are one or more links shoppers can click to view all offers of the same product available through other sellers. These offers include both new and used products, Prime and non-Prime products, and those that are Fulfilled by Merchant.

>> **Your Amazon Store page:** Amazon shoppers who choose to shop in your Amazon Store essentially bypass the general product details page and its buy box, ensuring that you make the sale, assuming the shopper chooses to buy the product.

TIP You can also secure sales by linking to your product listing from outside Amazon, for example, from your own website or blog. (See Chapter 11 for details.)

Obtaining High-Quality Product Photos

A picture is worth thousand words, but on Amazon, great product photos can be worth thousands of dollars in sales as well. Instead of trying to compete with other Amazon Sellers solely by offering the lowest price, try competing by offering superior product photos. Great photos can go a long way to impress buyers and convince them to buy from you instead of another seller.

In this section, we present various methods for procuring great product photos and offer some tips and techniques for improving photo quality if you decide to take your own photos.

Amazon provides eight image slots for every product listing, giving you eight opportunities to impress shoppers. Use them all!

Brushing up on Amazon's product photo rules and restrictions

To maintain quality standards on its platform, Amazon requires that product photos meet certain specifications, which vary depending on whether the photo is the main product image or another image.

The main product image must meet the following criteria:

>> The image must be the cover art (as for a book or package) or a professional photograph of the product. Drawings or illustrations of the product aren't allowed.

>> The image must be of the product only; no other objects are allowed.

>> The image must be in focus, professionally lit, and photographed or scanned with realistic color and smooth edges.

>> Books, music, and video/DVD images should be the front cover art, and fill 100 percent of the image frame. Jewel cases, promotional stickers, and cellophane aren't allowed. All other products should fill 85 percent or more of the image frame.

>> The full product must be in frame.

>> Backgrounds must be pure white (RGB 255,255,255).

>> The image must not contain additional text, graphics, or inset images.

>> Pornographic and offensive materials are prohibited.

Any additional images must meet the following criteria:

>> The image must be of, or pertain to, the product being sold.

>> The image must be in focus, professionally lit, and photographed or scanned with realistic color and smooth edges.

>> Other products or objects are allowed to help demonstrate the use or scale of product.

>> The product and props should fill 85 percent or more of the image frame.

>> Cropped or close-up images are permitted.

- **»** Backgrounds and environments are permitted.
- **»** Text and demonstrative graphics are permitted.
- **»** Pornographic and offensive materials are prohibited.

TIP

Make sure your images are high-quality and at least 1,000 pixels or larger in either height or width to enable the zoom function. Larger, higher quality images enhance sales and search ranking.

Procuring manufacturer photos

When selling branded products, procuring high-quality product photos is a snap (usually). Most manufacturers have product photos they're happy to provide to retailers who sell their products. To obtain product photos from a manufacturer, try the following techniques:

- **»** **Visit the manufacturer's website.** Look for a link for retailers, partners, or the press, click the link, and look for a link to product photos. If there is no such area, you can check the product page for the item you're selling to find suitable photos. Right-click a photo and click Save Image As to download it. (Control-click on a Mac to access the Save Image As option.)

- **»** **Email a request for photos to the manufacturer.** You can usually find an email address for contacting the manufacturer on its website. Request photos for the product you're selling. The manufacturer will usually send the photos or provide instructions on how to download them from its website.

- **»** **Scan product photos in a catalogue.** If you have a catalogue that contains an image of the product, you can scan the image to create a digital copy.

REMEMBER

Whenever a manufacturer updates or upgrades its product and you start to sell it, be sure you update your product photos accordingly.

TIP

Obtain all the information you can about each product you sell from the manufacturer, including product descriptions and specifications. This info will come in handy when the time comes to create a product listing.

Taking your own photos

Whether you're selling your own private label products or another manufacturer's wares, we encourage you to include at least a few of your own unique photos — product photos that no other seller offers. If you're a relatively good photographer, you can take the photos yourself; otherwise, hire a professional, as we discuss in the next section.

If you decide to snap your own product photos, here are tips on how to take product photos that sell:

>> **Use a decent camera.** A digital single-lens reflex (dSLR) camera is best, but a high-quality smartphone camera does the trick in a pinch. The benefit of a dSLR camera is that the photo is identical to what you see through the viewfinder. With a standard point-and-shoot camera, photos are offset and often differ from what you see through the viewfinder.

>> **Use a tripod for greater stability during the shoot.** You want sharp, crisp photos. Unfocused photos are worse than useless; they'll drive customers away and hurt your product's search ranking.

>> **Use a white background.** For product-only photos, as opposed to in-context or in-use photos, use a white background, which makes it easier to edit photos and provides consistency across your product line and the Amazon marketplace.

>> **Get the lighting right.** Natural light is usually best. You can take photos outside or in a room that gets plenty of sunlight. Another option is to purchase a light tent or light box specifically made for shooting product photos or build your own (you can find instructions and instruction videos online). Ideally, you want lighting to be uniform around the product with *no* shadows.

>> **Take mostly product-only photos with one or two in-context photos.** An in-context photo shows the product being used — for example, somebody wearing the dress you're selling or camping near the tent you're selling. You may also want to include photos that highlight a product's top-selling features, such as the no-spill lid on a travel mug.

TIP

For additional guidance on taking photos of all kinds, check out the latest edition of *Digital Photography For Dummies*, by Julie Adair King (John Wiley & Sons, Inc.).

Outsourcing product photos

One way to get great custom product photos is to hire a third-party firm that specializes in product photoshoots. This option is likely to be the most expensive in terms of both the photography and the cost of shipping the products to the agency or paying a photographer for travel and time to shoot photos onsite. These firms typically charge per product or per image, but they charge more if the photographer has to travel (with equipment), set up, and shoot onsite.

Before you decide, weigh the cost against these potential benefits:

>> The image quality is likely to be superior to your homemade snapshots, which is likely to translate into higher conversion rates.

>> The agency handles any modifications required to use the photo on different platforms. If you sell in multiple marketplaces, accommodating the technical requirements of every platform can be challenging.

>> A professional photographer can probably produce quality product photos faster than you can.

>> You don't have to hire someone to do product photos in-house, which can save you money.

>> You free up your time and energy to focus on higher level business tasks.

Checking out Amazon Imaging Services

If you use FBA, you can use Amazon Imaging Service to take professional product photos. Prices range from $50 to $150 depending on the product type for at least two images, maybe more depending on the product. To use Amazon Imaging services, take the following steps:

1. **In Seller Central, open the Inventory menu, choose Manage Inventory, and filter your inventory list by Fulfilled by Amazon.**

2. **Open the Edit menu to the right of each product and choose Manage Images.**

3. **Select the Images tab and select Let Us Image Your Products.**

   A pop-up page appears displaying a FAQ and a terms-and-conditions link along with an order total.

4. **Review the FAQ, terms and conditions, and order total, and if you agree with everything, click Buy Now (One-Click) to request Amazon Imaging Services for the selected item(s).**

   A green box appears confirming your work order submission.

   If your order can't be placed for whatever reason, a message appears in place of Buy Now (One-Click) to inform you.

REMEMBER

After you place your order, FBA ships the product from a fulfillment center to an Amazon imaging studio for the photos to be taken. When your product photos are available, the studio uploads them to your Seller Central account and collects charges against your sales proceeds or charges the credit card account you have on file if charges exceed your sales proceeds balance.

TIP

For additional details about Amazon Imaging Services, select the magnifying glass icon near the top Seller Central, click in the Search bar, type **imaging services**, and press Enter, or visit https://www.amazon.com/b?ie=UTF8&node=18369505011 .

Creating a Product Listing

When you're ready to start selling a product, the time has come to list the product for sale on Amazon. In this section, we guide you through the process of creating a product listing by matching to an existing listing, creating a new listing, listing multiple products in bulk, and offering bundles and subscriptions.

Before you create a product listing, we encourage you to read through all the following sections, so you're better prepared to select the method that's best for each product you're selling.

Matching to an existing product listing

If a product you want to list is already being sold on Amazon, don't waste your time doing what's already been done. You can save a lot of time by matching your product to the existing listing.

To match to an existing listing, first find the product's Amazon Standard Identification Number (ASIN) or universal product code (UPC). To find the product's ASIN, locate its product details page on Amazon and scroll down to the Product Information section of that page. The ASIN is typically displayed below the manufacturer.

Knowing the product's ASIN or UPC, you're ready to create a product listing based on the existing listing. Take the following steps to list your product:

1. **After logging into Seller Central, open the Inventory menu and click Add a Product to display the Add a Product submenu.**

2. **Type or paste the ASIN or UPC from the existing product listing into the search box just below the "List a New Product" header and press Enter.**

   Amazon displays the details of the product matching the ASIN you entered. If the product is in a category that requires Amazon's approval to sell in that category, you see a Request Approval button. Otherwise, you see a Sell Yours button.

3. **If the product is in a category that requires Amazon's approval to sell in that category, click the Request Approval button and follow the on-screen instructions to complete the process.**

   After you obtain approval, you'll be able to list your product for sale.

4. **If you're approved to sell in the specified category, click the Sell Yours button.**

   The product listing page appears, prompting you to enter details specific to your product listing.

5. **Type the requested details into the appropriate fields.**

   The information requested pertains only to details specific to your listing, such as the following:

   - Price

   - Seller SKU

   - Quantity

   - Fulfillment channel — whether you want to have the order FBA or fulfill it yourself (Fulfilled by Merchant).

   Because the product already has a listing, you're not allowed to change most of the product details such as title, images, description, and bullet points, and you cannot update these details unless you own the brand.

6. **Click the Save and Finish button.**

   It's that simple: With just a few steps, you're selling on Amazon!

PIGGYBACKING ON SUCCESSFUL LISTINGS

Piggybacking involves finding hot selling products, getting their ASINs, and listing the same product for a lower price. Using this tactic, you take advantage of the popularity of the well-established product without going through the entire process of creating your own listing and trying to win the buy box.

Assuming you follow Amazon's rules, piggybacking is ethical and legitimate. However, the practice has become controversial due to the misuse of the option by some sellers offering counterfeit products of popular brands, thus undermining the integrity of the Amazon marketplace.

To piggyback on existing products without crossing the line, be sure to offer the same exact product in original condition sourced from manufacturers and authorized distributors only.

When practiced ethically, piggybacking can be a great way to generate sales fast and build a good standing on Amazon when you haven't yet had a chance to establish yourself.

Creating a new product listing

To create a new product listing (for a product that's not already for sale on Amazon), first gather the following details:

>> **SKU:** This is your internal product identifier that helps you keep track of different products in inventory. Think of an identifier that clearly describes your product, such as iPhoneXS-max-6.5-64gb or iPhoneXS-max-6.5-256GB.

>> **Product ID:** Obtain the universal product code (UPC), European article number (EAN), or international standard book number (ISBN) from the manufacturer, if possible. If you want to sell an item that has no such product ID, such as a handmade product, you can request an exemption from Amazon, but you can't list the product until your request is approved. See the later section "Requesting a GTIN exemption" for details.

>> **Offer details:** Offer details include the product's condition (new or used), price, quantity, and shipping options. You can change these details at any time.

>> **Product details:** Product details include the product name (in the title), brand, category, description, and product photos or other relevant images. The product details describe the product so shoppers can make a well-informed purchase decision.

>> **Keywords and search terms:** These are words or phrases you think shoppers will use to find this product. Choosing these keywords and terms wisely can make your products easier to find, hence resulting in more sales. See the later section "Using keywords to your advantage" for details.

When you have all the information required to list a product, take the following steps to create your product listing:

1. After logging into Seller Central, open the Inventory menu and click Add a Product to display the Add a Product submenu.

2. Search or browse for the category that best matches the product type, choose the category, and click the Select Category button.

3. Enter the information requested, ensuring that you fill in all required fields.

4. Click Save Changes to save the new listing and post it on Amazon.

In the following sections, we explain the key information required to list a product on Amazon in greater detail. We also explain how to request a global trade item number (GTIN) exemption to sell a product that has no UPC, EAN, or ISBN.

Requesting a GTIN exemption

A global trade item number (GTIN) is a UPC, EAN, or ISBN. You may not need a GTIN if the product you want to sell matches a product already being sold on Amazon. In such a case, you can sell through the existing product listing (see the earlier section "Matching to an existing product listing" for details). If that's not an option, you can request a GTIN exemption. GTIN exemptions are commonly approved for selling the following items:

» Private label or handmade products for which the manufacturer or publisher doesn't provide a GTIN or a bar code

» Parts or accessories, such as auto parts or cellphone accessories that don't have a GTIN

» Bundles of two or more products

Prior to requesting a GTIN exemption, gather the following information:

» Product name

» Two to nine images showing all sides of the product and its packaging

» Support letter from the brand owner, manufacturer, or publisher in Word, PDF, or an image format containing the following details:

- Name and contact info of the brand owner or other person authorized to write the letter

- A statement that the brand doesn't issue a GTIN and the reason for not doing so

- The physical address of your business and your phone number, email address, and website address

With the required items and information in hand, take the following steps to request a GTIN exemption:

1. **After logging into Seller Central, go to the GTIN Exemption Page at** https://sellercentral.amazon.com/gtinx.

2. **Type the brand or publisher name in the Brand/Publisher field or type Generic (case sensitive) for unbranded items or bundles.**

TIP

You can request up to ten exemptions at once. To do so, click + Add More Brands/Publishers to add requests for exemptions in the same category or + Add More Categories to add requests for products in different categories.

3. **Click the Check for Eligibility button.**

   An Eligibility Summary appears with a checkmark in the Status column if the product is eligible and no checkmark if the product is ineligible (in which case, you won't be able to proceed).

4. **If your product is eligible for exemption, click the Continue to Submit Proof button.**

5. **After the Provide Proof page appears, follow the on-screen cues to upload your support letter and product images.**

6. **Click Submit Request.**

Adding a title

Every product listing must have a title of the product being listed. Titles for all non-media products must meet the following criteria:

>> No longer than 200 characters, including spaces

>> Must include product identifying information, such as "hiking boots" or "vacuum cleaner"

>> No promotional phrases, such as "free shipping" or "satisfaction guaranteed"

>> No decorative characters such as ~ ! * $? _ ~ { } # < > | * ; ^ ¬ ¦

REMEMBER

Amazon doesn't specify the same criteria for media products because certain characters and symbols might legitimately be part of the media product titles such as books and movies.

WARNING

Failure to comply with these requirements may cause a product to be suppressed from Amazon search results. See the later section "Using keywords to your advantage" for tips on using keywords strategically in the product title.

Composing a product description

Every product listing on Amazon must have a detailed and accurate product description (up to 2,000 characters, including spaces) that enables shoppers to make a well-informed purchase decision. Amazon encourages sellers to go beyond the manufacturer's description to include the following details:

>> A description of the product in your own words

>> A concise, honest, and friendly overview of the product's uses and where it fits in the category in which it's listed

>> Features and benefits of the product, especially those that highlight its unique properties

>> Best applications for the product — for example, a vacuum cleaner that's especially suited for vacuuming a car

See the later section "Using keywords to your advantage" for tips on using keywords strategically in the product description.

WARNING

When composing your product description, be careful not to mention competitors. Also, check spelling and grammar before submitting it.

Adding bullet points

Bullet points provide an opportunity to highlight key features and benefits of a product, so be sure to take full advantage of them. Some shoppers may not even read the product description; they may merely skim the bullet points and base their purchase decision solely on that content. Make your bullet points as brief but descriptive as possible, and include your most important keywords, as we explain in the later section, "Using keywords to your advantage."

REMEMBER

Technically, you can a list a product on Amazon without bullet points, but we can't imagine any seller doing so. Bullet points provide a golden opportunity to highlight the best your product offers and to increase your search ranking and sales.

Including product photos and related images

Amazon allows you to include up to eight images in your product listing, and we recommend that you fill all eight slots. Make sure your photos and other images are high quality and relevant to the product. Images may include the following:

>> **Product-only photos:** Amazon requires only one photo — a main product photo, which must be cover art or a quality photo of the product. Consider including additional product photos to show the product from different angles.

>> **In-context photos:** Photos of the product in use, such as a lawnmower being pushed across a lawn. Keep these to a minimum — only one or two.

>> **Illustrations:** Drawings that may be helpful in describing the product, illustrating its use, or highlighting a feature or benefit.

>> **Printed content:** For example, a label showing the ingredients of a supplement.

Refer to the section, "Obtaining High-Quality Product Photos," earlier in this chapter, for more photo-specific information.

Increasing product visibility with search optimization

As you create product listings, one of your primary goals is for your listing to appear at or near the top of the list whenever a shopper searches for your product or similar products. You accomplish this goal via search optimization sometimes also referred as *listing optimization*. When creating a product listing, identify keywords and phrases that shoppers are likely to type to find the product and then use these keywords and phrases in your listing, specifically in:

>> Keywords

>> Listing title

>> Product description

>> Bullet items

>> Any text included with product photos

See the later section "Increasing Your Product Search Ranking on Amazon" for additional guidance on how to boost your product search ranking on Amazon.

Experiment with different product listings

If your existing product listing isn't resulting in satisfactory sale performance, experiment with the listing to see whether certain changes can improve results. Revisit the listing title, product description, bullet items, price, product images, and all other facets of your listing, and reconsider your choice of keywords (see the later section "Using keywords to your advantage").

Listing multiple products in bulk

If you have a large number of products to list, creating product listings individually can be extremely time consuming. To streamline the process, Amazon enables Professional Sellers to post product listings in bulk — listing hundreds or even thousands of product listings simply by uploading a spreadsheet that contains the details for every product you want to list. Amazon even provides bulk listing templates (inventory files) to simplify the process. The key to success is choosing the right inventory file template for the appropriate product category.

In the following sections, we lead you through the process of listing products in bulk.

WARNING

Be careful when using Amazon inventory files. Uploading a completed inventory file that contains errors or omissions may introduce errors in existing product listings or eliminate one or more listings altogether.

Lay the groundwork

Before you can list products in bulk, attend to the following preliminaries:

>> Purchase and install Microsoft Excel, which is required to open and edit Amazon's inventory files. (Another option is to use a free spreadsheet program that is Excel compatible, such as Apache OpenOffice Calc or LibreOffice Calc, which you can find and download online.)

>> If you're using Excel, enable macros. Click the File tab, Options, Trust Center, Trust Center Settings, Macro Settings, Enable All Macros, OK, OK. Macros will appear on the Excel Add-Ins menu in the toolbar above the Amazon template. Macros include Validate, Upload File, Import File, and Update Template.

>> Request approval, if necessary, to sell in the desired product category. See the next section for details.

>> Match as many of your products as possible to existing product listings on Amazon, and then record the ASIN number for each. See the earlier section "Matching to an existing product listing" for details.

Request approval to sell in specific product categories

Amazon may require that sellers meet additional qualifications to sell certain brands or list products in certain categories. To determine whether approval is needed and to apply for approval if required, take the following steps:

1. **After logging into Seller Central, open the Inventory menu and click Add a Product.**

2. **Search for the product you want to sell.**

3. **In the search results, check to see whether a Listing Limitations Apply link is next to the product you want to sell.**

   If no link appears, you're free to list the product. Otherwise, click the Listing Limitations Apply link.

4. **Click the Request Approval button and follow the on-screen instructions to submit your request.**

   Sometimes you get lucky, and the resulting screen simply indicates "Congratulations, you're approved to list."

Downloading an inventory file

To create and download an Amazon inventory file (a bulk listing template), take the following steps:

1. **After logging into Seller Central, open the Inventory menu and click Add Products via Upload.**

   The Products via Upload page appears.

2. **Click the Download an Inventory File tab.**

   The first section on this page contains Amazon's product classifier.

3. **Take one of the following steps:**

   - Click in the Search Tool box, type one or more words to describe the category you think would be best, click Search or press Enter, and in the search results list click the Select button next to the category that's the most appropriate.

   - Click a category in the Product Classifier list, continue to click down the tree of subcategories until you see the best match, and then click the Select button next to that subcategory.

   Clicking a category's Select button adds it to the Summary of Your Selected Products list just below the product classifier. (You can remove one or more categories from this list by clicking the X to the left of the category you want removed.)

4. **Repeat Step 3 to classify all products you want included in your inventory file.**

5. **Scroll down to Step 3: Select the Type of Template, and click one of the following:**

   - **Lite:** To create a simple file that contains only the minimum information required to list products.

   - **Advanced:** To include all the attribute fields you can populate for each product.

   - **Custom:** If you want to add your own attributes.

6. **Click Generate Template.**

   Amazon creates the inventory file according to your specifications, and your web browser downloads the file to your computer.

TIP

Move your downloaded inventory file to a folder on your computer exclusively for inventory files. Whenever you edit the file in your spreadsheet program, use the File, Save As command to save the new version under another name, such as "Inv_020221_v2." That way you have a history of changes for your records.

Completing the inventory file

After downloading your inventory file, open it in your spreadsheet program and check out the different sheets that comprise the inventory file. You can click the desired tab near the bottom of the screen to switch to the sheet you want:

>> **Instructions** includes instructions for entering product details into the template.

>> **Images** specifies Amazon's image requirements.

>> **Example** provides an example of a completed template.

>> **Data definitions** define each attribute within the inventory template. For each attribute, this sheet presents its name, definition, use, acceptable values, an example, and whether it's a required field. Turn to this sheet if you're having trouble figuring out what to enter in each field on the Template sheet.

>> **Template** is the sheet on which you'll enter your product information.

WARNING

Don't edit any of the top three rows of the Template sheet. If you change any of the labels in the top three rows, your inventory file won't be processed correctly when you upload it to Amazon.

>> **Valid values** provides a list of fields that require specific entries along with a list of valid entries for each field.

To complete the inventory file, click the Template tab, and enter the attributes for one of your products in the first row below the existing labels. Continue in subsequent rows, so you have the attributes for each product in a separate row. You don't need to type an entry in every field for each product, but certain fields are required. After you enter (choose) the product's type in the leftmost field in the row, required fields are outlined in red. You can also consult the Data Definitions sheet to determine which fields are and aren't required.

Note that fields requiring a valid value are drop-down lists. You simply click the field and select one of the values from the list. By choosing an item from a list, you avoid the possibility of mistyping an entry.

When you're done entering attributes for all the products you want to list, save the inventory file.

Uploading the completed inventory file

After you've completed your inventory file, you can check it and upload it to Amazon to list your products. Take the following steps to check and upload your inventory file:

1. **After logging in to Seller Central, open the Inventory menu and click Add Products via Upload.**

   The Add Products via Upload page appears.

2. **Click the Check and Upload Your Inventory File tab.**

3. **Under Step 1 – Check Your File, click Choose File and choose your inventory file, which is stored on your computer.**

4. **Enter your email address in the Email Alert box, to receive an email notification when the upload is complete.**

   Depending on the file size, uploads can take minutes to hours.

5. **Click the Check My File button.**

   Amazon uploads the file and checks it for errors. You can click the Monitor Upload Status tab to check progress. When the file check is complete, the upload status notifies you of any errors. You can click the Download Your Processing Report link for details about any errors.

6. **Click the Check and Upload Your Inventory File tab.**

7. **Scroll down to the Step 2 – Upload File section.**

8. **Click the File Type button and choose the inventory file type.**

9. **Click Choose File and choose your inventory file, which is stored on your computer.**

10. **Enter your email address in the Email Alert box, to receive an email notification when the upload is complete.**

11. **Click the Upload button.**

12. **Click the Monitor Upload Status tab to keep track of the upload progress and check to make sure the file you uploaded has no errors.**

    If the upload status indicates any errors, click the Download Your Processing Report link for details about them, correct the errors, and upload the file again.

TIP

One of the benefits of uploading listings in bulk is that you can edit your inventory file at any time and upload it again to update any attributes in your product listings. For example, if you change a product's price, simply make the change in your inventory file and upload it to Amazon.

Listing variations and bundles

Product listings become a little more complicated when you're offering variations or bundles. A *variation* is a product option, such as a T-shirt available in different colors or a smartphone with different storage capacity, such as 64GB or 128GB. A *bundle* is a group of products that are typically related, such as a mobile phone charger, a mobile phone cover, and a screen protector that would probably cost more if bought separately.

In the following sections, we explain how to create listings for variations and bundles.

Listing variations

Before you can create a variation, the following conditions must be met:

>> **The product must have a *parent listing:*** A main non-buyable product to which the variations relate, such as a T-shirt that can't be purchased until the size and color are specified.

>> **The product must have *child listings:*** Specific products related to the parent listing, such as multiple listings for T-shirts in a variety of sizes and colors.

>> **A variation theme must be specified:** A *variation theme* defines how variations differ, such as by size or color.

You can create a variation by matching to an existing variation listing, by combining existing product listings in your account, or by creating a new variation listing. To match to an existing variation listing, take the following steps:

1. **In Seller Central, open the Inventory menu, select Manage Inventory, and select Add a Variation.**

   Seller Central displays the Variation Wizard.

2. **Select Add to or Update an Existing Variation Family.**

   Seller Central prompts you to search for the ASIN of the variation you want to list.

3. **Search for the variation ASIN or parent ASIN you want to list.**

   Seller Central presents a list of all the variations of the selected product family currently in the Amazon catalog. In the Actions column, you have the option to edit a variation if it's already in your account or "Sell Yours" if the listing isn't yet in your account.

4. **Select Sell Yours, because you're choosing to list an existing variation.**

   The Variation Wizard prompts you to enter details about your product.

5. **Enter requested details about your product into any blank fields, including Condition, Quantity, and Price.**

TIP

If the variation you're trying to add doesn't exist in the variation family, you can add your own variation by selecting "Add Variation," just under the variation list, and supplying all the requested details.

6. **Press the Save and Finish button.**

If you have standalone listings in your account that qualify for being variations, you can combine them to create a variation family. Take the following steps:

1. **In Seller Central, Open the Inventory menu, select Manage Inventory, and select Add a Variation.**

2. **After the Add a Variation Wizard appears, select Create a Variation Family by Combining Existing Stand-Alone Listings within Your Catalog.**

   The Wizard prompts you to search for a variation or product parent ASIN.

3. **Search for the variation ASIN or parent ASIN you want to list.**

   Amazon presents a list of all the variations of the selected product family currently in the Amazon catalogue.

4. **Follow the Wizard's guidance to create a new variation family using category-specific templates.**

Creating a variation listing for a product that's not already listed on Amazon is a more involved process. Take the following steps to create a new variation listing:

1. **In Seller Central, open the Inventory menu and click Add a Product.**

2. **Click I'm Adding a Product Not Sold on Amazon.**

3. **Search for or browse the category that matches the product you want to list and click the Select Category button.**

4. **On the Vital Info tab, fill in all the required fields (those marked with an asterisk) and click Continue.**

5. **Click on the Variation tab, open the Variation Theme drop-down list, and select the appropriate theme.**

   After you list a product with the selected variation theme, you can't change it. Amazon prompts you to enter values for the chosen theme.

6. **Enter values for the selected theme.**

   For example, if you chose color as the theme, you can enter "blue," "red," "green," "yellow," and so forth.

7. **Click Generate Variations.**

A Variations Matrix appears, allowing you to add details for each variation, such as the following:

- A product identifier such as a UPC (required)

- A seller SKU, which is automatically generated if you don't specify one

- Offer details, such as condition, price, and quantity

You can delete variations at this point. To delete a variation, click the box next to it and click Delete Selection.

8. **Click Continue.**

9. **Use the remaining tabs to add images, a product description, keywords, and other product attributes that you want to include for all variations.**

You can edit this information at any time via the Manage Inventory page.

10. **Click Save.**

REMEMBER

You can use a category-specific inventory file to create variations when listing multiple products at once. Refer to the previous section "Listing multiple products in bulk," and follow the instructions on the first sheet in the file to complete the fields for the variations you want to create.

Listing bundles

The process for creating a bundle is nearly the same as that for creating a listing for a product that's not already listed on Amazon. (See the earlier section "Creating a new product listing" for details.) However, a listing for a bundle includes product images of all the bundled items, and the product's title must include the title of the main item followed by "Bundles With" and the titles of the other items.

Creating product subscriptions

The Amazon Subscribe & Save program lets customers sign up for scheduled deliveries of certain products to earn a discount of 5 to 20 percent along with free shipping. Subscribe & Save offers are also available to registered Amazon Business customers for a discount of 5 percent regardless of product category or number of subscriptions.

REMEMBER

Any coupons and promotional discounts you offer are added to Subscribe & Save discounts. For example, if you run a Lightning Deal on a product in the Subscribe & Save program, you must offer the deal price and award the buyer the Subscribe & Save discount. Be sure to account for these discounts when setting your product price.

WHY BUNDLE?

As an Amazon Seller, you really should consider bundling products when it makes sense to do so. Bundling offers several advantages, including the following:

- **Enhanced value to shoppers.** Bundled products typically cost less than if the same products were purchased separately. As a result, you may be able to beat your competitors on price without completely crushing your profit margin.

- **Increased differentiation for you.** A unique bundle is a great way to avoid stiff competition from multiple sellers offering the same products only purchased separately. For example, dozens of Amazon merchants may be selling the same iPhone, but if you bundle yours with a case and a screen protector, you set yourself apart.

To be eligible to offer Subscribe & Save, you must meet the following minimum requirements:

» Be registered with an FBA account and selling in FBA for at least three months

» Be in good standing with Amazon

» Have a customer feedback rating of at least 4.7

To activate Subscribe & Save for your account, take the following steps:

1. **Click Settings (upper-right corner of Amazon Seller Central), click Fulfillment by Amazon, and scroll down to Subscription Settings.**

2. **Click the Edit button (upper-right corner of the Subscription Settings box).**

3. **Click Enable and then Update.**

4. **Read the FBA Subscribe & Save program agreement, and if you consent to the terms, click Agree.**

Amazon uses the following criteria to determine product eligibility for Subscribe & Save:

» Fulfillment history and in-stock rate

» Sales performance

» Product category

» Average selling price

All eligible products are automatically enrolled in the program. To opt out of automatic enrollment, or to enroll a new product that hasn't been automatically enrolled in Subscribe & Save, email your request to fba-sns-help@amazon.com.

To access the Subscribe & Save dashboard for managing enrolled products, take the following steps:

1. **From the Seller Central main menu, select Programs and then Fulfillment Programs.**

2. **Under My Programs, click Subscribe & Save.**

   The Subscribe & Save dashboard appears.

REMEMBER

Enrollment of new products in Subscribe & Save is limited to brand owners. Any products enrolled before December 18, 2019, remain eligible for Subscribe & Save regardless of whether you're a brand owner.

Increasing Your Product Search Ranking on Amazon

Every seller has the same goal on Amazon — to increase sales. It's the same game in every retail venue, whether online or on the street, but on online, you achieve that goal by ranking higher than everyone else and placing consistently near or at the top of the search results when shoppers search for the products you sell.

Although there's no single, clearly defined path to success in the Amazon marketplace, successful Amazon Sellers have developed and practice several methods to beat the competition and stay on top. In this section, we present several approaches to gaining a competitive edge, especially when struggling to find initial success in the Amazon marketplace.

Harnessing the power of the A9 algorithm

The key to getting your products ranked higher in Amazon searches is to understand the *A9 algorithm* — Amazon's automated system for ranking product listings in search results. Even though Amazon doesn't explicitly reveal the criteria it uses to rank product listings, how A9 works is evident based on observations and experimentation.

Key factors impacting the rank of product listings in search results include the following:

» **Sales performance:** The more you sell of a particular product the higher its ranking. To win the top spot, you need to increase your sales velocity beyond that of the top seller of that product. One way to do this is to point all your internal and external sales traffic to your Amazon product listing.

» **Text relevancy:** All text contained in your product listing must align with what shoppers search for when looking for the product. Text includes keywords, listing title, product description, and bullet items. We explain how to keyword-optimize these text items later in this section.

» **Price:** All other things being equal, low price wins. You don't want to compete on price alone, because that strategy reduces the profit margin for all sellers; however, you do need to price your products competitively.

» **Availability:** Before A9 will rank you near the top, it wants to make sure you have plenty of product in stock to fulfill orders. Using FBA and keeping your FBA inventory well-stocked is the best way to show A9 that product is available.

Other factors may also impact a product listing's search ranking, including the following:

» **Fulfillment method:** Fulfilled By Amazon (FBA) trumps Fulfilled by Merchant (FBM).

» **Customer reviews:** Higher customer product reviews can give your product listing a bump in search ranking. A liberal return policy and superior customer service, including after-sale product support when it makes sense, helps.

» **Answered questions:** Answered questions are listed above customer reviews and play an important role in sales conversions and the ranking of product listings.

» **A+ content:** A+ content, formerly known as *Enhanced Brand Content (EBC)*, enables sellers to showcase their products using additional images and more creative copy (and with A+ Premium), videos, testimonials, comparison charts, and more. Think of A+ content as a professionally designed multimedia ad embedded in the product listing. (See Chapter 11 for more about A+ content.)

» **Pay-per-click (PPC) ads:** Amazon PPC, also known as *Sponsored Products,* enables you to essentially pay Amazon for a higher search ranking. With Amazon PPC, you set your daily budget for ads. The more you're willing to pay for an ad, the greater your chances of having it displayed, and the higher its placement. For more about Amazon PPC, see Chapter 12.

>> **Images:** When creating a product listing, use all eight image slots and be sure to use high-quality images that are at least 1,000 pixels in height or width. Smaller images fail to enable the zoom feature, which hurts both search ranking and sales.

>> **Promotions:** Offering special deals and promotions can boost your products in the search rankings. See Chapter 12 for details.

In the following sections, we explain various ways to improve a product listing's search ranking that give you the "most bang for your buck."

Checking out the competition

Researching the competition is a great way to ride a competitor's success to increasing your own search rankings. When researching a competitor, examine the following:

>> **Keywords:** Several tools are available to help you peek behind the scenes of competitors' product listings to find out which key words and phrases they use; for example, JungleScout's Keyword Scout (www.junglescout.com/features/keyword-scout/) and Sonar's keyword tool (http://sonar-tool.com/us/).

>> **Product listings:** Examine the competitor's product listings, including the title, product description, image use, questions answered, and customer reviews.

>> **Price:** Look at the way your competitors price products and change the price over time to figure out their pricing strategy. How are your competitors pricing and repricing products to win the price game while increasing sales and still earning a profit?

Using keywords to your advantage

Amazon shoppers aren't window shoppers. They usually know the type of product they want, and they search for it by name. Often, they even have a specific brand in mind. You want to make sure that the keywords you use in your product listing match the words and phrases shoppers are likely to enter into Amazon's Search box to find the product you're selling.

Amazon offers the following tips for optimizing your search terms:

» Use no more than 250 bytes. (You can type in all lowercase or mix upper and lowercase.) A *byte* is a group of usually eight binary digits (zeros and ones) that act as a unit. Each alphanumeric character (a–z, A–Z, 0–9) is one byte, but complex characters such as ö may be two bytes, and some Chinese and Japanese characters can be three or four bytes.

The Search Terms field has a built-in counter that stops accepting input as soon as the byte limit is reached.

» Separate keywords with spaces, not commas or other punctuation.

» Include synonyms but not misspellings.

» Include abbreviations and alternate names.

» Don't repeat words.

» Don't include the product's brand name or any brand name in your search terms.

» Don't include the product's ASIN.

» Don't waste characters on words such as "a," "an," "the," "and," "or," "by," "for," "of," and "with."

» Use singular or plural — no need for both.

» Avoid temporary statements such as "new" or "on sale now."

» Don't make subjective claims, such as "best" or "cheapest" or "amazing."

» Don't use offensive or abusive terms.

To edit search terms in a listing, take the following steps:

1. **Open the Inventory menu and click Manage Inventory.**

2. **Click Edit (to the right of the product whose listing you want to edit).**

3. **Click the Keywords tab.**

4. **Click in the Search Terms box and type the desired keywords.**

5. **Click Save.**

You can also update keywords by making changes to your inventory file and uploading it to Amazon. See the earlier section "Listing multiple products in bulk" for details.

In the following section, we offer a couple tips for finding effective keywords and how to use keywords in your product listing's title, product description, and bullet items.

Digging up effective keywords

To find effective keywords, try one or more of the following methods:

>> Find out which keywords your competitors are using, as we discuss in the earlier section "Checking out the competition."

>> Find out which keyword Amazon requires. Use Amazon's Product Classifier, as we explain in the earlier section "Downloading an inventory file" to find the required keyword for a specific product category, and be sure to include it in your list of keywords and in your product listing title, product description, and bullet items.

>> Start typing a word or phrase in the Amazon Search box that describes the product you're selling. As you type, Amazon gives you a handful of suggestions based on the history of user searches. The items in the list are usually a good source for keywords.

>> Use a third-party tool such as JungleScout's Keyword Scout (www.junglescout.com/features/keyword-scout/) or Sonar's keyword tool (http://sonar-tool.com/us/) for analyzing keywords in Amazon, based on product category.

REMEMBER

What matters to the customers matters to the A9 algorithm, so when you're choosing keywords, put yourself in the shopper's shoes. What would a typical shopper type in the Search box to find your product? If you can answer that question, you've found the perfect keyword!

Using keywords in your product listing title

A typical customer types one or more keywords into the Amazon's Search box, and Amazon displays a list of products that it determines are most relevant to those words. The customer quickly scans the product titles and clicks the title that most accurately describes the desired product. To show up in that list, preferably at or near the top, make sure the title of the listing contains the keywords shoppers search for.

TIP

To optimize your product title, move the most important, most descriptive keywords to the beginning of the title. You typically want to include the brand name and model (if relevant) followed by the product type and any key details; for example, "Shark Navigator Lift-Away Deluxe NV360 Upright Vacuum Blue."

REMEMBER

Titles of product listings are truncated on mobile devices, which means stacking important keywords at the beginning of the title is even more important to win sales from mobile shoppers.

Using keywords in your product description

Your product description provides even more opportunity for the strategic use of keywords. As you compose your product description, be sure to pack it with keywords, especially important keywords that you couldn't include at the beginning of the title. However, make sure the keywords blend in smoothly with your narrative. Don't write a product description consisting entirely of keywords.

Adding keywords to bullet items

One additional way to take full advantage of keywords is to include them in the bullet items in your product listings. You can use the same keywords you used in the title and product description to reinforce the importance of those keywords.

Chapter **10**

Fulfilling Customer Orders

Many people start selling products on Amazon long before they give any consideration to filling orders. These mom-and-pop operations typically sell products and then pick, pack, and ship them to customers themselves. However, when the business begins to grow, they have less time to devote to these chores and discover that they can be more successful spending their time on higher level tasks, such as finding products with high sales and profit potential and optimizing their product listings, customer service, and other business functions.

Fortunately, options are available for outsourcing some of the work involved in running a retail business, including order fulfillment, especially when you're selling on Amazon. In this chapter, you explore your options and get up to speed on the basics of different order fulfillment methods.

Choosing an Order Fulfillment Method

Order fulfillment plays a big role in ecommerce success, especially on Amazon where more than one million Prime customers expect free two-day delivery or faster, and Amazon rewards sellers with higher product placement for satisfying its customers' delivery expectations.

One of your first decisions as an Amazon Seller is how to fulfill customer orders. You have four options (not mutually exclusive), as we explain in the following sections.

Fulfillment by Amazon (FBA)

With FBA, you send your products or arrange to have them sent from your suppliers to Amazon fulfillment centers in various locations in your marketplace(s) — the United States, Canada, Mexico, wherever. Your customers order from you on Amazon, and Amazon picks, packs, labels, and ships your products from its fulfillment centers to your customers and provides them with tracking information. Amazon's customer–service team manages customer inquiries and processes returns and refunds.

When considering FBA, weigh the pros and cons.

Here are the pros:

>> All FBA products receive two-day shipping to Prime customers, which improves your chances of closing sales. About half of Amazon's customers (101 million in the United States alone) are Prime, with each spending on average about $1,400 annually in products on Amazon.

>> Using FBA is hassle-free. All you need to do is get your products to Amazon fulfillment centers, and Amazon handles the rest.

>> You get reduced shipping rates to Amazon fulfillment centers and from those centers to your customers: Amazon negotiates high-volume shipping contracts with carriers, and you reap the benefits of lower shipping costs.

>> An FBA product has a greater chance than a Fulfillment by Merchant (FBM) product of winning the buy box (being the featured offer). Buy box placement accounts for more than 80 percent of all Amazon sales.

>> FBA can also be integrated into your other sales channels, so if customers purchase a product on your own ecommerce site (outside Amazon), FBA can fulfill the order (subject to a higher FBA fee).

>> Offsite product storage is much more convenient. If you're running your ecommerce business out of your home or garage, you avoid the clutter of having to store inventory onsite.

Meanwhile, here are the cons:

>> Amazon charges FBA fees to cover storage, fulfillment, and customer service, plus you pay for shipping products to fulfillment centers. (See the later section "Accounting for the costs" for details.) You may also incur a high-volume listing fee on some items and long-term storage fees if products don't sell within a year's time.

>> Preparing and shipping products to Amazon fulfillment centers requires some work. Each unit must be labeled with a bar code, so it can be picked and packed easily with outgoing orders. See the later section "Using Fulfillment by Amazon (FBA)" for details.

>> Access to your inventory is limited because it's stored in Amazon fulfillment centers.

REMEMBER

We strongly encourage you to use FBA as your primary fulfillment method, especially for high-volume, high-margin products, leveraging Amazon's industry-leading logistics and customer service to cater most effectively to Amazon customers and simplify the process of scaling your business. Reserve other fulfillment methods for specialty items, such as custom-made furniture that requires special packing or a more personal touch.

TIP

To compare the costs of FBA and FBM, use the Fulfillment by Amazon Revenue Calculator:

1. Go to https://sellercentral.amazon.com/fba/revenuecalculator/index?lang=en_US to access the Fulfillment by Amazon Revenue Calculator.

2. In the Find Your Product on Amazon.com text box, type the product name, UPC, EAN, ISBN, or ASIN and select Search.

   Amazon presents a collection of products that match your search term or phrase.

3. Below the product you're interested in, click Select.

4. In the Your Fulfillment column, type your fulfillment costs in the Item Price, Shipping, Cost of Seller Fulfillment, and Cost of Product fields.

5. **In the Amazon Fulfillment Current column, enter your numbers for Item Price, the per-item cost to ship the product to an Amazon fulfillment center, and the cost of the product.**

6. **Press the Calculate button.**

The calculator crunches the numbers and displays a comparison of your net profit and margin percentage for your fulfillment costs versus Amazon fulfillment costs. (See Figure 10-1.)

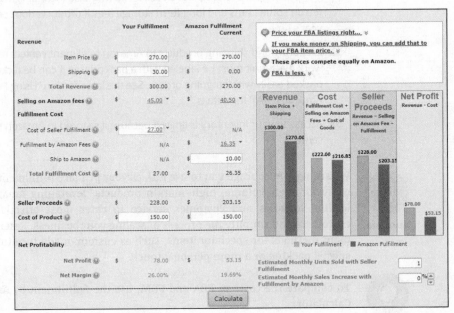

FIGURE 10-1:
Compare your fulfillment costs to those of FBA.

Fulfillment by Merchant (FBM)

If you're testing a product or selling low-volume, low-margin products, FBM may be the better choice. For comparison, check out the pros and cons of FBM.

Here are the pros:

>> Avoiding FBA fees may help to lower your costs, which can boost profit margins. Crunch the numbers, though, to determine whether Amazon's lower shipping fees offset other FBA fees.

>> Fulfilling orders yourself gives you greater control over inventory, packing, and shipping, which can be beneficial when selling custom products or adding a personal touch to outgoing packages.

And the cons:

>> With FBM, you spend more time and effort to pick, pack, label, and ship products and process customer service requests, returns, and refunds.

>> FBM products aren't automatically eligible for Prime. You may be able to qualify for Seller Fulfilled Prime, as we discuss in the next section.

>> You have less opportunity to win the buy box (and be the featured offer).

>> Although profit margins may be higher with FBM, sales volume is likely to be lower.

>> You need to store products in your home or garage or procure warehouse storage.

>> Overhead costs, including shipping fees, are generally higher.

Seller Fulfilled Prime

With Seller Fulfilled Prime, you store and ship products from your own warehouses, while committing to delivering products to Prime customers within Amazon's required two-day delivery window. If approved for Seller Fulfilled Prime, you're allowed to display the Prime badge for products shipped from your warehouses. In addition to other benefits, Amazon provides access to discounted transportation solutions to help meet the two-day Prime delivery promise.

In the following sections, we explain Seller Fulfilled Prime basics and how the program works.

REMEMBER

During the time of this writing, Amazon wasn't accepting new registrations for Seller Fulfilled Prime, but you can join the waitlist at https://services.amazon.com/services/seller-fulfilled-prime.html.

Recognizing the benefits of Seller Fulfilled Prime

Seller Fulfilled Prime offers several benefits, including the following:

>> You pick, pack, and ship products from your warehouses, so you have greater control over your own inventory and operations.

>> You can list products as Prime, which is very appealing to Amazon's most loyal customers. Prime customers often filter product listings so as to display only Prime products. To have a chance to win this business, your products must qualify as Prime offerings.

>> Prime listings have a greater chance of winning the buy box.

>> By offering free two-day guaranteed shipping, you improve your chances of repeat and multiple orders.

Seller Fulfilled Prime is generally best suited for high value items, seasonal products with unpredictable demand, slow moving goods, items with variations, and inventory that requires special handling or preparation.

Meeting Seller Fulfilled Prime requirements

Being able to deliver products from your warehouse(s) to Prime customers within Amazon's two-day window is only one of several Seller Fulfilled Prime requirements. To qualify for and maintain good standing in this program, you must meet the following requirements:

>> Offer premium shipping options.

>> Ship more than 99 percent of the orders on time (the same day you receive the orders).

>> Maintain order cancellation rate of less than 0.5 percent.

>> Buy Amazon shipping services for at least 98.5 percent of Amazon orders; for the most part, you buy shipping labels from Amazon-approved carriers, who deliver orders to customers.

>> Allow Amazon to handle customer service queries.

>> Agree to and comply with Amazon Returns Policy.

Successfully navigating the trial period

To participate in Seller Fulfilled Prime, you must successfully complete a trial period, which traditionally consists of filling a certain number of orders within a set period of time — for example, 50 orders in 90 days or fewer. Products aren't listed with the Prime badge during this time, and all orders must be processed with a zero-day handling time.

Assuming you successfully complete the trial period, you're enrolled in the program, and the Prime badge is displayed for participating ASINs.

Participating in Seller Fulfilled Prime

To meet your Seller Fulfilled Prime obligations, take the following steps:

1. **Maintain sufficient inventory in your warehouse(s) to fill customer orders.**

2. **Buy shipping labels from Amazon-approved carriers.**

    In Seller Central, select Orders and then Manage Orders and press the Buy Shipping button for the order you want to ship. Follow the on-screen instructions to complete the process.

3. **Pick, pack, and ship the orders the same day they're received, typically by 4 p.m.**

    Orders will be delivered within two days by Amazon-approved carriers.

WARNING

Inspect shipping costs closely prior to deciding whether to "Buy Shipping" from Amazon-approved carriers. Seller Fulfilled Prime free shipping options may be cost-prohibitive for certain products or product categories.

For questions about Seller Fulfilled Prime, email sfp-enrollment@amazon.com.

Managing Seller Fulfilled Prime orders

To manage Seller Fulfilled Prime SKUs, log on to Seller Central, open the Inventory menu, and select Manage Seller Fulfilled Prime. The Manage Seller Fulfilled Prime dashboard appears providing the tools you need to manage orders.

Drop-shipping

Drop-shipping is the ultimate in look-ma-no-hands order fulfillment and low-cost, low-risk startups and product testing! You build a store and list products that the drop-ship supplier has available. Customers order products through your store, and the order goes to the drop-shipper, which fulfills the order for you. (Most drop-shippers merely act as a conduit between sellers and numerous suppliers that offer their own drop-shipping services.) Because you don't have to stock up on inventory, you can start selling without having to buy any products up front.

Although drop-shipping may strike you as the ideal option, consider a couple potential (and significant) drawbacks:

>> Although drop-shipping is a low-cost, low-risk approach to testing the waters with customers, as your sales and business grow, the costs eat into your profit margins. If you're selling high-volume or low-margin items, drop-shipping may not be the best choice for selling any product long term.

>> If the drop-shipper drops the ball on an order, you suffer the consequences of disappointing a customer.

>> You're at the mercy of the drop-shipper regarding inventory. If your drop-shipper runs out of stock or discontinues a product, you're out of luck.

Even though Amazon generally accepts drop-shipping to its customers, it enforces certain criteria to maintain a high-quality shopping experience. All the sellers who intend to fulfill the orders through drop-shipping must meet the following criteria:

>> Be the seller on record

>> Identify as the seller of the products on all the packaging material, invoices, and any other documentation

>> Remove any mention of the drop-shipper from invoices, packaging, products, and anything else sent to customers

>> Be responsible for all the product returns

>> Comply with all other seller policies and Amazon policies

TIP

Drop-shipping is a great way to test the market for any new, unproven products. You can list the product without investing in inventory. If the product takes off, you can switch to FBA or FBM.

To find out more about drop-shipping, check out some of the top drop-shipping suppliers:

>> AliExpress at https://home.aliexpress.com/dropshippercenter/dashboard.htm

>> Doba at www.doba.com

>> Oberlo at www.oberlo.com

>> SaleHoo at www.salehoo.com

>> Sprocket at www.spocket.co

Using Fulfillment by Amazon (FBA)

The big challenge you face with FBA is getting your products to Amazon fulfillment centers with the proper packaging and bar codes. In this section, we lead you through the process. But first, we discuss the costs involved in this valuable service.

Accounting for the costs

Amazon charges a per-unit product fulfillment fee based on weight and package dimensions plus a monthly storage fee based on cubic feet. In this section, we break down those fees into three categories: per-unit order fulfillment fees, storage fees, and long-term storage fees.

Per-unit order fulfillment fees

The Amazon per-unit order fulfillment fee covers picking and packing orders, shipping and handling, customer service, and product returns. This fee varies according to whether a package is standard-size or oversize, as Table 10-1 shows.

TABLE 10-1 **FBA Per-Unit Fulfillment Fees**

Standard-Size			
Tier	Weight	Package Dimensions	Charges ($)
Small	10 oz or less	Longest: 15 inches or less Shortest: 0.75 inches or less Median: 12 inches or less	$2.41
Small	10+ to 16 oz	Longest: 15 inches or less Shortest: 0.75 inches or less Median: 12 inches or less	$2.48
Large	10 oz or less	Longest: 18 inches or less Shortest: 8 inches or less Median: 14 inches or less	$3.19
Large	10+ to 16 oz	Longest: 18 inches or less Shortest: 8 inches or less Median: 14 inches or less	$3.28
Large	1 to 2 lbs	Longest: 18 inches or less Shortest: 8 inches or less Median: 14 inches or less	$4.76
Large	2 to 3 lbs	Longest: 18 inches or less Shortest: 8 inches or less Median: 14 inches or less	$5.26
Large	3 to 21 lbs	Longest: 18 inches or less Shortest: 8 inches or less Median: 14 inches or less	$5.26 +$0.38/lb above first 3 lbs

(continued)

TABLE 10-1 *(continued)*

Tier	Weight	Standard-Size Package Dimensions Oversize	Charges ($)
Small	71 lbs or less	Longest: 60 inches or less Median: 30 inches or less Longest + Girth: 130 inches or less	$8.26 + 0.38/lb above first 2 lbs
Medium	151 lbs or less	Longest: 108 inches or less Longest + Girth: 130 inches or less	$9.79 + $0.39/lb above first 2 lbs
Large	151 lbs or less	Longest: 108 inches or less Longest + Girth: 165 inches or less	$75.78 + $0.79/lb above first 90 lbs
Special	More than 151 lbs	Longest: More than 108 inches Longest + Girth: More than 165 inches Or any product that requires special handling or delivery	$137.32 + $0.91/lb above first 90 lbs

Theses FBA fees are subject to change. Visit `https://services.amazon.com/fulfillment-by-amazon/pricing.html` for current fees.

Additional fees may apply to specific items, such as the following:

>> **Clothing:** $0.40/unit

>> **Lithium batteries:** $0.11/unit for items containing lithium batteries

Storage fees

Storage fees are based on daily average volume for the space occupied in Amazon fulfillment centers. Monthly storage fees for regular goods are charged per calendar month between the 7th and 15th of the following month. Rates vary according to regular storage, season, storage of dangerous items, and long-term storage, as Table 10-2 details. (For more about dangerous or hazardous items, see the later section "Knowing what to send and not send to FBA.")

Amazon charges a minimum per-unit storage fee of $0.15 or the cubic foot fee, whichever is greater.

REMEMBER

Amazon may randomly verify product dimensions using samples. When a seller's information differs from Amazon's measurements, Amazon's measurements are considered final for calculating the charges.

TABLE 10-2

Storage Fees

Regular Storage		
Month	Standard Size	Oversize
January to September	$0.69 per cubic foot	$0.48 per cubic foot
October to December	$2.40 per cubic foot	$1.20 per cubic foot
Dangerous Goods		
January to September	$0.99 per cubic foot	$0.78 per cubic foot
October to December	$3.63 per cubic foot	$2.43 per cubic foot

TIP

To calculate cubic feet of storage needed, take the following steps:

1. **Multiply length by width by height in inches to get the volume.**

2. **Divide the volume by 1,728 (cubic inches per foot).**

For example, a unit measuring 47-by-12-by-10 inches takes up 5,640 cubic inches of space: 5,640 cubic inches divided by 1,728 cubic inches per cubic foot = 3.26 cubic feet.

Long-term storage fees

Amazon charges long-term storage fee for all units stored more than 365 days in its fulfillment centers. The inventory cleanup date is the 15th of each month. If on the 15th of the month items have been in storage for longer than 365 days, Amazon charges $6.90 per cubic foot or a minimum of $0.15 per item, whichever is larger.

The long-term storage fee for items enrolled in the FBA Small and Light program are different. To be eligible as Small and Light, products in new condition must measure 16-by-9-by-4 inches or less, weigh 10 oz or less, and be priced at $7 or less. Refer to Amazon Seller Central resources for current charges on these products and information on how to enroll products in the Small and Light program. (Click the magnifying glass icon in the Seller Central toolbar and search for "FBA small and light.")

TIP

To avoid having to pay long-term storage fees, consider taking one or more of the following precautions:

>> Submit an inventory removal order prior to the 365-day mark. The deadline for submitting a removal order is 11:59 p.m. Pacific Time on the 14th of the month.

>> Set up automated inventory removals subject to long-term storage fees.

See the later section "Removing inventory from FBA" for instructions on how to have inventory removed from FBA fulfillment centers or to set up automated inventory removals.

Knowing what to send and not send to FBA

Amazon places restrictions on some products to protect customers and fulfillment center staff from any dangers, so honor these restrictions. Failure to do so can lead to loss of inventory or account suspension. Amazon reserves the right to refuse or dispose of any restricted items that reach its fulfillment centers without proper preauthorization and isn't required to reimburse sellers for the cost.

In the following sections, we break down products into four categories: used/damaged goods, generally prohibited, hazardous, and date- and temperature-sensitive products.

Used or damaged goods

You can send used or damaged products to Amazon fulfillment centers as long as the products are accurately labeled to indicate their condition.

Generally prohibited products

WARNING

Don't send any of the following generally prohibited products to Amazon fulfillment centers:

>> Alcoholic beverages or non-alcoholic beer, wine, champagne, and so on

>> Fireworks, sky lanterns, or floating lanterns

>> Gift cards, gift certificates, and other stored-value instruments

>> Products that require refrigeration or air-conditioning

>> Products with unauthorized marketing materials, such as pamphlets, price tags, or non-Amazon stickers

>> Products that require preparation but that haven't been prepped according to FBA packaging and prep requirements (see the later section "Prepping products to ship to FBA" for more about packing and prep requirements)

>> Loose packaged batteries

>> Products that have been illegally replicated, reproduced, or manufactured (knock-offs)

Amazon won't accept pre-priced labels or products.

REMEMBER Apart from the list of prohibited products, Amazon restricts certain brands entirely that are more prone to get counterfeited or have exclusive licensing agreements in place.

Hazardous materials

Amazon categorizes certain products as hazardous and places them in dangerous goods category. In general, Amazon fulfillment centers prohibit most products considered dangerous by the U.S. Department of Transportation, including the following:

>> Aerosol sprays

>> Airbags and airbag inflators

>> Alcohols

>> Bacterium cultures

>> Bleaches

>> Car batteries

>> Fireworks, explosives, anything with gun powder

>> Fuels (gas, diesel, propane, kerosene)

>> Hydrofluoric acid

>> Items containing carbon tetrachloride, such as fire extinguishers, refrigerants, and cleaning agents

>> Items containing mercury

>> Lighters and matches

>> Paints and thinners

>> Pesticides

>> Products containing Bisphenol A (BPA)

Click the magnifying glass icon near the top of Seller Central and search for "FBA hazardous materials" to track down a comprehensive list of items considered dangerous.

TIP

To ensure compliance with Amazon's rules governing the sale of safe products, whenever you create a new product listing or convert a listing to FBA, Amazon requires that you answer dangerous goods questions. Provide accurate and complete information, including, if required, a completed Safety Data Sheet (SDS) for your product, which should include a list of ingredients used in the product. If Amazon approves your request to sell the product, it processes any hazardous products in dedicated fulfillment centers properly equipped to address any dangers.

Date- and temperature-sensitive products

Amazon considers all tropical and consumable products intended for humans or animals subject to expiration, even if the expiration date isn't mentioned on the product or its packaging. As a seller, you must ensure that all packages are labeled with proper expiration dates or Amazon may refuse and dispose of the products without reimbursing you for their cost.

When choosing and preparing products for FBA, adhere closely to the following rules:

» Send only products that can withstand temperatures between 50 and 120 degrees Fahrenheit during the product's shelf life without impacting quality.

» Label all date-sensitive products with an expiration in the MM-DD-YYYY or MM-YYYY format, including those that require a best-by or sell-by date, which Amazon treats as the equivalent of an expiration date.

» Assume a shelf life for food and beverages of no longer than 90 days. Within 50 days after the labeled expiration date, Amazon disposes of products without reimbursement or returning items to the seller. However, if you have a letter from the manufacturer stating that a product can be stored at a maximum of 120 degrees Fahrenheit for an extended period of time, Amazon may agree to store the product for a longer period of time.

REMEMBER

Products requiring refrigeration or air-conditioning such as fresh fruits and vegetables are prohibited from FBA throughout the year.

Any temperature-sensitive products such as butters and chocolates are accepted into FBA only between October 1 and April 30. Any such inventory left after May 1 is marked as unfulfillable and disposed of. To avoid losing product, submit an inventory removal order before May 1. (See the later section "Removing inventory from FBA" for details.)

Signing up for FBA

Check to see whether you're already enrolled in FBA. In Seller Central, open the Settings menu, select Account Info, scroll down to Your Services, and select Manage. If you see Registered next to Fulfillment by Amazon, you're good to go. If not, follow the on-screen cues to sign up and agree to Amazon FBA's service terms.

Preparing and shipping products to FBA

Now for the challenging part — getting your products to FBA fulfillment centers properly packaged and labeled. In this section, we walk you through the process.

TIP

Unless you're exclusively into *retail arbitrage* (buying from other retailers and selling on Amazon), we strongly encourage you to negotiate with your suppliers to have your products shipped directly from their warehouses to Amazon fulfillment centers. Having products shipped to you so you can ship them to fulfillment centers is inefficient and sure to add to your costs. See Chapter 8 for guidance on working with suppliers.

Enrolling products in FBA

Enrolling products in FBA is easy. You can add products to FBA when creating your product listings, as we explain in Chapter 9. To add a product, log on to Seller Central, open the Inventory menu, and select Add a Product. Follow the on-screen cues to create your product listing and be sure to choose as the Fulfillment option: Amazon Will Ship and Provide Customer Service.

If you're uploading products in bulk, also explained in Chapter 9, you can specify your fulfillment method when completing the product listing template/spreadsheet for each product before uploading your completed template to Amazon.

You can also convert existing FBM product listings to FBA by taking the following steps:

1. **Open the Inventory menu and select Manage Inventory.**

2. **Select the products you want to sell through FBA.**

3. **Open the Actions drop-down menu and select Change to Fulfilled by Amazon.**

4. **Take one of the following steps:**

    - If you're ready to ship products to Amazon fulfillment centers, select Convert & Send Inventory.

    - If you're not ready to ship products to Amazon fulfillment centers, select Convert Only.

REMEMBER

Although you can create listings for products that haven't yet arrived at Amazon fulfillment centers, these products aren't available for purchase. All listings have zero inventory until the stock is processed into the fulfillment centers.

REMEMBER

When converting products from FBM to FBA, Amazon prompts you to answer product safety questions, including whether each product is a battery or includes batteries and whether any products may be considered dangerous or hazardous.

REMEMBER

You can use both FBA and FBM to fulfill customer orders. Just be sure to create a separate stock keeping unit (SKU) for each fulfillment method. Use the same Amazon Standard Identification Number (ASIN) for both FBA and FBM, but specify different SKUs. FBA will fulfill orders out of the FBA SKU, while you fulfill any orders against the FBM SKU.

Shipping products to Amazon fulfillment centers

When you're ready to ship products to Amazon fulfillment centers, you can initiate the process for individual products or create and submit a bulk shipping plan. (See Chapter 9 for details on creating and changing product listings individually or in bulk.) In this section, we provide additional guidance to navigate the process from the Manage FBA Inventory page or by creating and submitting a bulk shipping plan.

INITIATING SHIPMENT FROM THE MANAGE FBA INVENTORY PAGE

If you're shipping only a few products to FBA, consider using the Manage FBA Inventory page to initiate the process:

1. **Log in to Seller Central and do one of the following:**

   - Select Inventory and then Manage Inventory to access all inventory, including FBA and FBM.

   - Select Inventory and then Manage FBA Inventory to access only FBA inventory.

2. **Select the checkbox next to the listing for each product you're ready to send to Amazon fulfillment centers.**

3. **Select Send/Replenish Inventory from the resulting drop-down menu on the top left section of the page.**

   Seller Central redirects you to a page for specifying your preferences and providing additional information.

4. **Follow the on-screen cues to supply the requested details.**

   Seller Central displays the main shipment page.

5. **Continue the process by skipping ahead to the section "Set quantity."**

INITIATING SHIPMENT VIA A BULK SHIPPING PLAN

If you plan to ship tens or hundreds of products to Amazon fulfillment centers, you can save time and reduce complexity by creating and submitting a bulk shipping plan. Take the following steps:

1. **In Seller Central, open the Inventory menu and select Manage FBA Inventory.**

2. **In the sub-menu that appears just below the primary menu, select Shipping Queue.**

   The Shipping Queue dashboard appears.

3. **Select Upload Shipping Plan File.**

4. **Press the Download Template button.**

5. **Open the downloaded template in a program that supports Excel (XLS) files.**

6. **Follow the instructions on the Instructions tab to complete the template and save it as a text (tab delimited, .txt) file.**

7. **Return to Seller Central, click the Upload Now button, and follow the on-screen cues to upload the template.**

8. **Under Review File Status and History, click Refresh; review the resulting report for any additional information, errors, or warnings; and address any outstanding issues.**

REMEMBER

After uploading the completed shipping plan file, you can access it from Seller Central by opening the Inventory menu, selecting Manage FBA Shipments, and then selecting the Shipping Plans tab. Open the desired plan and enter additional details, as we explain in the following sections.

The shipping plan consists of six subsections. After you complete these subsections, your products will be ready to be sent to Amazon fulfillment centers. Press the Continue button after completing each section to move to the next section. If you need to interrupt the process, you can revisit a section by clicking on its name.

SET QUANTITY

Under Set Quantity, enter requested details for all products in the shipment (individual listings and case packed), including quantity, package dimensions, and weights, if not already provided. If any essential details are omitted or any listing is ineligible for FBA, FBA won't allow you to proceed to the next step in the process.

REMEMBER

Amazon distinguishes between one box of different products (individual) and boxes that contain all of one identical product (case packed). When creating your shipping plan, be sure to distinguish between individual and case-packed items because they'll be handled differently at Amazon fulfillment centers.

PREPARE PRODUCTS

This section provides an opportunity to indicate whether any products you're shipping to fulfillment centers require special preparation, packaging, or handling. Also, specify who will be preparing the products — you or Amazon. If you choose to have Amazon do any of the product preparation, Amazon will quote a per-unit fee after you specify the preparation required.

LABEL PRODUCTS

REMEMBER

All products must have a bar code. If your product is eligible for tracking with the manufacturer bar code, you don't need to print and apply Amazon labels to your items. If your product is not eligible, then it must have an Amazon bar code. To print and apply Amazon bar code labels, open the Who Labels? drop-down menu and select Merchant, then click Print Labels for This Page. To have Amazon print and apply the labels (for a fee), open the Who Labels? menu and select Amazon. In either case, specify the number of labels needed (typically one per item) and the label size.

REVIEW SHIPMENTS

The Review Shipments page displays the following details:

- ≫ All costs for product preparation, labeling, and handling
- ≫ A list of distribution centers where products will be sent, which is helpful for determining how to pack products and cases for shipment

REMEMBER

After verifying all the details entered so far, select Approve & Continue. Though you have the option to edit the shipment contents one more time in the next step, usual practice is to approve the shipment. After orders are approved, FBA creates one or more shipments depending on the number of locations the products are being sent.

PREPARE SHIPMENT

"Prepare shipment" is a bit of a misnomer. You're not actually handling the product here; you're just adding details about how products will be shipped. To prepare the shipment, take the following steps:

1. **For one of the shipments FBA created in the previous section, select Work on Shipment.**

   FBA displays the shipment's contents.

2. **Review the shipment contents.**

   Check and, if necessary, modify the shipment quantities. Note that quantity modification can't exceed more than 5 percent or six total products. For larger quantities, cancel the existing shipment plan and submit a new one.

3. **Select shipping service.**

   Select Small Parcel (individual boxes) or Less Than Truckload (LTL for pallets of at least 150 lbs) and a carrier (Amazon partner UPS or other available carrier).

4. **Specify shipment packing details**.

   Details include how the contents of the shipment will be packed into the *master boxes* (bigger boxes containing more than one SKU according to the details provided during the shipment creation process), number of boxes, box weights, and box dimensions. You can provide packing information here, on the shipment page, or by uploading it via a template file. After you provide the shipping details, FBA presents estimated shipping charges based on box weights and dimensions.

REMEMBER

   Make sure the weight of any box containing multiple units doesn't exceed 50 pounds. For single units, if the weight exceeds 50 pounds, label each item "Team Lift" on the top and sides to ensure safe handling.

5. **Review and approve or reject the proposed shipping charges.**

   If you approved the charges, proceed to Step 6 to prepare your boxes.

6. **Arrange your boxes and products for the different Amazon distribution centers they'll be shipped to, so you'll have a clear idea of the shipping labels you'll need.**

7. **Select the option to print the labels for the boxes you'll be shipping to Amazon's fulfillment centers and use the labels as follows:**

   - Affix your shipping label to the outside of the box. (You don't need to put the printed packing labels inside.)

   - Don't photocopy, reuse, or modify the labels. Each shipping label is unique and is used to track the box and its contents.

You have up to 24 hours to void the charges if you change your mind. You can delete the shipping plan by clicking on the "Delete shipment" button on the bottom left of the page.

PREPPING PRODUCTS TO SHIP TO FBA

With your boxes, products, and shipping labels on hand, you're ready to pack. Be sure to adhere to all FBA packaging guidelines, including the following:

>> Apply a unique product label (or bar code) to each product box for easy scanning at Amazon fulfillment centers.

>> Create a unique SKU for each product item.

>> If the product has an existing label, cover it with an Amazon printed label wherever required.

>> Don't include any marketing materials or flyers with packaging or products.

>> If you're selling sets or bundles, pack them together and label them something along the lines of "Sold in sets; don't separate."

>> Make sure any box containing a product can survive a three-foot drop on all sides. If a box is likely to fail the drop test, pack it in a polyurethane (poly) bag according to the following guidelines:

• Use 1.5 mil thick clear polyethylene bag, so the bar code on the box clearly shows through for scanning. If the bag is likely to obscure the bar code, affix the bar code sticker to the outside of the bag.

• Add a suffocation warning sticker to any plastic bag with an opening of more than five inches.

• Pack any adult products in black opaque poly bags with the bar code affixed to the outside of the bag.

Removing inventory from FBA

To avoid paying long-term storage fees on products that aren't selling, request that Amazon remove your inventory from its fulfillment centers and return it to you.

Removal order fees vary by service type (return or dispose of item) and product size (standard or oversize); the return fee is a flat fee charged per item to return products to the specified location:

Service	Standard-size (per item)	Oversize (per item)
Return	$0.50	$0.60
Disposal	$0.15	$0.30

You can submit an order to have products removed from fulfillment centers or set a date on which products will automatically be removed.

Submit an inventory removal order

To submit an inventory removal order, follow these steps:

1. **Take one of the following steps:**

   - On Seller Central, open the Inventory menu and select Manage Inventory. Choose the items you want to remove, open the Action on Selected drop-down list, and select Create Removal Order.

   - On Seller Central, open the Reports menu, select Fulfillment, scroll down to Removals (in the navigation bar on the left), select Recommended Removal, and click Begin Removal Process.

2. **On the Provide Details page, under Method of Removal, take one of the following steps:**

   - Select Ship-to Address and enter the address where you want the inventory shipped (your address or the address of a supplier, for example).

   - Select Dispose of to have inventory disposed of at the fulfillment center(s).

3. **In the Set Order ID field, enter the customer order ID you want to use to track this transaction or leave the field blank to have an order ID generated automatically.**

   Save the removal order ID for tracking purposes.

4. **Under Specify Ordered SKUs/units, enter a title, MSKU, ASIN, or FNSKU in the Search and Add Items text box, click Search, select the products you want removed from inventory, and select Add Selected.**

5. **Under Fulfillable Qty. enter the number of fulfillable units to remove from inventory.**

   Fulfillable quantity is the number of items that can be sold. The number of items you specify represent excess inventory to remove to avoid storage fees.

6. **Under Unfulfillable Qty. enter the number of unfillable units to remove.**

   Unfulfillable quantity is the number of items that can't be sold for whatever reason, such as damaged product or packaging.

7. **Click Continue.**

The Review and Place Order page appears. Check the details to ensure everything is correct and that you're satisfied with the shipping speed and estimated removal fees.

8. **Select Place Order to submit the inventory removal order.**

REMEMBER

An inventory removal may take up to 30 days to process, but as long as you meet the inventory removal request deadline, Amazon won't charge you a long-term storage fee.

Set up an automated inventory removal

To have inventory removed from Amazon fulfillment centers automatically prior to sitting in storage for more than a year, schedule in advance to have the inventory removed:

1. **Take one of the following steps:**

   - Open the Settings menu and select Fulfillment by Amazon.
   - Open the Inventory menu, select Manage FBA Inventory, Remove Unfulfillable Inventory, and Auto Removal Settings.

2. **On the Fulfillment by Amazon Settings page, locate Automated Unfulfillable Removal Settings, and next to that option, click Edit.**

3. **On the Automated Unfulfillable Removal Settings page, click Enable and select one of the following:**

   - Return to have products returned to you
   - Dispose to have products disposed of at the fulfillment centers

4. **Select your preferred schedule:**

   - Immediate
   - Weekly (on the 8th, 15th, 22nd, and 28th)
   - Twice a month (on the 15th and 20th)
   - Once a month (on the 1st)

5. **In the Email Address box, enter your preferred email address for receiving notifications about the inventory removal.**

6. **If you chose to have products returned to you (in Step 3), enter your address and phone number.**

7. **Select Update.**

Shipping Products Yourself: Fulfillment by Merchant (FBM)

Although FBA is a great option for its convenience and speedy delivery, you may be better off shipping certain products yourself. When deciding whether to list products as FBA or FBM, consult Table 10-3 for guidance.

TABLE 10-3 **Comparing FBA with FBM**

Choose FBA When . . .	Choose FBM When . . .	Because . . .
Products are fast movers (sell within one month).	Products are slow movers.	With slow-moving products, you'll rack up high fees for storing products in FBA distribution centers.
Products are expensive, small, and light.	Products are inexpensive, big, and heavy, especially oversize items (more than 20 pounds and measuring length + width >/= 130 inches)	Big, heavy products are expensive to store, and if the product is relatively inexpensive, you may not be able to recoup the cost with your markup.
You lack the time and personnel to ship products yourself and provide quality customer service.	You have the time or personnel to ship products yourself and provide quality customer service.	You must deliver products to customers quickly and provide quality customer service, whether you do it yourself or farm it out to a third party such as FBA.
Commingling products is okay. FBA gives you the option of allowing or prohibiting the *commingling* of products (shipping your product with one or more products from other sellers).	Commingling products has the potential to damage the brand — for example, having your genuine product packed and shipped with a counterfeit product.	You don't want your reputation tainted by other Amazon Sellers who don't follow the rules.
You don't have sufficient space for storing products.	You have sufficient space for storing products.	You need enough storage space to maintain sufficient inventory for fulfilling all customer orders.
You don't have a great seller feedback rating (four stars or higher).	You have an excellent seller feedback rating.	Shoppers are reluctant to order from a seller with a low rating, but FBA compensates for a low rating to some extent because shoppers trust that Amazon will deliver.

(continued)

TABLE 10-3 *(continued)*

Choose FBA When . . .	Choose FBM When . . .	Because . . .
Sales aren't near the end of the year holiday season.	Sales aren't so great near the end of the year or holiday season.	Storage fees are higher than average in Q4. If your Q4 sales volume doesn't rise to the level of covering the added cost, you may need to fulfill orders yourself.
You're selling standard items with no assembly required.	You're selling custom products or products requiring assembly.	You're probably more careful in packing and shipping products.
FBA shipping fees are competitive with shipping fees you can negotiate with individual carriers.	You can ship products for less than Amazon can.	You want to avoid tacking on a high shipping cost to a sale, which can drive away shoppers and get you into trouble with Amazon.

REMEMBER

You may want to offer the same product as FBA and FBM whenever it makes sense to improve the chances of maximizing sales. For example, some shoppers may be willing to pay a premium to have a product assembled or packed and shipped a certain way, whereas others may be more comfortable knowing that the product is fulfilled by Amazon.

WARNING

When fulfilling orders yourself (FBM), keep a close eye on shipping costs to avoid violating Amazon's Fair Pricing Policy. Specifically, you want to avoid the following practice known to damage customer trust:

> Setting a shipping fee on a product that is excessive. Amazon considers current public carrier rates, reasonable handling charges, as well as buyer perception when determining whether a shipping price violated our fair pricing policy.

REMEMBER

Typically, shipping rates that exceed standard carrier rates by more than 25 percent are considered unfair, though the policy might be revised time to time as with any other Amazon policy.

Chapter **11**

Helping Shoppers Find You and Your Products

N ewbies are at a distinct disadvantage in the Amazon marketplace, having to compete against giants, including Amazon and other big brands, many of which restrict or prohibit third parties from selling their products. Making the marketplace even more competitive are more than two million active sellers worldwide, many of whom already have years of experience and a considerable amount of positive feedback to help drive sales.

As a newcomer, you're probably wondering, "How do I gain traction on Amazon?" In this chapter, we present several techniques to answer that question.

Gaining Traction with Product and Seller Ratings and Feedback

Your visibility and sales success and that of the products you sell are impacted by product ratings and reviews and by your seller rating and feedback. Knowing the differences among these important metrics is a key first step in using them to drive sales:

>> **Product ratings and reviews** are about the product, not about you. A product's rating impacts its ranking in relevant product search results on Amazon. Products with more reviews and higher ratings are generally ranked higher in their product category than comparable items with few or no reviews or a very low overall product rating.

>> **Seller rating** is all about you, not the product. Your seller rating is a reflection of your performance based on shipping time, order cancellations, credit card chargebacks, customer inquiries, A-to-Z Guarantee claims against you, and other metrics. Your seller rating impacts your ability to win the buy box and, if it gets too low, your ability to do business on Amazon.

>> **Seller feedback** consists of comments that buyers share about your service and products. Seller feedback may have an impact on your seller rating but is only one of many factors that do. Savvy sellers use this feedback to transform a customer's negative shopping experience into a positive one and to improve customer service overall.

In the following sections, we provide guidance on how to obtain more product reviews for new product listings and how to improve your seller rating and feedback.

Encouraging customers to review products

Product reviews are key to Amazon's success. A large part of the reason people shop on Amazon is that they want to see what other customers have to say about a product before they buy it (or choose to buy a competing product). Even people who don't shop on Amazon come to check out the customer reviews before buying the product elsewhere, which gives Amazon an opportunity to win their business.

Generally, products with more reviews sell better, and products that sell better have more reviews; it's a chicken-and-egg scenario — which came first? On Amazon, the reviews often come first. Without at least a few reviews, a new product in a given category may not appear on the first couple pages of a shopper's search results. To raise a new product's visibility, you need to encourage people who buy the product to post reviews about it, but you need to do it without violating Amazon's product review policies.

REMEMBER

This advice applies only to new product listings that have few or no customer ratings. If you start to sell a product that's already listed on Amazon, has dozens of ratings and reviews, and is already a top seller in its category, you don't need to solicit product reviews.

Understanding the rules of the road

In the heat of competition, unethical sellers post bogus reviews to make their products look better and competing products look worse. In an attempt to ensure fair play and assure shoppers that the ratings and reviews are authentic, Amazon has established the following product rating and review policies:

>> Don't post reviews of your own or a competing product.

>> Don't offer any financial incentives, discounts, free products, or any other compensation to any third parties to post product reviews or engage a service provider to post reviews of your own or a competing product.

>> Don't offer or provide a refund or reimbursement after the buyer posts a review of your product.

>> Don't offer or issue a refund, payment, or reimbursement in any form to a customer in exchange for posting, revising, or removing a product review.

>> Don't ask a reviewer to change or remove a product review.

>> Don't engage friends, family members, employees, or any other associates to post reviews of your own or a competing product.

>> Don't use any tools or mechanisms to divert negative reviews to other platforms while routing positive reviews to products listed on Amazon.

>> Don't ask or prompt buyers in any way or through any means, including a product's packaging, to post only positive reviews of your products.

>> Don't create variations with unrelated products with the intention of aggregating the product reviews for those items.

>> Don't use a customer account to post, revise, or remove a product review.

Amazon has a zero-tolerance policy toward any violation of these policies and will take immediate action against any sellers found violating these policies. Penalties include but aren't limited to the following:

>> Removal of any product reviews posted in violation of the policies or removal of all reviews associated with your product and potential suspension of all future reviews for that product

>> Permanent removal of your product from the Amazon marketplace

>> Permanent removal of selling privileges and withholding any payments or funds

>> Legal action, including lawsuits and referral to civil and criminal enforcement authorities

>> Public disclosure of your name and other related information

For additional information about Amazon's customer product review policies, click the Search button near the top of Seller Central, search for "customer product review policies," and use the search results to explore the topic.

TIP

If you're involved in the design or manufacturing of a product or are the brand owner, product reviews may serve as valuable feedback. Use insights gleaned from the feedback to improve the product and your product listing.

Enrolling new products in the Early Reviewer program

If you're a brand owner, Amazon allows you to use its Early Reviewer program to solicit up to five reviews from customers who've purchased the product. In exchange for posting a review (positive, negative, or neutral), the customer receives a $3 Amazon gift card.

To take advantage of this program, you must enroll a product and pay a $60 fee plus any applicable taxes. The enrollment covers all stock keeping units (SKUs) in a parent or SKU family or standalone SKU. After you enroll a product, Amazon chooses buyers at random and requests that they post a review of your product in exchange for a $3 Amazon gift card. Amazon continues to request reviews for up to one year or until five reviews are posted.

Eligibility for this program is based on the following requirements:

>> You must be the product's brand owner.

>> The product must have fewer than five reviews.

>> The product must be priced above $9.

>> The product must be sold in the United States (during the writing of this book, the Early Reviewer program was available only for products sold in the United States).

To take advantage of the Early Reviewer program and enroll one or more products in it, log in to Seller Central, open the Advertising menu, select Early Reviewer Program, and follow the on-screen directions.

Taking advantage of the Amazon Vine program

If you're an Amazon Professional Seller, you can enroll certain products in Amazon's Vine program to obtain reviews from trusted reviewers called Vine Voices. These select reviewers are invited by Amazon to participate in the program due to the quality and helpfulness of their past reviews (based on feedback from other Amazon customers). Amazon sends the product to review to Vine Voices, who use the product for a period of time and post their unbiased review. Sellers are prohibited from influencing, modifying, or editing the reviews.

To participate in the Vine program, you must meet the following criteria:

» Be a Professional Seller

» Have your brand registered in Amazon's Brand Registry

» Have eligible FBA offers

To be eligible for consideration in the Vine program, a product must meet the follow criteria:

» Be registered in Amazon's Brand Registry

» Have fewer than 30 reviews on the product's detail page

» Have a buyable FBA offer in new condition and be available in inventory

» Not be an adult product

» Be launched at the time of the enrollment (no pre-launch products)

» Have a product description and image

To enroll in the Vine program, log in to Seller Central, open the Advertising menu, select Vine, and following the on-screen directions.

REMEMBER

During the writing of this book, the Vine program was free, except for the cost of free products supplied to Vine reviewers, but Amazon reserves the right to revise the program terms at any time.

Improving your seller rating and feedback

Just as a product rating can impact the search rank of a product, your seller rating can impact the search rank of your listings and your ability to win the buy box. To improve your seller rating, be aware of the metrics it's based on, including the following (refer to Chapter 13 for more information):

» **Shipping:** You're rated on how quickly you ship an order relative to the dates promised and how soon you confirm shipment.

- **Order defect rate (ODR):** ODR is a key measure of your ability to deliver quality customer service. An order is deemed defective if it results in one of the following:

  - **A-to-Z Guarantee claim:** You can't resolve an issue with a customer, so the customer files an A-to-Z Guarantee claim against you with Amazon.

  - **Chargeback:** Your customer contacts his credit card company to dispute a charge for one or more of your products he purchased and the company issues a credit for that amount to the customer's account, essentially refunding the purchase price.

  - **Negative seller feedback:** The customer posts a negative rating or review of the shopping experience.

- **Responsiveness:** Amazon expects you to respond to any buyer inquiries within 24 hours.

- **Order cancellations:** If you (the seller) cancel the order for any reason, it counts against you. Order cancellation initiated by a shopper doesn't count against you.

- **Inventory performance index:** This metric reflects how well you drive sales by stocking popular products and how efficiently you manage on-hand inventory. Your seller rating is likely to suffer if Amazon has to suspend a listing because the product is out of stock.

Harnessing the Power of Search Engine Optimization (SEO)

Most Amazon shoppers find products by searching specifically for what they want. They enter a few keywords in the Search bar, press Enter, and skim through the search results. *Search engine optimization (SEO)* is the use of various techniques to present users with search results that most accurately match what they're looking for.

On Amazon, you can leverage the power of SEO in your product listings to have them appear when shoppers are looking for products identical or similar to the ones you're selling. If your product isn't search engine optimized, it may not appear in a list of relevant search results even if it's rated higher than competing products.

REMEMBER

According to one estimate, more than half of all shoppers start their new product search on Amazon. Furthermore, products listed in the first page of search results account for nearly three quarters of all sales on Amazon. SEO is crucial for reaching shoppers and getting your product in front of them when they're ready to buy. Additionally, all online marketing efforts, including pay-per-click (PPC) advertising on Amazon (see Chapter 12), perform best when they're search engine optimized.

On Amazon, SEO boils down to catering to Amazon's search algorithm, commonly known as A9. As we explain in Chapter 9, the A9 algorithm considers a wide range of factors to determine each product's ranking in any given search with the goal of presenting the customer with the product that's most suitable to what he wants or needs.

Jazzing Up Your Listings with A+ Content

Admittedly, Amazon product listings are a little on the drab side, consisting merely of text and a few product photos. If you're a brand owner enrolled as a Registered Brand, you can jazz up your listings by taking advantage of Amazon's A+ Content (formerly known as Enhanced Brand Content).

With A+ Content, you stitch together a collection of modules to create your very own multimedia brand story. It also enables you to highlight your product's features and benefits and address any questions or concerns that may be holding a customer back from making a purchase decision. One additional perk is that it gives you the chance to introduce customers to a range of other products.

REMEMBER

According to Amazon, A+ Content increases conversions by 3 to 10 percent and reduces returns and negative reviews. To create an A+ page to add to your product listing, take the following steps:

1. **Log in to Seller Central.**

2. **Open the Advertising menu and select A+ Content Manager.**

3. **After the A+ Content Manager page appears, select Start Creating A+ Content.**

   The A+ Content Manager displays a page with two options:

   - **Self-Service Modules:** For creating your own A+ page using a template

   - **Amazon Builds for You:** To upload your content and have Amazon create your A+ page

4. **Press the Build Your Own button to create your own A+ page.**

(To have Amazon build the page for you, press the We Build for You button and following the on-screen directives.) When you click the Build Your Own button, A+ Content Manager prompts you to enter the product's ASIN.

5. **In the Step 1: Enter ASIN box, type or paste the ASIN of the product for which you're creating the A+ page and then choose the product from the pop-up that appears.**

6. **Click in the Project Name box and type a descriptive name for the new A+ page.**

7. **Press the Continue button.**

The A+ Content Manager displays the Build Layout page with a list of modules on the left and a work area on the right.

8. **Drag selected modules from the left and drop them into the work area on the right to create the desired page layout.**

You can drag modules up or down in the work area to rearrange them. To delete a module, hover the cursor over it in the work area and click the red X in the upper right of the module.

9. **Click Continue.**

The A+ Content Manager displays your page layout with placeholders for text, images, bullet items, and so on.

10. **Replace the placeholders with the text, images, and other content you want to use.**

11. **Press the Preview button.**

A+ Content Manager displays a preview of your completed A+ page. (You can use the buttons above the preview area to see how the page will look on a desktop computer or mobile device. You can use the Back button in the lower-left corner to go back and edit your page.)

12. **When you're happy with your A+ page, press the Checkout button and follow the on-screen directions to pay for your A+ page.**

REMEMBER

When writing this, A+ Content was free, but Amazon still required you to go through the checkout process.

Driving Web Traffic from Outside Amazon to Your Product Listings

One way to drum up business on Amazon is to drive traffic from the web to your Amazon Store or listings. It's sort of like hiring a guy to stand on a street corner with a spinner sign to divert traffic from a busy thoroughfare to your local business. This technique is great if you already have a popular website, blog, or Facebook page, but if you don't, it's pretty easy and inexpensive to get started.

In this section, we explain three ways to drive web traffic from outside Amazon to your product listings — by using social media, a website landing page, and off-Amazon pay-per-click advertising.

WARNING

Simply driving traffic from the web to your product listings can backfire by reducing your conversion rates and hence your seller rating. You want to drive prospective customers to your listings who are ready to make a purchase. Be sure the content you post on social media or a web landing page prepares shoppers to buy your product.

Generating buzz via social media

Social media is a great way to generate buzz around a product, especially a great new product, because everyone will want to share the news with their friends and family members. If this idea appeals to you, consider targeting the largest social media sites first, including the following:

>> **Facebook:** On Facebook, you can create separate Facebook pages for your ecommerce business and any products you sell. You can then add the Shop Now button and link it to your Amazon Store or to a specific product listing.

>> **Instagram:** You can use the Amazon Associates (affiliate) program to create URLs for your Amazon Store or for individual product pages and add these to your bio, captions, and stories. Visit `affiliate-program.amazon.com` for more about Amazon Associates. You may not be able to create clickable links, but the URLs are typically short enough to remember.

>> **Pinterest:** You can use the Amazon Associates program to create links to your Amazon Store or to individual product detail pages. You'll need a business account to add affiliate links to your boards, and be sure to read and follow Pinterest's terms of use regarding affiliate links.

>> **YouTube:** Product videos are a great way to showcase the features and benefits of products and instruct users on the proper use of certain products.

You can use YouTube in the following two ways to help market your Amazon Store and products:

- Host your product videos on YouTube and then embed the videos in web pages, social media pages and posts, blog posts, and so on. On YouTube, you simply pull up the video you want to embed and click Share below the video to display various options for sharing the video.

- Join Amazon Associates and use it to add affiliate links to your YouTube channel and videos. This is a complicated process, but you can find instructions by searching the web.

» **Your blog:** If you manage your own blog, you can post content related to the products you sell and use your blog posts to promote your products. For example, if you frequently post about fashion topics, you can link your posts to your Amazon Store or to specific products you recommend.

WARNING

Whenever you recommend your store or a product on a social media site or a web page, be sure to disclose that you're an affiliate and will earn money from any sales. Otherwise, you could end up in legal trouble with the U.S. Federal Trade Commission (FTC). Here's an example of an affiliate disclosure:

This is an affiliate link. If you click it and make a purchase, I will earn a commission at no additional cost to you.

TIP

Consider offering your social media followers and fans exclusive promotional deals on Amazon. To create a social media promotion code for a product you're selling on Amazon, take the following steps:

1. **Log in to Seller Central, open the Advertising menu, and select Promotions.**

2. **Click the Create Promotion tab and choose Social Media Promo Code.**

3. **Click Create.**

4. **Follow the on-screen instructions to create your promo code and enter your preferences and restrictions.**

   When you're done creating your promo code, Amazon displays a URL that you can copy and paste into your social media posts and pages and any outgoing email to share the promotion with your followers and fans.

Creating a website or landing page

Brands often host their own websites or landing pages to promote their products and services. They may create a webstore on the site where customers can place orders or link to one or more ecommerce stores. Regardless of whether you're a brand owner, you can use a website or landing page to attract prospective customers and promote your products.

You can use your website or landing page just as you would use your social media accounts to promote your webstore and products — by including on your web pages relevant links to Amazon.

As an added bonus, you can use your website as a sales funnel to lead a prospective customer through the journey of making a well-informed purchase decision. A sales funnel generally leads a prospective customer through the following six stages in this order:

>> Awareness

>> Interest

>> Consideration

>> Intent

>> Evaluation

>> Purchase

Leading prospective customers through these stages instead of simply directing them to your Amazon Store or a product page will generally increase your conversion rate. You send customers to Amazon only at the Purchase stage, when they're ready to make a purchase.

The sales funnel concept is beyond the scope of this book, but the general idea is to give prospective customers the information and insight they need at each stage of the process, such as the following:

>> Images and infographics

>> eBooks, white papers, and reports

>> Educational videos or webinars

>> A coupon, promotional code, or other discount

You may want to offer some of these freebies on your website in exchange for the person's email address. Capturing valid email addresses is a great way to stay in touch with people who've demonstrated an interest in your products and keep them posted concerning any new products to drive future sales.

One drawback to the sales funnel approach is that it draws out the sales process. As a result, some prospective customers are likely to lose interest or patience and drop out. Ideally, these are the same people who would never buy the product, even if you offered it practically for free. However, you could also lose some very good prospects. To minimize the loss, provide engaging, informative content throughout the process.

Using pay-per-click advertising

Pay-per-click (PPC) advertising involves paying an ad publisher every time a user clicks your ad and is redirected to your destination of choice — typically your website, webstore, product page, or order form. In Chapter 12, we explain how to use Amazon's Sponsored Products, which is a PPC program that displays PPC ads only on Amazon. You can also use PPC ads outside Amazon, typically on online search sites, such as Google, Bing, and Yahoo!.

With PPC, you create an ad, complete with a small amount of text, an image, and a list of keywords that trigger the ad to appear. You also specify how much you're willing to pay per click and your total budget for the ad campaign. When a user conducts a search using words that match one of your ad's keywords, your ad bids against other ads using the same keyword. If your ad wins, it appears at the top of the search results (or in another prominent location on the page). If the user clicks your ad, you pay the search engine company for that click. (Even if you're not the high bidder, your ad may appear on the page, though in a less prominent location.)

Because Google is the most popular search engine, if you're interested in PPC, we suggest you start with Google Ads at ads.google.com, where you can find out more about PPC and discover how Google Ads work before spending any money.

IN THIS CHAPTER

» Increasing visibility with Amazon ads

» Giving your items top billing as sponsored products

» Strutting your stuff as a sponsored brand

» Increasing conversions with special deals and promotions

» Driving external traffic to your product listings and Amazon Store

Chapter **12**

Boosting Sales with Marketing and Advertising

Selling on Amazon involves more than just buying, listing, and shipping products; you need to get your business and products in front of shoppers. Unless you're the only one selling a unique product that's in high demand, getting your business and products in front of shoppers is a huge challenge, especially when you're just getting started.

To increase your visibility on Amazon, take advantage of its marketing and advertising tools, including Sponsored Products, Sponsored Brands, Deals, and Coupons. With these tools and other techniques presented in this chapter, you can start to build the momentum to drive current and future sales.

Exploring Different Ad Types

Amazon is not only the largest marketplace in the United States and one of the largest in the world, it's also a very popular online advertising platform. Its advertising products enable you to market your products inside and outside Amazon to boost sales, increase brand recognition, and expand your reach.

In this section, we introduce you to the different Amazon advertising tools, so you can decide which is best for you.

REMEMBER

You can access all your advertising options through the Amazon Advertising console at advertising.amazon.com.

Sponsored Products

The advertising tool of choice for most sellers on Amazon is Sponsored Products. These ads appear at the top of the first page of search results and in various locations on certain product pages to call attention to the products that sellers want to promote.

With Sponsored Products, you choose the product you want to promote, enter the keywords that trigger the ad's appearance, and specify how much you're willing to pay per click and per day. When a shopper's search phrase includes one of the keywords you specified, you bid against other sellers for premium ad placement, and Amazon automatically places ads based on the bid amounts. If the shopper clicks one of your ads, you pay Amazon the amount you bid for that click, which is why this form of advertising is referred to as *pay-per-click (PPC)*.

Sponsored Products offers the following benefits:

>> **Enhanced targeting:** With Sponsored Products, you can target your ads to shoppers who are more likely to buy your product by specifying keywords best suited to your product or to specific product categories or brands. You can even narrow the criteria to target a certain price range, Prime-eligible products, or star ratings. Also, you can specify *negative keywords* — words in search phrases that tell Amazon not to display your ad.

>> **Increased visibility:** Even if you don't win the buy box (see Chapter 9), your advertised products are sure to be seen by customers.

>> **Increased sales:** Increased visibility generally results in increased sales by driving more traffic to your product's listing.

Determining Sponsored Product eligibility

You can run a Sponsored Product ad only if you're a Professional Seller, a vendor (or book vendor), a Kindle Direct Publishing (KDP) author, or an agency representative. In addition, the product must be in one or more of the following eligible categories and be buy-box eligible:

Eligible Categories

Apparel	Cellphones and Accessories	Grocery and Gourmet Food	Musical Instruments
Appliances	Clothing and Accessories	Handmade	Office Products
Arts, Crafts, and Sewing	Collectible Coins	Health and Personal Care	Outdoors
Automotive Parts and Accessories	Computers	Home & Kitchen	Patio, Lawn, and Garden
Baby	Electronics	Industrial and Scientific	Pet Supplies
Batteries	Entertainment	Luggage	Shoes
Beauty	Collectibles	Movies and TV	Software
Camera	Fine Art	Music	Sports
Sports Collectibles	Tools and Home Improvement	Toys and Games	Video Games

The following product types aren't eligible to be advertised as Sponsored Products:

>> Adult products

>> Used products

>> Refurbished products

>> Products in closed categories (see Chapter 5 for more about closed categories)

Controlling your spending

You don't need deep pockets to start advertising on Amazon. You're charged only when a shopper clicks one of your Sponsored Product ads, and you can specify your maximum bid amount and daily budget and suspend or cancel your ad at any time:

>> **Set a maximum bid amount:** The higher your bid price, the better your ad placement, but the fewer clicks you get for your daily budget. Amazon presents you with a suggested bid range, which is calculated based on winning bids for similar product ads.

>> **Ad budget:** You can set a daily budget for each Sponsored Product ad, which you can adjust at any time in response to your campaign's performance.

For guidance on how to run a Sponsored Product ad, see the later section "Optimizing Your Search Rank with Sponsored Product Ads."

Sponsored Brands

Sponsored Brands enable Professional Sellers enrolled in Amazon Brand Registry (see Chapter 17), vendors, book vendors, and agency representatives to increase brand awareness and showcase a small selection of products. Each Sponsored Brands ad features the brand's logo, a headline, and up to three products. Sponsored Brands ads appear when a shopper conducts a search that contains one or more of the keywords specified to trigger the ad.

Four Sponsored Brands ad placement spots are available on every search results page, all of which are considered prime real estate for brand visibility:

>> One at the top of a shopper's search results page

>> One on the left side of the page

>> Two at the bottom of the page

Sponsored Brands are a great way to generate some initial buzz around a newly launched brand and to showcase a small selection of products. When shoppers click your brand logo, they're redirected to your store or a custom landing page. If they click a product, they're taken to that product's listing.

As with Sponsored Products, you must set a bid amount and daily budget, and you pay the bid amount only when a shopper clicks your ad. Sponsored Brands are allowed for any brand and products that meet nearly the same eligibility requirements as those for Sponsored Product ads.

For guidance on how to run a Sponsored Brands ad, see the later section "Boosting Brand Awareness with Sponsored Brands."

Sponsored Display

Sponsored Display ads are very similar to Sponsored Products. The ads are typically small, consisting of a product image, a brief description of the product (including its price and product rating), and a Shop Now button that links back to the product's detail page on Amazon. The big difference is that Sponsored Display ads appear on and off Amazon — on third-party websites and ads. Another big difference is that you don't need to specify keywords; Amazon uses information about a person's browsing and buying habits to target your ads to people who are likely to be interested in the product you're promoting.

REMEMBER

Sponsored Display ads are available only to Professional Sellers enrolled in Amazon Brand Registry, vendors, and agencies with clients who sell products on Amazon in the United States.

Amazon demand-side platform (DSP)

Amazon DSP is a platform that provides an easy way for advertisers to buy advertising space from publishers of relevant content. For example, you can create a video ad for a plumbing tool, and Amazon DSP will display that ad whenever someone views a relevant plumbing video on YouTube or article on a plumbing website.

REMEMBER

Amazon DSP is available to advertisers regardless of whether they sell products or services on Amazon. To find out more about Amazon DSP and to get started using it, visit advertising.amazon.com/products/amazon-dsp.

Amazon DSP supports display and video ads, as we describe in the following sections.

Display ads

Display ads are very similar to A+ Pages (see Chapter 11) in that they enable you to create more professional-looking ads than what's possible with Sponsored Products. In addition, display ads appear on or off Amazon, and instead of being charged per click, you're charged by cost-per-thousand (CPM) of impressions, and prices vary according to ad format and placement.

Video ads

Video ads enable you to showcase your brand or demonstrate your products and services. Like display ads, video ads appear on or off Amazon and are available to advertisers regardless of whether they sell anything on Amazon. Video ads enable advertisers to extend their video ad campaigns from TV to digital. Pricing varies depending on format and placement.

Custom ads

Custom ads are typically multimedia ads consisting of text, graphics, audio, and video, and they're designed to engage consumers online and offline, wherever they may be. These ads are available to advertisers regardless of whether they sell on Amazon.

REMEMBER

Unlike Display and Video ads, which are self-serve, custom ads require working with an ad consultant. For more about custom ads and to launch a campaign using custom ads, visit advertising.amazon.com/products/custom-ads.

Deals and coupons

Almost every shopper gets excited when they see coupons and hot deals, and Amazon knows it better than everyone. As an Amazon Seller, you have the opportunity to boost sales by enticing customers with special promotional offers and coupons.

In the following sections, we describe these two options. In the later section "Giving Your Shoppers an Added Incentive to Buy: Deals and Coupons," we explain how to create deals and coupons.

Deals

Deals are limited time promotional offers. The big advantage of deals is that they appear on the Today's Deals page, which is a popular page among Amazon shoppers.

To be eligible to offer deals, you must be a Professional Seller with at least five seller feedback ratings in a month and an overall rating of 3.5 stars. In addition, the product you're promoting must meet the following criteria:

>> Have a sales history in Amazon Stores with at least a 3.5-star rating

>> Include as many variations as possible

>> Not be a restricted or offensive product

>> Be eligible for Prime in all regions

>> Be new

>> Comply with customer review policies

>> Comply with pricing policies

>> Comply with deal frequency policies (you have to wait a certain number of days before you can offer another deal on the same product)

All eligible products satisfying the preceding criteria are automatically displayed on your Deals dashboard, so you can easily select a product to promote. To access the Deals dashboard, open the Advertising menu and select Deals.

If a product is approved for a deal and later found to be violating any of the preceding criteria, the deal will be cancelled and any deal charges may be forfeited.

Deals discounts are combined with any other discounts or promotions running on the same ASINs at the same time. For example, if you're offering 25 percent off a product that normally sells for $100 and the same product has another promotional offer of 10 percent off, you have to sell the product for 35 percent off, so consider other discounts running on a product before offering your own discount.

Coupons

Amazon coupons enable you to offer shoppers a percentage or dollar discount on individual products. The discount is applied during checkout. Like Sponsored Products and Sponsored Brands, coupons appear in shoppers' search results and on product detail pages.

Coupons have certain features that make them appealing to sellers, including the following:

>> **Multiple placements:** Coupon discounts appear on the Amazon homepage, in search results, on product detail pages, on the Offer Listings page, and in the shopper's cart.

>> **Ability to create a coupon for multiple products:** You can offer the same dollar or percentage discount on up to 30 products, so you don't have to create a separate coupon for each one.

>> **Ability to set the discount amount and budget:** The discount can be a dollar amount or percentage, but it must be between 5 and 80 percent off the item's lowest price in the last 30 days. As soon as your budget is used, the coupon is discontinued.

>> **Ability to schedule and target coupons:** You can schedule your coupons to run a maximum of three months to cover year-end festival seasons and can target the customer segment of your choice.

>> **Performance tracking:** You can track the performance of each coupon to see which coupons work best.

To be eligible for a coupon discount, a product must meet the following criteria:

>> Be in new condition.

>> Have zero (0) reviews, one to four reviews with an average rating of 2.5 stars or better, or five or more reviews with an average rating of three stars or better.

>> Be fulfilled by Amazon, seller, or seller-fulfilled Prime.

Coupons can't be created for the following products:

>> Collectibles or products in used or certified refurbished condition

>> Any of the following product types: Adult, sexual wellness, hunting and fishing, guns and gun accessories, books, music, video, or DVD

>> Product's listing must not contain any offensive content

WARNING

Don't use coupons as an incentive to get reviews.

Optimizing Your Search Rank with Sponsored Product Ads

To succeed as a seller on Amazon, your products must appear on the first page of search results, but they need to sell well to earn a top spot, so new sellers barely have a chance. Sponsored Product ads provide a way to break the logjam and move your products to the very top of the search results. With a Sponsored Product ad, you essentially buy one of the top spots.

Amazon provides two options for creating Sponsored Product ads: You can have Amazon target the ads for you based on relevant keywords or choose to target the ads yourself. In the following sections, we explain each method and then provide guidance on how to evaluate the success of your ad campaign.

Letting Amazon target your Sponsored Product ad for you

Amazon can create your Sponsored Product ad campaign for you and take on the hardest part of the job — the keyword research. To have Amazon create and target your Sponsored Product ad campaign for you, take the following steps:

1. **Log on to Seller Central, open the Advertising menu, and select Campaign Manager.**

2. **After the Campaigns dashboard appears, press the Create Campaign button.**

   Amazon prompts you to select the desired campaign type.

3. **Select Sponsored Products.**

   Amazon displays a screen prompting you to add details about your Sponsored Product campaign.

4. **Follow the on-screen prompts to enter the following information:**

   - Campaign name

   - Portfolio name: You can create a portfolio in the Campaigns dashboard to organize campaigns, set the budget cap per portfolio, and track performance of each portfolio.

   - Start date and end date: You can omit the end date, but if you want to end the campaign, you'll need to return to the Campaign Manager and cancel it manually.

   - Daily budget: The most you're willing to spend on this campaign per day.

   - Targeting preference: Choose Automatic to have Amazon target your ad for you.

   - Campaign bidding strategy: Dynamic bids - down only, Dynamic bids – up and down, or Fixed bids

5. **Create at least one ad group and add the products you want included in each group.**

6. **Set the default (maximum) bid for the entire ad group.**

7. **Press the Launch Campaign button.**

Targeting your own Sponsored Product Ads

Creating and targeting your own Sponsored Product ad campaign gives you more control over the keywords used in targeting your ads to shoppers' interests and allows you to bid on each keyword separately, so you can bid higher for top-performing keywords.

To create and target your own Sponsored Product ads, take the following steps:

1. **Log on to Seller Central, open the Advertising menu, and select Campaign Manager.**

2. **After the Campaigns dashboard appears, press the Create Campaign button.**

   Amazon prompts you to select the desired campaign type.

3. **Select Sponsored Products.**

   Amazon displays a screen prompting you to add details about your Sponsored Product campaign.

4. **Follow the on-screen prompts to enter the following information:**

   - Campaign name

   - Portfolio name: You can create a portfolio in the Campaigns dashboard to organize campaigns, set the budget cap per portfolio, and track performance of each portfolio.

   - Start date and end date: You can omit the end date, but if you want to end the campaign, you'll need to return to the Campaigns dashboard and cancel it manually.

   - Daily budget: The most you're willing to spend on this campaign per day.

   - Targeting preference: Choose Manual, so you can choose the keywords you want to bid on.

   - Campaign bidding strategy: Dynamic bids - down only, Dynamic bids – up and down, or Fixed bids.

5. **Create at least one ad group and add the products you want included in each group.**

6. **Set the default (maximum) bid for the entire ad group.**

7. **Select keyword targeting or product targeting.**

   Keyword targeting enables you to specify the keywords that trigger the appearance of your ad. Product targeting enables you to specify products, categories, or brands that trigger your ad to appear.

8. **Specify the keywords or the products, categories, and/or brands you want to trigger your ad's appearance and specify the desired match type: broad, phrase, or exact.**

9. **Adjust the maximum bid for each keyword, product, category, or brand.**

10. **If desired, select Negative Keywords and specify any negative keywords you want to use.**

    Negative keywords prevent your ad from being displayed if the negative keyword is included in a shopper's search.

11. **Press the Launch Campaign button.**

Evaluating and adjusting your ad campaigns

Whether you choose to target your own ads or have Amazon target them for you, monitor your ad's performance and make adjustments to optimize its performance. To see how your ad campaigns are doing, log in to Seller Central, open the Advertising menu, and select Campaign Manager. The Campaigns dashboard appears. Examine the following metrics:

>> **Impressions:** Number of times the ad was displayed to the shoppers.

>> **Clicks:** Number of times the ad was clicked or the product page was visited through the ad.

>> **Conversions or orders:** Numbers of orders placed within a week from the time the ad was clicked. (Note that orders include other products not advertised.)

>> **Turnover:** Total turnover generated from the orders.

>> **Click-through-rate (CTR):** The percentage of impressions that resulted in a shopper clicking the ad.

>> **Conversion rate (CR):** The percentage of clicks that resulted in a shopper ordering the product.

>> **Advertising Cost of Sales (ACoS):** The ratio of advertising cost to sales revenue. The lower this ratio, the more profitable or successful the ad is.

TIP

To ensure that your ad campaign is earning you more money in sales than the ad is costing you, make sure your ad campaign's ACoS is lower than your profit margin. For example, if your profit margin is 25 percent and your ACoS is 15 percent, you can still make 10 percent profit after accounting for the cost of the ad.

TIP

When you're running an ad campaign that Amazon is targeting, consider making the following adjustments to improve the profitability of the campaign:

>> If the ACoS is too high, lower your default bid.

>> If the ACoS is too low, raise your default bid.

>> If you're manually targeting your ad and the number of impressions is too low, check to see whether your campaign is missing any important keywords or try increasing your bid.

>> If Amazon is targeting your ad, generate a search terms report in Seller Central (via the Reports menu), identify the high-converting customer search terms, and use only those terms to create a new advertising campaign with manual targeting.

>> Identify all the search terms that are costing you money but not leading to conversions and add them to the campaign's negative keyword list.

>> If the campaign is profitable, consider increasing the campaign's daily budget.

TIP

Here are some additional tips to get the most bang for your buck with Sponsored Product ads:

>> Use the same keywords in your product listings as you do in your ads. Amazon displays an ad only if the product listing has the same or similar keywords. One of the best approaches is to run an Amazon-targeted ad for a week, generate a search terms report, and then add the keywords with the higher conversion rates to your product listing.

>> To increase the conversion rates for your ads, create great product listings (see Chapter 9) and work on getting more positive reviews for your products. A successful ad campaign can drive shoppers to your product listing, but the listing and ratings still need to sell the product.

>> Monitor your ad campaign performance by tuning your ad campaigns and tweaking your product listings to optimize your conversion rates (CRs). By doing so, you give even a newly launched product a chance to beat a product that's well-entrenched in a given category. CR is an important metric in Amazon's ranking algorithm. A poorly optimized ad campaign results in a low CR, which drives down a product's ranking, thereby driving down sales.

>> Use automatic targeting and manual targeting in tandem. Automatic targeting enables you to identify high-performing keywords, which you can then use to your advantage in manually targeted campaigns. For best results, make sure your automatic and manually targeted campaigns are for the same set of products.

Boosting Brand Awareness with Sponsored Brands

If you're a Professional Seller and you added your brand to the Amazon Brand Registry, you can use Sponsored Brands to increase your brand recognition. A Sponsored Brands ad features your brand logo, a custom headline, and up to three products you want to showcase. If a shopper clicks your brand, he's taken to your Amazon store or a custom landing page with a selection of your products. If he clicks a product, he's taken to that product's details page.

To create a Sponsored Brands ad campaign, take the following steps:

1. **Log in to Seller Central, open the Advertising menu, and select Campaign Manager.**

2. **Press the Create Campaign button.**

   Amazon prompts you to select the desired campaign type.

3. **Select Sponsored Brands.**

   Amazon displays a screen prompting you to add details about your Sponsored Brands campaign.

4. **Follow the on-screen prompts to enter the following information:**

   - Campaign name

   - Portfolio name: You can create a portfolio in the Campaigns dashboard to organize campaigns, set the budget cap per portfolio, and track performance of each portfolio.

   - Start date and end date: You can omit the end date, but if you want to end the campaign, you'll need to return to the Campaign Manager and cancel it manually.

   - Daily budget: The most you're willing to spend on this campaign per day.

5. **If you have more than one brand, open the Brand list and choose the brand you want to promote.**

6. **Choose the landing page for your brand: Amazon Store or New Product List Page.**

   Vendors have a third option; they can choose to link to a custom website address.

7. **Choose the Amazon Store you want to link to or the products you want to include on your new product list page.**

   You're then taken to the creative section, where you can customize your Sponsored Brands ad.

   If you create a new product list page, add at least five of your most popular products to the page for best results.

8. **Use the options in the creative section to customize your ad with your brand name, a custom headline, your logo, and up to three products you want to showcase.**

   If you chose to link to your Amazon Store, the product images are preselected for you, but you can choose to change them.

   For your ad's headline, use a call to action and a brief description of what the user will find after clicking the link, such as "Save on office supplies."

9. **Enter your default keyword bid (the maximum amount you're willing to pay each time a shopper clicks your ad).**

10. **Turn automated bidding on or off.**

    With automated bidding on, Amazon optimizes your bids for best placement without exceeding your maximum bid amount.

11. **Specify the keywords that will trigger the appearance of your ad, and choose the match type for each keyword: Broad, Phrase, or Exact.**

    Amazon suggests some keywords, which you're free to use, and you can enter your own keywords.

    Type each keyword or phrase on a separate line.

12. **Enter any other preferences.**

13. **Press the Submit for Review button.**

    Your campaign is sent to Amazon moderators for review. The review can take up to 72 hours before your campaign is approved and running.

Here are a few tips to get the most bang for your buck with Sponsored Brands:

>> **Optimize keywords:** Use generic (unbranded) keywords that are highly relevant to the three products you choose to showcase in your ad, such as "winter skincare products." Avoid using competitive brand names, so you're not wasting advertising money on customers who are unlikely to switch their brand allegiance.

>> **Check your Sponsored Product ads for top-performing keywords:** If you're running Sponsored Product ads for items that are the same or similar

to those showcased in your Sponsored Brands ad, check the performance of Sponsored Products keywords and use those that are performing best in your Sponsored Brands ad.

>> **Monitor the performance of your Sponsored Brands ad:** To access advertising reports in Seller Central, open the Reports menu and select Advertising Reports. Compare the performance of different keywords and make adjustments to optimize the performance of your ad overall.

>> **Run A/B tests to experiment with different ads:** *A/B testing* involves creating two versions of an ad and seeing which performs best. Try running your campaign with two or more versions of a Sponsored Brands ad. Experiment with different headlines, products, and keywords. Amazon offers the following advice for A/B testing:

- Identify the criteria for testing based on your objectives, and identify the variables you want to experiment with.

- Set up multiple campaigns, changing only one variable at a time.

- Run tests for at least a couple of weeks.

- Track the performance of each campaign to gain insight into how your changes impact your objectives.

Giving Your Shoppers an Added Incentive to Buy: Deals and Coupons

Amazon provides a couple options sellers can use to offer discounts to customers — deals and coupons. Deals are limited-time offers. Coupons are codes provided to shoppers that enable them to claim their discount during the checkout process. In this section, we explain how to create deals and coupons.

Offering special deals

Every savvy shopper is looking for the best deal, and Amazon enables you to offer shoppers special deals. A deal typically runs for a week or until the limited number of products are no longer available.

To create a deal, take the following steps:

1. **Log in to Seller Central, open the Advertising menu and select Lightning Deal.**

   The Deals dashboard appears, showing a list of products recommended for a deal.

2. **Click the Advanced Edit button below the product you want to offer in your deal.**

   Amazon prompts you to enter details about the deal.

3. **Enter the following information:**

   - Internal description: For your reference.

   - The week during which you want the deal to be offered: When you choose a week, Amazon displays the fee charged for that week.

   - Deal price: The maximum to charge for the item.

   - Quantity for deal: The maximum number of items you want to sell at the deal price.

4. **Carefully review all details about the deal and make any changes before submitting it.**

5. **Press the Submit button.**

   The deal you created is scheduled to run during the specified week.

WARNING

If you decide to cancel a deal, do so at least 25 hours before it's scheduled to start to avoid paying the fee and being blacklisted from offering deals in the future. To cancel a deal, return to the Deals dashboard, select Upcoming and Active (on the left), press the View button for the deal you want to cancel, and press the Cancel button.

When creating deals, follow these guidelines:

» If the product has variations, such as size and color, offer as many variations as possible, so customers are less likely to be disappointed if a variation they want is unavailable.

» Carefully consider the maximum deal price, because you're not allowed to change it when the deal is running.

» The deal's title comes from the product title of the ASIN participating in the deal or that of a parent ASIN if the product has variations. To change the deal title, change the product title before creating the deal.

>> At least seven days prior to the scheduled start date, make sure you have enough items in stock to cover the specified deal quantity.

>> The deal image comes from the existing product image and must be on a white background without any logo or watermark text that's not part of the product. Any violation may result in cancellation of the deal.

>> Monitor your deal's status via the Deals dashboard to avoid any cancellation or suppression of the deal which could lead to overstocking.

Offering coupon discounts

Coupons enable you to offer shoppers a percentage or dollar discount off one or more select products. To create a coupon, take the following steps:

1. **Log in to Seller Central, open the Advertising menu, and select Coupons.**

2. **After the Coupons dashboard appears, press the Create a New Coupon button.**

3. **If this is your first coupon, select the Create Your First Coupon option.**

4. **Using the menu on the left, search for and select the products you want to add to the coupon and select Add to Coupon.**

   The selected products move to the product list on the right side of the screen.

5. **To remove any variations from the coupon, select Manage Variations in the selected product's box, select the variations you want to remove, click Remove, and click Continue to Next Step.**

6. **Choose Percentage Off or Money Off and enter the percentage or dollar discount you want to offer.**

   Coupons must offer between a 5 and 80 percent discount.

WARNING

   If you're offering any other discounts, such as a deal, be sure to account for it. Your coupon discount will be combined with other discounts being offered at the same time, including deals, promotions, sale price, business price, and giveaways. If you're not careful, you can end up giving away products and losing money on each sale.

7. **Enter a budget for your coupon and click Continue to Next Step.**

8. **Enter a title, a start and end date, and any preferences specifying how to target your coupon to customers, and click Continue to Next Step.**

9. **Review your coupon, and if everything looks okay, press the Submit Coupon button.**

You can edit a coupon up to six hours before its scheduled start time, at which time it's locked down. After it's locked down, you can't edit it until it goes live, at which time you can only increase the coupon's budget or extend its duration. However, you can cancel a coupon at any time by returning to the Coupons dashboard and pressing the Deactivate button next to the coupon you want to cancel. If a customer is in the process of using the coupon, that coupon will remain valid for up to 30 minutes or until the time the customer checks out.

Creating promotions

Promotions are special offers, such as free shipping, percentage off, buy one get one free, and giveaway. They're a great way to increase brand recognition, introduce a new product, clear out excess inventory, and boost sales. To create a promotion, take the following steps:

1. **Log in to Seller Central, open the Advertising menu, and select Promotions.**

   The Promotions dashboard appears with the Create a Promotion tab selected.

2. **Press the Create button below the type of promotion you want to offer: Free Shipping, Percentage Off, Buy One Get One, External Benefits, or Giveaway.**

3. Specify the conditions for your promotional offer; conditions include the following:

   - **Buyer purchases:** Specify whether to apply this promotion only if the shopper buys a minimum or any quantity of the promoted product.

   - **Purchased items:** Select the products that the shopper needs to buy to be eligible for the promotion. You can choose to specify a group of products or offer the promotion if a shopper buys any item in your catalog.

   - **Buyer gets:** Specify what the buyer gets in exchange for making the purchase (this option isn't available for all promotion types).

   - **Applies to:** You can choose Purchased Items to have the promotion apply to the purchased items you specified or Qualifying Items to apply the promotion to the purchase of some other item, such as, if you purchase this power mixer, you get 25 percent off this mixing bowl.

   - **Advanced options:** You can create a product selection group to exclude individual products from the purchased items list if you chose to offer the promotion if the shopper buys any item in the catalog.

4. **Enter a start and end time for this promotion, an internal description, and a tracking ID.**

5. **Enter any additional preferences, including the following:**

   - **Claim code:** Select single use, group code, or no code required to claim the promotion. If you select group, you can use the default code that populates the field or enter the code of your choice. If you select single code, you can generate any number of single-use claim codes. After creating the promotion, go to View Promotion and press the Manage Claim Codes button to generate single use claim codes of the desired number.

   WARNING

     A group claim code has no quantity limits, so be careful. If the group code is posted on social media, your entire inventory can be sold off in a matter of minutes.

   - **One redemption per customer:** Check this box to prohibit any customer from claiming the discount multiple times.

   - **Claim code combinability:** Select either Preferential to prevent a customer from using more than one claim code in a single order or Unrestricted to allow more than one claim code per order. If you choose Preferential, a customer qualified for more than one claim code is allowed to use the code that provides the maximum discount.

   - **Custom messaging:** Enter any custom text you want to appear during checkout or on the product detail pages. Follow the on-screen directions to complete the fields.

6. **Press the Review button and make sure your promotion's settings and details are correct.**

7. **Press the Submit button to create your promotion.**

   A promotion is typically up and running within a few hours of being submitted.

Taking Advantage of External Marketing Options

Though Amazon provides powerful marketing and advertising tools for promoting products and brands inside and outside its marketplaces, you can also choose to work outside of Amazon to drive traffic to your Amazon Store or product. In this section, we present different ways to use social media and influencer marketing to promote your brand and the products you sell on Amazon.

Dipping into social media marketing

Social media are computer-mediated technologies that enable users to create and share content with one another in virtual communities. Social media platforms include Facebook, Twitter, Instagram, Pinterest, SnapChat, and YouTube, along with personal blogs. These platforms often provide a more affordable (or free) means of promoting products and brands and are especially useful for marketing to millennials.

Here we provide some cursory guidance on how to promote your products and brand on some of the more popular social media platforms.

WARNING

Don't be that person who attends parties for the sole purpose of selling raffle tickets. Your friends, family members, and colleagues on Amazon probably won't appreciate being sold to. However, with the right approach, social media market-ing can be both effective and welcome. To find out how to do it properly, check out *Social Media Marketing For Dummies* by Shiv Singh and Stephanie Diamond (John Wiley & Sons, Inc.).

Facebook

With more than two billion people on its platform, Facebook provides a unique opportunity to expand your brand's engagement. Facebook ads create one of the most effective tools for reaching a broader audience. In addition, Facebook provides several free features for promoting your brand and products, and pay-per-click advertising is generally much cheaper on Facebook than it is on Amazon.

Here are a few tips for using Facebook to promote your Amazon brand and products:

» Create a Facebook page for your brand or business (or both) and link it to your brand's landing page or Amazon Store.

» Use Facebook ads to drive traffic to your brand's landing page or your Amazon Store. One advantage of Facebook ads is that they enable you to build a contact list for future direct marketing efforts.

» Think twice about linking from Facebook directly to product listings, because if the traffic you generate doesn't lead to conversions, it lowers your conversion rate, which can negatively impact your Amazon product ratings and sales. Directing traffic to an intermediate destination enables you to filter out some of the traffic from people who are unlikely to buy something.

Instagram

Instagram is a great platform for generating buzz about a brand or product, because you can use visually appealing content to increase engagement. Instagram posts are estimated to generate 15 times the engagement as Facebook posts and 20 times the engagement as Twitter tweets. With its support for hashtags, Instagram enables you to target active discussions that are relevant to your brand and the products you sell. As you develop a following on Instagram, trust in your brand grows, thereby increasing conversion rates.

Here are a few tips on how to use Instagram to achieve your marketing objectives.

>> **Project an engaging personality.** Express your brand's personality, values, and culture through your posts. Everyone is attracted to someone who's fun, energetic, and generous. Be the person and the brand everyone is attracted to.

>> **Use Instagram's shopping feature.** Tag your products in your posts to make it convenient for people interested in the products you're posting about to find them on Amazon.

>> **Tell compelling stories.** Use high quality visual content to connect your audience emotionally to your brand and products.

>> **Use hashtags to link your content to trending stories.** By connecting your posts to trending topics, you can attract more people to your posts and increase your chances of making a sale.

>> **Use Instagram Insights to analyze the effectiveness of your Instagram marketing efforts.** By examining certain metrics, you gain insight into what works and what's doesn't and which changes are likely to improve the effectiveness of your efforts.

YouTube

As the world's most popular video streaming site, YouTube can serve as a powerful tool for increasing brand recognition and driving sales on Amazon. Here are a few suggestions for marketing successfully on YouTube:

>> **Create your own YouTube channel using a brand account instead of your personal account.** Consult YouTube's help system to find out how to create a brand account and set up a YouTube channel.

>> **Customize your channel.** Customize your banner, icons, video description, and about us page to reflect your brand.

>> **Post engaging and relevant videos.** Post how-to videos, product demos, repair videos, and so on, designed to provide prospective customers with something of value. Don't use videos merely to try to sell products.

TIP

For more about using YouTube to drive sales and increase brand recognition, check out *YouTube Marketing For Dummies* by Will Eagle (John Wiley & Sons, Inc.).

Harnessing the power of influencer marketing

Influencer marketing is a form of social media marketing that involves endorsements and product placement with people and organizations whose opinions are trusted by a large audience. You can use influencer marketing in two ways to increase brand awareness and drive sales on Amazon:

>> If you're an influencer, you can join the Amazon Influencer program. With this program, you can create your own influencer page with a custom URL and use your page to recommend hundreds of products, earning money on each product sold. To qualify, you need to have a YouTube, Instagram, Twitter, or Facebook account with a sufficient number of followers. Visit affiliate-program.amazon.com/influencers for details about the program.

>> Partner with an influencer and convince her to promote your products. You don't need a celebrity to vouch for your products; you can partner with anyone who has a large social media following and is likely to be interested in the products you're selling.

Influencer marketing tends to be especially effective in the following product categories:

>> **Electronics:** YouTube in particular has been a successful platform for marketing electronics products. Millions of people subscribe to hundreds of channels to view videos about the latest, greatest electronics products hitting the market.

>> **Diet, weight loss, and fitness products:** Influencers in this product category are generally trainers who help others or people who have traveled their own journeys toward improving their health and fitness.

>> **Toys:** Parents, teachers, and even children can influence the sales of toys by demonstrating how fun and educational certain toys can be. When people are shopping for toys to give as gifts, an expert opinion can be very helpful.

>> **Beauty and fashion:** Consumers of beauty and fashion products have always looked to people who are considered beautiful and fashionable for their opinions on what to wear and how to look their best.

Firing Up Your Email Marketing Machine

Email is one of the quickest and most effective ways to capture consumer attention. Cleverly executed, an email marketing campaign can help you boost sales, score more reviews, and build brand recognition. However, with so much junk mail cluttering recipients' inboxes, email marketing can go unnoticed or even backfire, causing more harm than good. Here are a few tips to make your email marketing campaigns more successful:

REMEMBER

>> **Address the recipients' needs and desires.** Imagine telling friends or family members about a product or brand you discovered that will significantly improve their lives. Avoid coming across as a salesperson pitching a product.

It's not about the product; it's about the person.

>> **Plan a series of email messages.** If you're launching a new product, build the customer's interest in it over time. Instead of sending one email message, plan on sending three over the course of several weeks:

- First, send a starter email to peak the recipient's curiosity, making her eager to receive your next message.

- Second, send out the launch email, with the actual product details and a call to action with a link to purchase the product or sign up for your service.

- Finally, send a post-launch email with product testimonials and social proofs to back up your product claims and show recipients what they're missing out on.

>> **Create professional, branded email templates.** Include your brand's logo and color scheme and keep your templates uncluttered.

>> **Create engaging, entertaining, and informative content.** Include a mix of text, graphics, and perhaps video that captures and keeps the recipient's attention. Maintain a consistent tone throughout your email campaign.

>> **Automate your email campaign.** Email automation enables you to schedule your email messages so that they reach each customer at the right stage of the sales cycle.

>> **Track the metrics.** Examine the metrics to understand shoppers' behaviors and adjust your email campaigns for maximum impact.

TIP

Use a reputable email marketing platform, such as Mailchimp or Jump Send to manage your email marketing campaigns and track metrics such as click-through-rate, purchase history, bounce rate, device used, and so on.

IN THIS CHAPTER

» **Recognizing why quality customer service is so important**

» **Meeting or exceeding customer expectations**

» **Taking quality customer service personally**

» **Addressing key customer service issues**

» **Turning negative customer feedback into a positive outcome**

Chapter **13**

Focusing on Customer Service

Many consumers are drawn to Amazon primarily because of its product ratings and reviews. Knowing what other consumers deem are the best products, and most trustworthy sellers enables shoppers to make well-informed purchase decisions and buy with confidence. As a result, Amazon and its most successful sellers make customer satisfaction their number one priority. After all, satisfied customers are more likely to become return customers and to recommend Amazon and the products they purchased on Amazon to their friends and family members.

In this chapter, we do a deeper dive into why customer satisfaction is so important on Amazon and highlight the key areas you need to focus on before, during, and after a sale.

Understanding Why Customer Satisfaction Is So Important

As an Amazon Seller, customer satisfaction should be your number one priority for two reasons: because it's important to Amazon shoppers and because it's important to Amazon. Amazon has invested considerable time and effort building a thriving marketplace and a very large and loyal consumer base. It has opened this marketplace to third-party retailers like you on one condition — that they uphold Amazon's commitment to stellar customer service. Those who do are rewarded with better product placement. Those who fall short are penalized with negative customer ratings and reviews, poor product placement, and seller account suspension or cancellation. Specifically, here are seven reasons why you should prioritize customer satisfaction:

» **Positive ratings and reviews boost your listing's placement in Amazon's search results and increase your chance of winning the buy box.** Positive ratings and reviews are a reflection of quality products and service. The more ratings/reviews you have and the more positive those reviews are overall, the greater the visibility of your products. (See Chapter 9 for more about product placement and the buy box.)

» **Positive ratings and reviews increase your conversion rate.** Shoppers are more likely to purchase products with higher ratings and more positive reviews due to satisfaction with the product, customer service, or both.

» **Buyers are more likely to post reviews if the product or customer service rises far above or sinks far below their expectations.** The more positive reviews you get, the better your chance of outcompeting another seller for product placement, such as the buy box. On the other hand, too many poor ratings or negative reviews will hurt product visibility and sales.

» **The only way to receive positive reviews is to earn them.** Technically speaking, you can buy positive reviews, but doing so breaches Amazon's rules, and if you get caught, your seller account could be suspended or cancelled. Customers are more likely to post positive reviews if the product or customer service they receive exceeds their expectations.

» **Positive ratings and reviews are a form of free advertising.** Positive ratings and reviews are the biggest drivers of product placement and sales on Amazon, and they cost you nothing.

» **Product reviews and ratings engage customers.** When a product or seller spurs numerous buyers to post their ratings and reviews, a product page becomes a mini discussion forum that takes on a life of its own, which can help to increase interest in your products.

>> **If you upset too many customers, Amazon may suspend or cancel your seller account.** Amazon has the power to suspend or cancel your account if too many customers post negative ratings or reviews. Suspension could result in having any money in your seller account frozen until the issue is resolved.

REMEMBER

Amazon encourages shoppers to post honest feedback to create a community in which shoppers help to guide one another to the best products and most trustworthy sellers. The best way to succeed on Amazon is to focus less on what you need to be successful and more on meeting the needs and exceeding the expectations of shoppers. Satisfy your customers, and success will follow.

Laying the Groundwork for Quality Customer Service

Quality customer service is built on a foundation of solid ecommerce business fundamentals, including the following:

>> **Follow Amazon's program policies.** Amazon has very detailed policies to govern buyer and seller behaviors on its marketplace. Click Help, scroll to the bottom of the page, and click Program Policies to access links to Amazon's Seller Code of Ethics, Communication Guidelines, Conditions of Use, Anti-Counterfeiting Policy, Fair Pricing Policy, Product Detail Page Rules, and more. You can often avoid conflicts with shoppers by knowing and adhering to Amazon's program polices.

>> **Make sure your shipping settings are correct.** Shipping settings enable you to determine whether and how much you charge customers for shipping. Amazon provides a number of tools to automate your shipping calculations, enabling you to charge for shipping based on product size, weight, shipping location, the total dollar amount of an order, and more. To avoid any misunderstandings with customers about shipping costs, be sure your shipping settings are correct. See Chapter 3 for details.

>> **Establish customer-friendly return policies.** Amazon has a very liberal return policy that charges customers for return shipping only on discretionary returns (those that are clearly the buyer's fault, such as changing his mind after the purchase). We recommend that you adopt the same return policy and factor in return costs when setting product prices. See Chapter 3 for details on checking and changing your return settings.

Most shoppers won't check your return policy before placing an order, instead assuming that your policy is the same or better than Amazon's. If you set a more restrictive policy, for example by requiring a restocking fee, you're likely to upset customers resulting in negative ratings/reviews.

>> **Provide convenient access to your contact info.** Give shoppers an easy means to contact you via phone or email. Click Settings, Account Info, Your Seller Profile, and to the right of Customer Service Details, click Edit. Enter your email address in the Customer Service Email and Customer Service Reply-to-Email boxes and your phone number in the Customer Service Phone box. Click Submit.

>> **Create accurate product listings.** To prevent buyers from feeling disappointed when they receive a product, create accurate product descriptions, being careful not to embellish the title or description. Check the title, images, and product description for accuracy. Having the buyer pleasantly surprised that the product is better than the listing presented it is preferable to having a customer disappointed.

>> **Anticipate problems and address them proactively.** If you're selling a product that may cause confusion or misunderstanding, try to address the issue in the product description. For example, if an article of clothing runs small, consider adding guidance to the product description advising buyers to order the next size up.

>> **Manage expectations.** Underpromise and overdeliver. For example, if you're not sure you can meet the promise to ship an item the same day, promise to ship it in a more realistic time frame, say three or four days. If you're able to ship it sooner, your customer will be delighted to receive it early, but if you don't make it, your customer won't be disappointed.

Managing and Shipping Orders

Low product ratings and negative reviews are often related to fulfillment issues — products not delivered on time, sometimes because they weren't shipped on time. By using Fulfilled by Amazon (FBA), as we discuss in Chapter 10, you can avoid most of these problems. Products are picked, packed, and shipped from the Amazon fulfillment center closest to the buyer, so they almost always arrive at the right destination within the designated time frame.

Of course, mistakes do happen. The Amazon fulfillment center can drop the ball and ship the wrong product to the wrong address, the carrier might lose the package or deliver it to the wrong address, or a busy holiday season or a natural or human disaster could cause shipping delays. Whatever the cause, you can often avoid problems or address them more effectively by managing orders closely and, if you're handling fulfillment yourself, by putting an impeccable fulfillment process in place and choosing reliable carriers.

To manage orders, log in to Seller Central, open the Orders menu, and select Manage Orders. Use the options on the left or above the orders list to filter and sort the list according to your preferences. For example, you can choose to filter the list to show only those orders that need to be shipped by today, so you can focus your efforts in fulfilling high-priority orders. Monitor orders and contact customers immediately if you encounter a fulfillment issue that is likely to delay delivery.

REMEMBER

If you're going to miss the promised ship-by or deliver-by date, contact the buyer to let her know and to inform her of her options, such as canceling the order or returning the merchandise for a full refund. You may also want to offer a discount or some other perk for the inconvenience.

If you pack and ship orders yourself, monitor your late shipment rate (LSR) to see how you're doing. To view your LSR from Seller Central, select Performance (in the main menu bar near the top), choose Account Health, and scroll down to Shipping Performance. Choose Late Shipment Rate to view your LSR report.

WARNING

Amazon expects sellers to maintain an LSR below 4 percent of total orders over both a 10- and 30-day period. Orders that are shipped late negatively impact the customer experience and lead to low ratings, negative reviews, and increased claims. An LSR above 4 percent may result in having your seller account deactivated.

Responding to Customer Questions, Concerns, and Complaints

Customers are usually understanding as long as they're not unpleasantly surprised. When you become aware of a problem on your end, own it and, when possible, communicate the issue to the customer before she becomes aware of it. When communicating with customers, follow these guidelines:

>> **Assume that the customer is right.** Even if the customer is wrong, she is right in her own mind and will respond more productively if you demonstrate understanding and empathy. Don't argue with the customer or try to prove her wrong; in most cases, this approach will cause the customer to dig in and become more combative. Instead, try to de-escalate.

>> **Remain calm, concerned, and respectful.** If talking to a customer on the phone, maintain an even tone of voice. Model the desired customer behavior, and the customer will be likely to follow your lead.

>> **Listen and ask questions to clarify your understanding.** Customers often need to vent, so start by listening and then follow up with questions until you fully understand why the customer is upset. Don't try thinking about or offering possible solutions; focus first on hearing and understanding the customer.

>> **Take a problem-solving approach.** Every customer question or complaint reveals a problem that needs to be addressed. Identify the problem and work with the customer to identify potential solutions. Engage the customer in the process of resolving the problem, so she feels as though she has had some input. Possible solutions include the following:

- Tracking a product that hasn't arrived when promised and providing the customer with status updates

- Providing guidance on how to assemble or use the product (technical support)

- Sending a replacement product (if the product received is damaged or defective)

- Providing a full refund, contingent or not upon the buyer returning the original product (see the next section, "Processing Returns, Refunds, and Cancellations," for details)

- Offering a different product that may be a better match for what the buyer needs

- Directing the customer to the Amazon help system or providing Amazon customer service contact information, if the problem is with Amazon

Processing Returns, Refunds, and Cancellations

If you use FBA exclusively to fulfill orders, you can safely skip this section because Amazon processes all your returns, refunds, and order cancellations. If you fulfill orders yourself (Fulfilled by Merchant, FBM), read on to find out how to handle these transactions.

Handling returns

Generally, Amazon allows buyers to return merchandise up to 30 days after delivery, although this window varies for different product categories; for example, baby items can be returned up to 90 days after shipment. We encourage you to read Amazon's Returns Policies (`www.amazon.com/gp/help/customer/display.html?nodeId=201819200`) for details. If you're a Professional Seller, Amazon automatically authorizes returns that fall within its returns policies. If you're an Individual seller or the buyer's return request falls outside Amazon's returns policies, Amazon sends you the return request via email stating the reason for the return, so you can choose how to respond.

In the following sections, we explain how to check and adjust your return settings and how to respond to return and refund requests and order cancellations.

Checking and adjusting your return settings

If you choose to fulfill orders yourself (Fulfilled by Merchant, FBM), you can adjust your return settings. In Seller Central, choose Settings (upper-right corner of the page) and then Return Settings. On the General Settings tab, you have the following options:

> » **Email Format:** Turn on Receive Return Request Emails with Links to Authorize, Close, or Reply, so that you'll be notified via email as soon as a customer submits a return request.

> » **Default Automated Return Rules:** You can choose to require that you authorize each request, that Amazon automatically authorize all requests that comply with its returns policies, or that Amazon automatically authorize all return requests. We recommend having Amazon automatically authorize only those requests that comply with its returns policies because doing so saves you valuable time while giving you the option to review any unreasonable or questionable return requests.

> » **Return Merchandise Authorization (RMA) Number Settings:** You can choose to have Amazon generate an RMA for you or have Amazon prompt you to supply an RMA for each request. Again, to save you time and effort, we recommend having Amazon generate RMAs for you.

The Return Settings page has three other tabs to consider:

> » **Returnless Refund:** For certain items that may cost you more in return shipping and handling than the item is worth, you can set up rules that issue a refund without requiring the buyer to return the product. Just enter a name of the rule, specify a price range and return window, and choose the product category(ies) and reason(s) for the return.

>> **Return Address Settings:** On this tab, you can set the default return address and override it for different markets (such as Canada and Mexico).

>> **Return Attribute Overrides:** Choose this option to access a return attribute template that enables you to enter return settings that override your standard return settings. Note that return attribute overrides only apply if you're part of Amazon's prepaid labels program.

Responding to a return request

To respond to a return request, log on to Seller Central and select Orders and then Manage Returns. A list of all return requests appears. Select the return request to which you want to respond. You can then respond in one of the following ways:

>> **Accept and authorize the return.** After authorizing the return, you can specify whether you want to use the Amazon-generated RMA or assign an RMA of your own. By default, Amazon issues the buyer an unpaid shipping label. If you're enrolled in Amazon's prepaid labels program, you can choose to issue a prepaid mailing label to the buyer.

WARNING

If the buyer will be required to pay for return shipping or pay a restocking fee, contact the buyer prior to authorizing the return to be sure she's aware of the costs.

>> **Close the return request.** Choose to close the request if you're denying the return request or issuing a refund without requiring that the merchandise be returned. When you choose to close a return request, you must select a reason for doing so, which is then sent to the buyer.

>> **Issue a refund.** After authorizing the return, you have the option of issuing a refund or waiting until you receive the returned merchandise before issuing a refund (refer to the next section).

>> **Contact the buyer.** You can choose to contact the buyer via email to discuss the issue and arrive at a mutually agreeable resolution.

REMEMBER

We recommend that you respond to any return request as soon as possible, and never more than 24 hours from receiving it. Buyers are often impatient and are more likely to post a low rating or negative review the longer they don't hear back from you.

Issuing refunds

After authorizing a return, you can come back to the Manage Returns page and issue a refund immediately or, if you are requiring the buyer to return the merchandise, after you receive it and evaluate its condition. To issue a refund, take the following steps:

1. **Log on to Seller Central.**

2. **Choose Orders and then Manage Returns.**

3. **Scroll down to the order for which you want to issue a refund and press the Issue Refund button.**

4. **Open the Reason for Refund list and choose the most accurate reason for issuing the refund.**

5. **Choose Refund Full Amount or enter specific amounts to refund for the product and any return shipping or other concessions.**

6. **In the Memo to Buyer box, type an explanation of any charges (such as a restocking fee or return shipping costs).**

7. **In the Memo to Seller box, type any information you want to retain for your personal records (such as a description of the returned item).**

   This step is optional.

8. **Press Submit Refund.**

   Amazon accepts the refund request, but it may appear as Pending for up to two hours.

TIP

As long as a refund request is pending, you can cancel it — for example, if you issued the wrong refund amount or issued a refund on the wrong order. To cancel a refund, open the Orders menu in Seller Central and choose Manage Returns. Next to the return authorization for the item you want to cancel, choose View Return and Refund Status and then Cancel This Return. A pop-up confirmation dialog box appears asking you to confirm your request; click Cancel This Return.

Following up on order cancellations

A buyer has up to 30 minutes after placing an order to cancel it. After 30 minutes, a buyer can request an order cancellation, but only the seller can cancel it. After an item is shipped, neither the buyer nor the seller can cancel the order. If you receive a cancel order request from a buyer, and the item hasn't shipped yet, take the following steps to cancel it:

1. **Log on to Seller Central.**

2. **Open the Orders menu and select Manage Orders.**

3. **Scroll down to the order referenced in the email notification you received and click Cancel Order.**

4. **Open the Reason for Cancellation list and choose Buyer Requested.**

5. **Press Submit.**

   Amazon cancels the order and sends an email message to the buyer notifying her of the cancellation.

If the item has already shipped, you won't be able to press the Cancel Order button. In this case, notify the buyer to return the item for a refund and let the buyer know of any charges that will be incurred, such as return shipping or a restocking fee.

WARNING

If you can't fulfill an order because an item is out of stock, resist the temptation to contact the buyer to submit a cancellation request so it won't be counted against you. Instead, choose as the reason No Inventory.

Managing Seller Feedback and Product Reviews

Negative seller feedback and product reviews from buyers can hurt sales and your reputation and, if negative seller feedback is frequent and serious enough, result in your Amazon seller account being suspended or canceled. (Negative product ratings and reviews don't impact your seller metrics or place your seller account at risk.) Some shoppers will even scroll down the list of product ratings and reviews to read the negative ones in an attempt to find a reason not to buy a product. The following sections explain what you can do to keep an eye on feedback and reviews.

REMEMBER

Buyers have 90 days from the date an order is confirmed to post feedback and 60 days from the time of posting feedback to remove it.

DISTINGUISHING PRODUCT REVIEWS FROM SELLER FEEDBACK

Amazon allows buyers to post product reviews and to post feedback for third-party sellers, and these two are entirely different:

- **Product ratings and reviews** enable buyers to rate and review products to help shoppers make well-informed purchase decisions regarding a product's quality and suitability. Product ratings and reviews don't reflect your performance as a seller and aren't used by Amazon to evaluate you.

- **Seller feedback** enables buyers to rate and review sellers to help shoppers make well-informed decisions regarding whom to buy from. Seller ratings and reviews do reflect your performance and may be used by Amazon to decide whether to suspend or terminate your seller account.

Monitoring and responding to seller feedback

We encourage you to monitor seller feedback daily or even more frequently using Amazon's Feedback Manager. To access Feedback Manager from Seller Central, open the Performance menu and choose Feedback. Feedback Manager displays two tables:

» **Feedback Rating:** This table displays a summary of your ratings for the past 12 months as well as your percentages and corresponding actual feedback counts for 30 days, 90 days, 365 days, and the entire time you've had a seller account.

» **Recent Feedback:** This table displays a running list, sorted by date and time, of ratings and reviews posted about products you sell. Feedback is associated with Order ID and rating. In the Recent Feedback table, you can take the following actions:

- View feedback comments.

- Post a public reply.

- Contact a customer privately.

- Notify Amazon of a comment in violation of its review policies and request that the comment be removed.

You can find several more sophisticated feedback management tools online, for example, tools that notify you via email or text whenever a buyer posts feedback.

If you receive negative seller feedback, first examine it to determine whether it's legitimate and reasonable. Competitors may post fake feedback themselves or hire someone to do so to steal market share from reputable sellers. After evaluating the feedback, take one of the following approaches in response:

>> **Contact the buyer to resolve the issue.** If the feedback is legitimate, contact the buyer via Amazon's Buyer-Seller Messaging Service (see Chapter 4). Thank the buyer for taking the time to post feedback and ask whether you can do anything to resolve the issue, such as replacing a product or issuing a full or partial refund.

Never ask a buyer to remove or revise seller feedback because such a request is a breach of Amazon policies. Focus on resolving any issues you can in the hopes that afterward the buyer will remove or revise the feedback on her own.

>> **Post a public reply.** If you can't resolve the issue with the buyer privately or if the buyer doesn't remove or revise her feedback, post a public reply to the buyer's feedback. In your reply, do the following:

- Thank the buyer for taking the time to provide feedback.

- Explain the interaction from your perspective without being defensive or argumentative or attacking the buyer.

- Describe the action you took to resolve the issue, including any changes you've implemented to prevent the same issue from recurring.

- Convey your commitment to customer satisfaction.

>> **Report feedback in violation of Amazon's policies.** If the seller feedback is clearly in violation of Amazon's feedback policies, contact Amazon to report the violation and request that the feedback be removed. Amazon only removes feedback in the following cases:

- The feedback contains obscene language.

- The feedback includes specific details that could be used to personally identify the seller.

- A comment posted as seller feedback is actually a product review or vice versa.

Approach negative seller feedback as a learning experience and an opportunity to turn a negative customer experience into a positive experience. Feedback provides the insight you need to become a better seller. In addition, it gives you the opportunity to transform a disgruntled buyer into an advocate and generate some positive word-of-mouth advertising. By treating negative feedback as beneficial, you're more likely to respond to customers in a positive way.

Monitoring and responding to product ratings and reviews

Unfortunately, Amazon doesn't provide a tool that enables you to monitor product ratings and reviews, nor does it provide an option to be notified (via email or text) when a rating or review of a product you sell is posted. To monitor product ratings and reviews (your own and your competitors'), you need to visit the product's page or use a third-party tool, such as ReviewMonitoring.com, FeedbackExpress, or Salesbacker.

If product rating or review appears suspicious or is more like seller feedback than a product review, select Report Abuse (below the review) and to confirm press Report Abuse again. (You aren't given the option to explain why you think the product rating or review is in violation of Amazon's policies.)

If a buyer posts a negative review, contact the buyer via Amazon's Buyer-Seller Messaging Service (see Chapter 4). Thank the buyer for taking the time to post the product review, apologize (assuming the review is from one of your customers), and ask whether you can do anything to resolve the issue, such as replacing the product or offering a full or partial refund.

Later, if you can't resolve the issue directly with the buyer or if the buyer doesn't change or remove the low rating or negative review, post a comment to the review. Thank the buyer for taking the time to post a product review, explain what you did to resolve the issue, and convey your commitment to customer satisfaction.

Check out Amazon's Customer Product Review Policies to get up to speed on what constitutes a violation. Specifically focus on the following five don'ts:

>> *Don't* post a review of your own or a competitor's product.

>> *Don't* offer anyone any sort of reward, compensation, or refund/reimbursement for posting a review of your own or a competitor's product or hire an individual or firm to do this.

>> *Don't* ask a friend or family member to post a review of your own or a competitor's product.

- >> *Don't* ask a reviewer to remove or change a review.

- >> *Don't* hack a reviewer's Amazon account or hire someone to do so to write, change, or remove a review.

Amazon automatically sends emails to buyers to ask them to post product reviews, so you don't need to. You're permitted to contact buyers and ask them to post reviews, but you're prohibited from asking the review to be positive or from offering compensation in any form.

Fielding A-to-Z Claims

Amazon provides its customers an A-to-Z Guarantee that covers the timely delivery and condition of products sold and shipped by third-party sellers. Amazon requires that customers try to contact you, either by submitting a return request or via the Buyer-Seller Messaging Service, at least 48 hours before filing an A-to-Z claim. If a customer files an A-to-Z claim, you have 72 hours to respond. If you don't respond within that time frame, Amazon grants the claim, issues a refund to the buyer, and debits that amount from your Amazon Seller account. You have 30 days to appeal Amazon's decision.

WARNING

Check your email frequently to monitor A-to-Z claim activity. Unresolved claims contribute to your Order Defect Rate (ODR), which is a key measure of customer satisfaction. An ODR above 1 percent may result in deactivation of your Amazon Seller account. The following types of claims negatively impact your ODR:

- >> Amazon grants the claim and debits the refund amount from your account.

- >> You issue a refund to a customer after she submitted a claim.

- >> You or Amazon, not the buyer, cancelled the order.

- >> The claim is pending a decision.

Your ODR isn't impacted for claims granted and paid for by Amazon, denied to the buyer, or withdrawn by the buyer.

To manage A-to-Z claims, log on to Seller Central, open the Performance menu, and choose A-to-Z Guarantee Claims. The Manage A-to-Z Claims page appears, showing any claims that have been filed against you. You can respond to an A-to-Z claim in any of the following ways:

>> **Respond to Amazon** to resolve the issue through Amazon instead of directly with the buyer. You generally use this option if you have strong evidence that the buyer is in the wrong.

>> **Issue a refund to the buyer** to put the matter to rest. However, if you issue a refund after the A-to-Z claim has been filed, your ODR will take a hit.

>> **Contact the buyer** to find an agreeable solution, so the buyer withdraws the claim voluntarily.

TIP

An ounce of prevention is worth a pound of cure. Try to resolve any issues with disgruntled buyers before they reach the point of the buyer filing an A–to–Z claim. After a buyer files a claim, attractive options begin to dwindle.

Chapter **14**

Building and Managing Your Own Webstore

When you're selling *on* Amazon, you're selling *in* Amazon; that is, Amazon is like a huge store on the web, and you're selling products within that store. When customers buy your products, they remember they bought them on Amazon, but they usually forget they bought them from *you* (assuming it even registered in their brains).

However, when you have your own store — a separate store inside or outside Amazon — you can build your own recognizable brand and start generating repeat sales. By building and maintaining your own store, you give shoppers a choice — they can buy from you or from Amazon. In addition, when selling to repeat customers, you won't have to compete so much with other sellers on Amazon to win sales.

In this chapter, we explain how to build your own store on the web — inside or outside Amazon — and use it in tandem with Amazon to boost sales and build brand recognition.

Choosing Where to Build Your Webstore: Inside or Outside Amazon or Both

If you're thinking about building your own webstore, you have three options:

>> **Amazon Stores:** If you're a Professional Seller on Amazon and have your own brand in the Amazon Brand Registry (see Chapter 17), you can create your own branded store on Amazon and list and sell your products from that store. Amazon Stores provide Professional Sellers who are brand owners a free, self-service webstore builder and store address, such as Amazon.com/YourBrandName.

>> **Your own webstore:** You can build your own webstore outside Amazon, selling the same products you sell on Amazon. You can even use Fulfillment by Amazon (FBA) to have the products sold in your webstore packed and shipped from Amazon fulfillment centers. (See Chapter 10 for details.)

>> **Both an Amazon store and a separate webstore:** Many large brands have their own webstores outside Amazon and a store within Amazon to establish their brand presence in two places.

In the following sections, we weigh the pros and cons of each option to help you decide which is best for you.

Weighing the pros and cons of building an Amazon Store

If you're a Professional Seller and an owner of a brand that's in the Amazon Brand Registry, and you have the time and other resources to build and manage an Amazon Store, we recommend you do so. As a registered brand owner, you can build your own store on Amazon for free, which can help in building brand recognition among Amazon shoppers. Building and managing your own Amazon Store is easy, and it doesn't complicate the ordering process for you or your Amazon customers.

REMEMBER

Nearly all the large brands that sell on Amazon have their own Amazon Store *and* a website or store outside Amazon.

The only drawback to having an Amazon Store is that few people are likely to visit your store. When most people shop on Amazon, they search for a product, click one of the product listings in the search results, add the product to their cart, and check out. Having your own Amazon Store probably won't boost sales much, because shoppers aren't likely to take the extra step to visit your Amazon Store. In addition, if someone searches for your brand on the web, they're probably more likely to find a link to your website or webstore outside Amazon than a link to your Amazon Store.

Weighing the pros and cons of building a webstore outside Amazon

Selling on Amazon certainly has its advantages in terms of providing instant access to a very large base of shoppers who spend lots of money. However, the one big drawback is that when you sell on Amazon, you're not exactly making a name for yourself or establishing your own base of loyal customers.

The most effective way to build brand recognition as a retailer is to have your own webstore. When people buy from your store, they remember it, and if they have a pleasant shopping experience, they'll likely return to your store and recommend it to others. In addition, when you have your own store, you can collect details about your customers, including their contact information, so you can keep in touch with them after the sale and let them know when you have other products they may be interested in.

Building and maintaining a webstore outside Amazon has three major drawbacks:

>> **Extra work:** A separate store nearly doubles your workload. You have product listings to create, orders coming in from Amazon and your webstore, and separate advertising to promote your store. In addition, you face a steep learning curve related to building, securing, and maintaining the webstore, unless you outsource those tasks, in which case they become extra costs.

>> **Extra costs:** Additional costs include domain registration, subscription to a separate ecommerce platform (or domain hosting and the costs for ecommerce software and services), and marketing costs to drive traffic to your webstore.

>> **Integration challenges:** With a separate webstore, you need to figure out how you're going to integrate your webstore operations with Amazon. For example, you need to decide how you're going to manage orders and inventory when you're selling through two channels. You also need to ensure that your product listings and other information are up-to-date and are consistent between Amazon and your store.

Creating two webstores

Building a webstore inside or outside Amazon doesn't necessarily need to be an either/or choice. If you have the resources, consider doing both. If you're going to be building a webstore outside Amazon, recreating a similar store on Amazon won't be too burdensome. After you tackle the difficult job of building a webstore outside Amazon, all you need to do is transfer your brand assets (graphics, font, color scheme, and so on) over to your Amazon Store. Amazon populates your store with your product listings, so you don't have to re-create those listings.

REMEMBER

Having a webstore inside and outside Amazon provides you with the best of both worlds. Your Amazon Store provides a way to build brand recognition on Amazon while complying with its content limitations. You can use your other webstore to do your own thing and engage in more self-promotion than what's allowed on Amazon. (Amazon has a long list of do's and don'ts that cover Amazon Store content, accessible at advertising.amazon.com/resources/ad-policy/stores#overview.)

Laying the Groundwork for Your Webstore

Laying the groundwork for your webstore involves figuring out how you're going to build it, where it's going to be hosted, what its web address will be, and the content it needs to include. It also involves gathering content, so you can simply copy and paste content when you're ready to start building your webstore.

In this section, we guide you through the process of preparing to build your own webstore, inside or outside Amazon.

Choosing a unique and recognizable domain name

If you build an Amazon Store, its domain name will be something like Amazon.com/YourBrand. If you build a stand-alone webstore, its domain name will be something like YourBrand.com. Either way, when you're choosing a domain name, follow these general guidelines:

>> **Keep it short, simple, and catchy.** A short, simple, and catchy name is easy for shoppers to remember, pronounce, and type. In addition, it can make a great logo for your brand. Try different combinations of short names or try tweaking a popular word or phrase to suit to your brand.

>> **Make it unique.** Your domain name should reflect the products and services you offer, but it should differ from whatever your competitors are already using. Think of something clever and maybe even funny depending on the look and feel of the brand you want to convey.

>> **Be creative.** In most cases, you want a domain name that ends in .com, but many companies have chosen to do something different that works very well for them, such as Goo.gl and bit.ly. Search a popular domain registrar, such as Bluehost or GoDaddy for ideas.

TIP

When you're struggling to come up with a unique, short, and catchy domain name, consider seeking inspiration from other cultures and languages. Google Translator at `translate.google.com` is a useful tool for identifying foreign words or phrases that may express your brand's identity.

>> **Avoid legal issues.** Make sure the domain name you're thinking of using doesn't violate any other individual's or organization's intellectual property rights. Research Google and the trademark registry at the United States Patents and Trademarks Office (`www.uspto.gov/trademarks-application-process/search-trademark-database`) to find out if the domain name you're thinking of using is too close to the name of an existing business or organization.

Deciding how to build your webstore

You have several options for building your webstore depending on where you want to host your store, how much money and time you want to invest in it, and a number of other factors. Your options basically boil down to the following four:

>> Build an Amazon Store on your own or with the assistance of a professional designer. If you're already selling on Amazon as a Professional Seller and registered brand owner, this is, by far, the easiest choice. Amazon provides everything you need to create and host an Amazon Store that's fully integrated with everything you're already doing on Amazon to build your ecommerce business. However, if you decide to open your own store outside Amazon, you'll need one of the other options listed here.

>> Hire an expert to build a stand-alone webstore for you. This option is the most expensive, typically costing thousands of dollars, but assuming you hire a competent web developer, you get a professionally designed and hosted ecommerce site that's fast, reliable, and secure and has all the features and functionality required in an ecommerce website. In addition, you have someone you can contact if anything goes wrong.

>> Register with an ecommerce platform such as Shopify, BigCommerce, WooCommerce, or Magneto and build your own webstore. An ecommerce

platform is a great choice, because it hosts your webstore, provides all the tools you need to build a branded webstore, provides all the features and functionality necessary to accept orders and process electronic payments, and secures your site and your customers' information. With this option, you have total control over your webstore's content and appearance.

>> Register with a web hosting provider such as Bluehost, HostGator, or Hostinger and use the provider's tools to build your own site. This approach is probably the least expensive but the most complicated and work-intensive. You need to use a number of tools to build your webstore, and you must configure your locale (to ensure proper currency and measurements — dollar or euros, pounds or kilos, and so on), set up shipping options and taxes, configure payment gateways (so you can accept credit card payments), secure your site and customer data, and more. If you don't already know how to build and configure websites for ecommerce, the learning curve is very steep.

Categorizing your products

Remember the last time your grocery store reconfigured its aisles? It probably took you weeks to reorient yourself before you could easily locate your favorite products. When you're planning your own webstore, keep in mind the importance of organizing products to make them easy for shoppers to find.

Organizing products in a webstore generally involves creating separate categories for related products, such as beauty, fashion, home, garden, sports, and toys. You can use the same categories Amazon uses or come up with your own product groupings. In the following sections, we offer a few suggestions for simplifying webstore navigation through the use of categories.

Use both parent categories and subcategories

When possible, create a list of general, parent categories with more specific sub-categories within each parent category, but keep the category–subcategory "tree" shallow. Using subcategories enables shoppers to focus their search for products, but if they need to go deeper than three or four levels, they're more likely to lose interest or get frustrated.

Make parent categories selectable

When a menu has a parent category with numerous subcategories, shoppers often try to click the parent category, which may or may not be selectable or, if it is selectable, clicking it opens a blank page. Be sure the parent category is selectable and that it links to a page that lists the parent category's subcategories.

Otherwise, some shoppers will get confused or frustrated, and your conversion rates will suffer.

Assign products to multiple categories, when relevant

Some products may belong in more than one category; for example, one shopper may look for backpacks under Sports > Hiking, whereas another looks for them under School Supplies. In such cases, feel free to be redundant; assign each product to each and every category in which it belongs. Likewise, feel free to include the same subcategory under multiple parent categories, when doing so makes sense.

REMEMBER

When creating categories and assigning products to categories, think about all the different ways shoppers may browse for products, then organize the categories so shoppers can find the product regardless of the path they choose to follow. You don't want customers leaving your store without purchasing a product just because they mistakenly think you don't carry it.

Keep category names short and simple but descriptive

When creating categories and subcategories, keep them as short and simple as possible, but also be sure they're easily recognizable and understandable to shoppers. If the customer has to think for more than a fraction of a second which products are included in a category based on the category's name, you run the risk of losing that customer.

WARNING

Don't get overly creative or clever in naming your categories or subcategories. Using standard, boring names that are recognizable to a majority of shoppers is far better than being creative and confusing. If you want to use more creative names, be sure to conduct A/B testing to determine the effect a certain category name will have on sales. (*A/B testing* involves trying out two versions of something to see which works better.)

Create separate What's New or What's Hot categories

Include at least one category to call attention to new or best-selling products or special deals. Chances are good that a sizeable number of your customers are looking for the latest or most popular products or the best deals. Providing quick and easy access to these products increases your chances of earning sales.

TIP

Consider using a product carousel on your homepage to showcase several products. A *product carousel* is a cross between a slide show and a merry-go-round that cycles through a collection of product photos automatically or when the user points and clicks or hovers the mouse pointer over the carousel. Some ecommerce platforms include a feature for creating product carousels. However, keep in mind that product carousels may improve or harm sales, so conduct A/B testing to determine how they affect sales before using them as a standard feature in your webstore.

Focus on filters

Filters are a great tool for enabling shoppers to narrow their search for specific products, so make use of all available filters — size, color, cost, brand, rating, age recommendation (for children products), and so on. When adding filters, try to think of all the attributes shoppers may consider when searching for a particular product.

TIP

If you're struggling to think of filters to include, check out the filters used on Amazon. You can use the same or similar filters for comparable products in your own webstore.

Use high quality category images

Most ecommerce platforms enable you to create your own product category menus and pages complete with images to portray the collection of products in each category. Be sure to use high-quality images that accurately represent the products in each category. You may want to use a photo of a single featured product or of a collection of products. What's important is that the image enables shoppers to instantly imagine all the products in the given category.

Gathering the essentials to build your store

Prior to building your store or even hiring someone to build it for you, gather all the content needed. Content consists of graphics (and perhaps video) for branding your webstore and for creating product listings, any text required for creating pages and product listings, and the UPC codes you need to track products. In the following sections we describe, in greater detail, what you'll need to create your webstore.

Graphics (including, maybe, videos)

Most shoppers are stimulated by visuals, so you want your store and product listings to be visually appealing and informative. As you gather content to include on your site, be sure to include the following graphic content:

- >> **Branding assets:** These items include your brand's logo, fonts, and color scheme, which all contribute to the overall appearance of your webstore.

- >> **High-quality product photos:** Because shoppers can't see or touch the actual product in your store, as they can in a physical store, you need to provide clear, detailed product photos that enable shoppers to see your products from every angle. According to one survey, about two-thirds of shoppers said high-quality product photos are more important than product descriptions in helping them make purchase decisions.

TIP

  360-degree photos and videos are a great way to showcase a product. You can hire a professional photographer to create 360-degree product photos for you or purchase specialize equipment, including a turntable, to create them yourself.

- >> **Product-demo photos or videos:** When relevant, include product photos or videos that show the product being used. For certain products, demonstrating how easy the product is to use or how well it works is a great way to increase sales conversions. For some products, you may also want to include assembly photos, illustrations, or videos.

- >> **Buyer-generated photos or videos:** Consider including, within individual product pages, a way for people who bought the product to share their product photos and videos. Amazon allows customers to share their product photos and videos when they post product reviews, and these photos and videos are a great way to showcase your products being used.

REMEMBER

When including any images or videos in your webstore, be sure to include meta tags that describe the content, so search engines can properly index the graphic content, and people with visual impairments can benefit from the visuals. (*Meta tags* are labels that describe content, providing search engines with additional information they need to properly index a website or webstore. For graphics they typically include the image or video title, a description, and a caption.) Be sure to include keywords that shoppers are likely to use to find the product depicted in the photo or video.

Text for pages and product descriptions

Every ecommerce website has a page for each product and service the business offers, but ecommerce websites have, or should have, additional pages to welcome shoppers, keep them engaged and informed, and enable them to find the information they need. Each of these pages requires both graphic and text-based content.

As you plan your ecommerce website, be sure to prepare text to populate the following pages:

- » **Homepage:** Your webstore's homepage should welcome shoppers and provide them an easy means to navigate your site and find what they're looking for. Include on your homepage the following:

  - A clear value proposition that communicates the benefits of your brand and the products you offer

  - Contact info, such as, email address, phone number, and a link to chat live

  - Call to action, such as a way to search for a product or check out one of your featured products

- » **Landing pages:** These pages showcase specific products or promotions and are specifically designed to sell something. These are pages linked to your email marketing campaigns and online advertisements. Consider including the following content on each landing page:

  - Details about the product or promotion

  - One or more customer testimonials

  - Time limit or quantity in stock limit to convey urgency

  - Call to action (typically a button to order the product)

- » **Product pages:** To create your product pages, you need the following text, which you can get from your existing product listings on Amazon:

  - Product title

  - Product description

  - Bullet points highlighting each product's features and benefits

  - Product reviews/ratings

- » **Collection pages:** A collection page is a category or group of related products, such as electronics, games, or videos; sale items; seasonal products; or makes/models, such as accessories for a certain model of cellphone. You may want to link to your collection pages from your webstore's homepage. (You don't need much additional content to create your collection page. You just need to decide on your product groupings.)

- » **Blog pages:** Blog posts are an excellent way to attract search engine traffic by establishing your blog as the go-to source for information about the products you sell. Search engines love sites with fresh, relevant content, and twice-a-week blog posts provide a constant stream of fresh content. In addition, blog posts encourage readers to post their own content, so your site can benefit from having fresh, relevant content that you don't have to create.

Be sure to include a way for your customers to subscribe to your blog to receive updates. When customers subscribe, they provide you with the opportunity to keep them posted about new products and services.

Universal product codes (UPCs) for tracking products

A universal product code (UPC) consists of a machine-readable bar code and a human-readable 12-digit number that identifies a product. UPCs were developed to help grocery stores increase the speed and accuracy of the checkout process, and they can do the same to help you as a retailer. Every product you sell should have a UPC to help you track inventory and sales. When you're creating product listings, be sure to include each product's UPC, which you can obtain from the following sources:

» The product manufacturer

» GS1 US (gs1us.org), where you can register to obtain a GS1 Company Prefix and use it to create your bar codes

Buying UPCs from GS1 US and using them to identify your products help to validate the authenticity of your products.

Creating Your Amazon Store

If you're a Professional Seller and registered brand owner on Amazon, you can use Amazon's self-service Store builder to create and edit your Amazon Store. Even without any design experience, you can easily create a branded store and populate it with your product listings. To create a new Amazon Store, take the following steps:

1. **Open the Stores menu and select Create Store (next to your brand name).**

2. **Enter your brand's name as you want it to appear in your Store's uniform resource locator (URL).**

    For example, if you use LugoBar as the brand name, the URL will be amazon.com/LugoBar, and shoppers will need to type "amazon.com/LugoBar" and not "amazon.com/lugobar" to access your store. (Amazon.com isn't case-sensitive, but everything after the forward slash is.)

3. **Follow the on-screen instructions to upload your brand logo, then press the Next button.**

   Amazon's Store builder displays controls for building a page, which consists of selecting a template on the left and then creating your page in the panel on the right.

4. **In the Page Description box (in the left panel), enter a brief summary of the page content.**

   This description will appear under the page title in search engine results.

5. **Select a template (in the left panel) to specify the desired layout for the page.**

   You can start with a blank page. After you choose a template, a page appears (in the panel on the right) showing the page structure without any content added.

   Each page consists of a collection of tiles, each of which can contain a different type of content:

   - Product
   - Text
   - Image (grid or carousel)
   - Video

6. **To add a tile, select + Add Tile on the page and, in the panel on the right, select the content type for the new tile.**

7. **To add content to a tile or edit a tile's existing content, click the tile.**

   A new panel appears on the right, which enables you to add or edit the tile's content.

8. **Use the controls in the panel on the right to add or edit the tile's content, then select Done (at the top of the rightmost panel) to save your changes.**

   Note that the rightmost panel includes a Delete button (near the bottom) to remove the tile from the page.

9. **Press the Preview Desktop button (above the center panel) to preview the page with the content you added.**

10. **To add a new page to your store, click the Add a Page button (in the leftmost panel) and repeat Steps 4 to 9.**

11. **After completing your Store, press the Submit for Publishing button (in the upper-right corner of the Store builder).**

12. **Amazon displays your publishing options, so choose the option that works best for you:**

- *Standard Publishing* makes your store available to shoppers as soon as your content is approved by Amazon's moderation team. To select this option, press the Submit button next to this option.

- *Scheduled Publishing* enables you to request the date and time you would like your store to be made available to Amazon shoppers. To use this option, check the Request Publish Date box, choose your desired date and time, and press the Submit button.

REMEMBER

Your requested date and time must be at least 24 hours in the future to accommodate for moderation review. If your store isn't approved, you will need to make corrections and resubmit your store and scheduling for publishing.

After you submit your store using either publishing option, it will be reviewed to ensure compliance with Amazon's policies. Amazon will notify you when the review is complete, and you can check the status in the status bar.

TIP

Use your Amazon Store as a landing page. You can then create ads inside and outside Amazon to drive traffic to your Amazon Store.

Creating a Stand-Alone Webstore

The process for creating a stand-alone webstore varies considerably based on the platform and tools you're using to build your store, so we can't provide you with step-by-step instructions. However, we can offer some general guidance for designing your storefront and for managing your store's launch and post-launch.

Designing your storefront

Although the tools for creating an ecommerce website vary considerably, the process typically starts with the overall design of the storefront, and this process begins with template or theme selection.

Choosing a theme

A *template* or *theme* is a collection of style and format settings that control the appearance of a website or webstore. Selecting a different theme changes the appearance of a site without affecting its content. When choosing a theme for your webstore, consider the following criteria:

>> **Great customer support and regular theme updates:** Before selecting a theme, make sure its creator is committed to the theme's success and updates the theme regularly. Regular theme updates are essential for maintaining compatibility with platform updates and ensuring website security.

>> **Mobile friendly (*responsive*):** Some themes are designed to be *responsive*, meaning the theme adapts to ensure that the website (or webstore) looks great and is easy to navigate regardless of the device the person is using to access the site/store, such as, whether a shopper is using a desktop computer, tablet, or smartphone to access the store. Make sure the theme you choose is not only responsive but that its responsiveness functions well; some themes designed to be responsive function better than others.

WARNING

If your webstore isn't responsive (mobile friendly), Google may decide not to include it in its search results, which negatively impacts your store's visibility and sales.

>> **Well-suited for your brand and target customers:** Themes typically have a look and feel that are more suitable for some brands and customers than they are for others. For example, one theme may be better suited for children and parents, whereas another is better suited to professionals. Choose a theme that reflects your brand, the types of products you carry, and the people who buy them.

>> **Search engine optimized (SEO):** SEO is important for your store to be able to rank high in web searches and grab shoppers' attention. Though SEO is mostly about publishing relevant content, a theme that includes options for including meta tags can make a webstore more search-engine friendly.

Customizing your theme

Even after you find a theme that fulfills your requirements, it may not be exactly what you want. Depending on the platform and tools you're using to create your webstore, you may be able to customize your theme or hire an expert to customize it for you.

If you're able to customize your webstore theme, be sure to adhere to the following guidelines:

>> Consider choosing a theme from a developer who offers customized themes and can handle the customization for you.

>> If you choose to customize the theme yourself, make a backup of the existing theme, so you can start from scratch if any changes to the theme render your site inoperable.

>> Exhaust the theme's built-in styles and customization features and functionality before opening and editing any of the theme files directly. Any mistakes you make in editing a theme's files can easily render your site inoperable and the mistakes can be difficult to find and fix.

>> Keep track of any changes you make and write down the names of any files you edit. (You can add comments to files next to any changes you make. Before editing any files, find out how to add comments so that they don't affect the file's function.)

>> Familiarize yourself with web browser plug-ins for developers, such as Web Developer for Google Chrome. These plug-ins enable you to preview your website in the browser, identify areas that don't function or look as you expect them to, and identify what's going on behind the scenes that's causing the problems.

>> Recognize the limitations of the platform and tools you're using. Every ecommerce platform, such as Shopify or BigCommerce, has limitations that prevent you from implementing certain customizations. Being aware of these limitations enables you to avoid wasting time trying to do something that's not possible.

Making sure you have everything in place

Before you publish your webstore and start offering products for sale, review the following pre-flight checklist to be sure everything necessary is in place and working properly:

>> **Payment gateway:** Make sure your payment gateway is working smoothly, so the checkout process is quick, easy, and reliable.

>> **Webstore pages:** Make sure all webstore pages are accessible and that they look and function properly.

>> **Navigation:** Check all links, buttons, and anything else that's clickable to ensure that they function properly.

>> **Shopping lists and notifications:** If your webstore enables shoppers to create their own shopping or wish lists, make sure this feature is working properly. Also check email notifications, such as confirmation that the customer placed the order, the order was shipped, and the order was delivered.

>> **Analytics integration:** Integrate your webstore with a good web analytics tool such as Google Analytics to monitor page visits, bounce rates, click-through rates, conversions, and other metrics than can guide you in improving your store's performance.

>> **Pre-launch marketing plan:** Create a marketing plan to promote your store. Elements of your marketing plan should include email marketing, social media marketing, and pay-per-click (PPC) advertising, among others. Create clever ads and videos that encourage people who see them to share them with their friends and family members, and link the ads and videos back to your webstore. Refer to Chapter 12 for more info about advertising.

>> **Configure your shipping settings:** Shipping settings are important for managing customer expectations pertaining to when items will be shipped and delivered. Check your settings to ensure that promised shipping and delivery times are realistic.

>> **Verify customer service functionality:** Check the contact information on your Contact Us page and the functionality of any features that enable customers to get in touch with you, such as email or live chat. Nothing is more frustrating for customers than when a contact us feature fails to connect them with a customer service representative.

TIP

Have an objective third party check your site and provide feedback prior to launching it. Even if you thoroughly check the site yourself, you may overlook something important, especially if you created the site yourself.

Chapter **15**

Managing Your Inventory

In the retail world, inventory management is an essential business function, ranking right up there with product selection, marketing and advertising, and customer service. Without enough inventory, you can't fill orders, and you lose business, whereas excess inventory results in higher costs of doing business.

In this chapter, we stress the importance of inventory management, give you several reasons to make it a priority, provide guidance on how to manage inventory more effectively, and reveal a few ways to buy inventory on credit to start or grow your ecommerce business even if you don't have the cash available to do so.

Grasping the Importance of Inventory Management

For many novice ecommerce retailers, inventory management is an afterthought. They think about inventory only when they run out of products or get stuck with a bill for products they can't sell and then receive another bill from Amazon for long-term storage.

Proper inventory management requires a more proactive approach, which involves close monitoring of inventory levels and regular adjustments to ensure that just enough stock is on hand to fill orders without tying up too much money in excess inventory and long-term storage fees.

To appreciate the importance of inventory management, consider the following problems you're likely to encounter with inventory mismanagement:

TIP

>> **Lost sales and revenue:** Obviously, when you run out of a product, you can't sell it. Amazon provides no option for shoppers to back-order items, so your product listing simply doesn't appear in search results, and another seller who has the item in stock gets the sale.

   You can work around a low inventory problem by increasing your order processing time for an item, but shoppers are more likely to order from a seller who can promise quick shipping and delivery.

>> **Lower search ranking:** Low-stock and out-of-stock items hurt your product's search ranking, which negatively impacts your sales and income.

>> **Lower seller rating:** If you need to cancel orders because you run out of a product, your seller rating is likely to get dinged, which can hurt your product search ratings and increase your risk of having your Amazon Seller account suspended or terminated.

>> **Fewer product reviews:** Fewer sales mean fewer product reviews resulting in a lower product search ranking and declining sales.

>> **Reduced market share:** Losing sales to the competition results in smaller market share for you and bigger market share for them.

>> **Higher inventory costs:** Overstocks result in higher inventory storage costs, losses from products you can't sell, and lost opportunity costs when you have money tied up in excess inventory and storage.

>> **Increased errors:** Poor inventory management leads to *mispicks* — shipping the wrong product due to poorly organized or improperly labeled inventory or to errors in inventory records.

Managing Inventory via Amazon's Manage Inventory Page

Use Amazon's Manage Inventory page to search, view, and update the inventory records for products you sell on Amazon. To access the Manage Inventory page, log in to Seller Central, open the Inventory menu, and select Manage Inventory.

The Manage Inventory page appears, as shown in Figure 15-1, where you can do the following:

Search listings   Filter listings   Inventory table

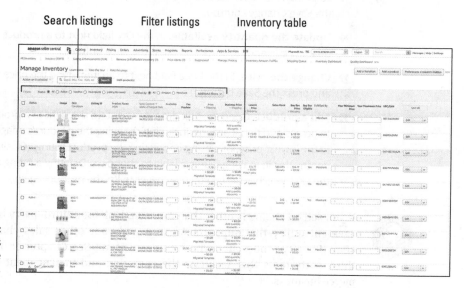

FIGURE 15-1:
Amazon's
Manage
Inventory page.

» **Search for a product:** To search for a specific product, click in the Search box, near the top of the page, type the product's SKU, Title, ISBN, or other attribute, and press the Search button.

» **Filter inventory:** Use the options above the table to view all products in inventory or only active or inactive inventory or to view all products or only FBA or only Fulfillment by Merchant (FBM) products. You may also see filters for displaying only those products with suppressed listings, quality issues, or price alerts — product listings that have specific problems you need to address before those products will appear in searches.

REMEMBER

One of the most common uses of the Manage Inventory page is to quickly identify suppressed listings and make corrections to those listings. Click Suppressed near the top left of the Manage Inventory page to display a complete list of suppressed listings. In the table of suppressed listings, select the Issue(s) to Fix box to find out why the listing is suppressed. Press the Edit button next to the listing, choose the option for correcting the issue, and follow the on-screen cues to complete the task. Click Save All to save your changes.

» **Sort inventory:** Select an inventory header attribute such as SKU or product name at the top of the inventory table to sort product listings according to that attribute.

- **Customize the inventory table:** Press the Preferences button, above and to the right of the inventory table, use the resulting options to specify the columns you want included in the table and other display options, and press the Save Changes button.

- **Update the quantity available:** In the Qty field next to a product, type the quantity currently in stock and press the Save button.

- **Change the price:** In the Price field next to an item, type the price of the item and press the Save button.

- **Edit a product:** Open the Edit drop-down list (to the right of a product listing) to access additional actions, including changing the product's image, matching to the lowest price, or closing or deleting the product listing. (Closing a listing deactivates it, making it unavailable to shoppers. Deleting a listing removes the SKU, which is best if you plan never to list the product again.)

TIP

If you sell on channels other than Amazon, look for a third-party inventory management utility that supports Amazon and your other sales channels, such as eBay, Shopify, and your own ecommerce store. See Chapter 18 for more about third-party tools that facilitate the operation and management of your ecommerce business.

Maintaining Sufficient Stock

As long as you have products listed for sale, you never want to run out, so you need to have a system in place to replenish inventory *before* you get to the point at which you don't have enough to fill an order. Having enough inventory comes down to math; you need to crunch the numbers to forecast total sales over a given period of time and then place an order to replenish inventory early enough for your supplier to deliver the goods before supplies run out.

In the following sections, we lead you through the calculations and provide additional guidance on how to automate the inventory replenishment process.

Forecasting sales

To avoid running out of stock, you first need to know the quantity of an item you sell over a given period of time. Calculating your average daily sales volume provides you with a number you can use to forecast sales for the coming weeks, months, quarter, and even year.

Use the following equation to calculate average daily sales volume for a product:

Quantity Sold divided by Number of Days = Average Daily Sales Volume

For example, if you sold 450 items in three months or 90 days:

450 divided by 90 = 5

Knowing the average daily sales volume simplifies the process of forecasting sales for any given period of time — a week, a month, a quarter, or a year. Just multiply the average daily sales volume by the number of days in the period, as shown in Table 15-1:

TABLE 15-1

Forecasting Your Sales

Period	Multiply Days in Period	By Average Daily Sales Volume	Equal Total Sales
Week	7	5	35
Month	30	5	150
Quarter	90	5	450
Year	365	5	1,825

TIP

After forecasting your total sales for a given period, add 25 to 30 percent to the quantity as a buffer. Also, be sure to consider the fact that sales volume of some products is likely to increase during certain periods of the year, such as Christmas, Black Friday, Cyber Monday, and Amazon Prime Day. Analyze your sales reports (accessible via Seller Central's Reports menu) to identify and better understand demand fluctuations for specific products.

Accounting for lead time

Suppliers need time to manufacture, pack, and ship products. Be sure to account for the time required, and place your order early enough so the products reach you or arrive at Amazon fulfillment centers before you run out of stock.

WARNING

Communicate with your suppliers to identify any potential supplier downtimes or other factors that may impact lead time, such as the following:

>> **Holiday seasons:** Holidays can impact lead times in two ways. First, if a number of employees take time off, the supplier may not have the workforce

required to fill orders. For example, most Chinese suppliers slow down or shut down for at least seven days (and some for several weeks) in late January and early February, in honor of Chinese New Year. Second, suppliers often are busier in the days leading up to holiday seasons, during which period they may need more time to fill orders.

>> **Order sizes:** Suppliers can typically fill small orders faster than large orders, so find out from your supplier how order quantity impacts fulfillment and then plan for these variations in lead times.

>> **Shipping/delivery:** Delivery times vary according to the location of the supplier and how the items are shipped, such as via air, land, or sea.

>> **Customs inspections:** If products need to cross borders, expect delays due to customs inspections.

>> **Inventory processing:** Whether items are shipped to you or to Amazon or other third-party fulfillment centers, they need to be logged in to inventory.

REMEMBER

With inventory planning, you need to think months in advance, not merely days or weeks. From the time you place an order with a supplier until the product is ready to be shipped (from you or an Amazon fulfillment center) generally requires at least 30 days and often longer.

Replenishing FBA inventory

If you use FBA, you can start the process of replenishing inventory from Amazon's Manage Inventory page:

1. In Seller Central, open the Inventory menu and select Manage FBA Inventory.

The Inventory Amazon Fulfills page appears, as shown in Figure 15-2.

2. Scroll down the product list to the product you want to replenish and select the check box to the left of that product.

3. Open the Actions menu and select Send/Replenish Inventory.

4. Follow the on-screen instructions to complete the process.

See Chapter 10 for additional guidance on how to prepare and send products to Amazon fulfillment centers.

1. Select product to replenish.

2. Select Send/replenish inventory

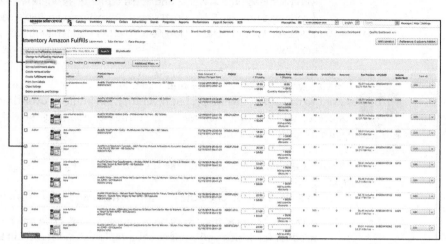

FIGURE 15-2: Start the process of replenishing FBA inventory.

Setting up replenishment alerts

Replenishment alerts notify you via email when the quantity of a product in inventory dips below the threshold you specify. With replenishment alerts, you don't have to constantly monitor your product listings via Amazon's Manage Inventory page. You simply set up an alert and then take action when you receive a replenishment notification.

REMEMBER

Replenishment alerts are available only for FBA products. For FBM products check the low stock alerts on your Seller Central homepage. These alerts are generated automatically based on sales over the past 30 days and the number of items in stock you entered when you first listed the product or most recently updated your quantity in stock.

When creating a replenishment alert for an FBA product, Amazon allows you to specify your replenishment threshold in terms of units or *weeks-of-cover* (the number of weeks' worth of inventory you have on hand based on sales over the past 30 days):

>> **Units:** To figure out when to replenish based on number of units in stock, multiply your lead time by your daily sales volume and add a buffer to ensure you don't run out of stock. (See the earlier sections "Forecasting sales" and "Accounting for lead time" for more about estimating average daily sales volume and lead times.) For example, if your lead time is 45 days and you sell an average of five units per day, you should set a replenishment alert for when you have a minimum of 225 items in stock. You would be wise to add a buffer of say 50 to 75 units to be sure you don't run short, such as 225 + 75 = 300 units.

>> **Weeks-of-cover:** To set a replenishment alert based on weeks-of-cover, start with your lead time in weeks and add a buffer of a couple weeks. For example, if your lead time is 75 days, that's about 11 weeks, plus two weeks equal 13 weeks. Every 13 weeks, you need to order enough items to cover the next 13 weeks.

REMEMBER

Revisit your alerts regularly and make adjustments when necessary. You don't want to run out of inventory, but inventory can build up over time leading to over-stock conditions that increase your storage costs and your risk of getting stuck with products you can't sell.

To set a replenishment alert, take the following steps:

1. In Seller Central, open the Inventory menu and select Manage Inventory.

2. After the Manage Inventory page appears, select the box next to each product for which you want to set a replenishment alert in the table of product listings.

3. Open the Action menu, select Set Replenishment Alerts, and press the Go button.

   The Set Inventory Replenishment Alerts page appears (see Figure 15-3).

4. In the When Do You Want to Be Alerted column, open the Apply to All list and select When Fulfillable Quantity Reaches (Units) or When Weeks-of-Cover Reaches (Weeks) to set the same replenishment level for all products listed or select the desired unit for each individual product.

5. Enter the desired alert threshold quantity in the Alert Threshold box at the top of the column to use the same threshold for all items in the list or enter the desired quantity in the Alert Threshold box for each product individually.

6. Press the Save button to save the alert.

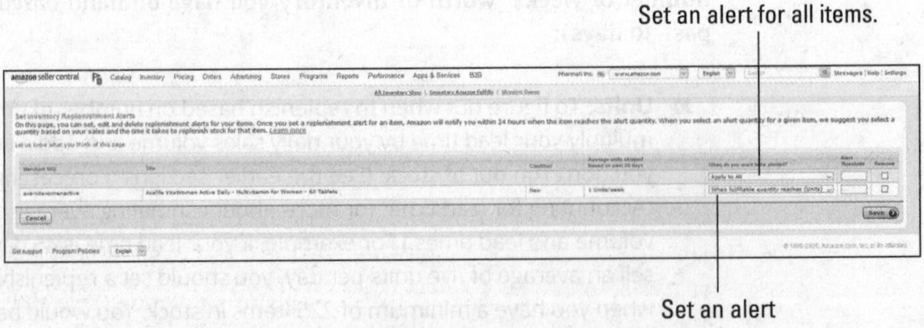

Set an alert for all items.

Set an alert

FIGURE 15-3:
Enter the desired
alert threshold.

TIP

Use Amazon's Restock Inventory tool to obtain recommendations on products to restock, replenishment quantities, and ship dates. To access the Restock Inventory tool, open the Inventory menu, select Inventory Planning, and select the Restock Inventory tab.

REMEMBER

Although Amazon will notify you via email when your fulfillment threshold is reached, you can check for alerts on Seller Central. Open the Inventory menu and select Manage FBA Inventory. A gold bell appears in the Available column next to the quantity when an alert has been set but not yet reached. A red bell indicates that the threshold has been reached.

Avoiding FBA's long-term storage fees

Inventory that has been in an Amazon fulfillment center is subject to long-term storage fees charged per item or per cubic foot, whichever is greater. To help sellers avoid these fees, Amazon features an inventory planner that enables you to monitor how long your products have been stored in Amazon fulfillment centers. To access the inventory planner from Seller Central, open the Inventory menu and select Inventory Planning. The inventory planner appears with the Inventory Age tab selected, as shown in Figure 15-4.

Check inventory age.

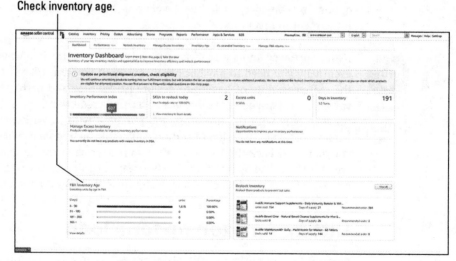

FIGURE 15-4:
Amazon's inventory planner.

For each product stored in FBA inventory, the inventory planner displays its name, sales rank, sales (units shipped in the last 90 days), FBA sell-through (in the last 90 days), inventory age, estimated long-term storage fees, your price, and the buy box price. Use these details to make informed decisions about each product; for example, you may want to avoid long-term storage fees by dropping a product's price to quickly sell any remaining units or have FBA ship any remaining items back to you and then close or delete the listing.

Getting Some Cash or Credit to Buy Inventory

To start and grow any business, you need cash or credit to cover expenses. With an ecommerce business, your direct costs and overhead are likely to be minimal. You don't have to build or rent buildings to serve as storefronts or warehouses or pay utilities to heat and light those buildings, nor do you need to hire and pay employees until you become profitable and so busy that you need help. Your costs are mostly related to buying inventory and paying ecommerce marketplace fees, such as the fees Amazon charges its sellers.

When you're thinking about starting or growing your ecommerce business on Amazon, the first hurdle you need to clear is coming up with the cash to purchase products to sell. You have several options, including using your savings and borrowing money from friends and relatives. In this section, we present a few more options to consider, including leveraging borrowed money to maximize your investment in inventory.

REMEMBER

Using borrowed money to finance a business venture is always risky because eventually you need to pay back that money. If you don't have it, you could face the real possibility of having to declare bankruptcy and perhaps even sell some valuable assets. When possible, use unsecured credit to mitigate the risk or secure the loan only with the inventory you purchase with it. With secured credit, the lender can take possession of certain collateral, such as your business or home, if you don't pay back the loan according to the terms of the agreement. Unsecured credit isn't backed by collateral, so the creditor can't take your property. However, unsecured credit usually comes with significantly higher fees and/or interest rate.

Hitting Amazon up for a loan

Amazon Lending offers qualified sellers 3-, 6-, 9-, or 12-month loans to meet their capital needs. To qualify, you need to have a proven track record of sales growth and superior customer service.

Assuming you qualify and receive an invitation to participate in the loan program, an Invitation Widget appears on the right side of your Seller Central homepage.

The widget describes the loan registration details. To apply for a loan, click the Apply Now button and follow the on-screen instructions. When you click the Apply Now button, Seller Central displays the loan details, including the interest rate, monthly payment amount, and terms of the loan.

REMEMBER

Getting an invitation from Amazon Lending doesn't necessarily qualify you to receive a loan. After you apply, Amazon Lending will check your credit history to determine whether you qualify. Even though you receive an invitation, your request for a loan may be denied.

Getting daily payouts with Payability

Amazon typically pays sellers every two weeks, and deposits from Amazon take three to five days to reach the seller's bank account. If your cash flow is tight, waiting 17 to 19 days for a payment may limit your ability to purchase more inventory. One way to regulate cash flow is to use a third-party service such as Payability. With Payability, you receive daily, next-day payouts from your Amazon seller account. During the time of this writing, Payability was charging 1 to 2 percent of gross sales in exchange for its services.

HOW AMAZON PAYS YOU

As you sell products, Amazon collects payments from buyers and deposits them into your account. Amazon also deducts fees from your account, including your per-item or monthly subscription fee (depending on whether you're an Individual or Professional Seller), any FBA shipping and storage fees, commissions, referral fees, closing fees, product refunds, and so on. (Advertising fees are typically charged to the credit card account you have on file with Amazon, but they may be deducted from your seller account balance.)

At the end of each two-week period, Amazon transfers the balance from your account to the bank account you specified when you registered to become an Amazon Seller. Depending on your bank, the deposit may not arrive in your bank account for another three to five business days.

Payments from certain sales transactions may experience additional delays because Amazon may hold back a portion of the buyer's payment for up to seven days in case the buyer chooses to return the item. As a result, you may be waiting up to 21 days from the time an item is purchased before Amazon transfers the money from that sale to your bank account.

REMEMBER

Visit Payability.com for more details about its daily payout service and other services the company offers, including inventory financing.

Making savvy use of credit cards

Credit cards are the staple of anyone who wants to buy what they can't afford, and they work equally well for buying inventory. Unfortunately, they typically come with steep interest rates, so use them intelligently. Here are a few tips for harnessing the power of credit cards without incurring huge finance charges:

>> Use credit cards that offer cash back for purchases. With these cards, you actually make money by charging your purchases.

>> Pay the entire balance when payment is due. Don't just make the minimum payment.

>> If you can't pay the entire balance when it's due, perform a balance transfer from a credit card that charges interest to one that doesn't charge interest for several months and doesn't charge a fee for the balance transfer.

WARNING

You can't float money forever, so don't get yourself so deep in credit card debt that you can't pay it off before you start getting charged high interest. Using credit cards to buy inventory is a risky, short-term solution. Keep in mind that if you don't sell that inventory, you still need to pay for it or forfeit the inventory if it's used as collateral.

Financing with loans or lines of credit

Depending on your credit score and other factors, you may qualify for a loan or line of credit to finance the purchase of inventory. With a loan, you get a lump sum of money and start accruing interest as soon as you receive the money. With a line of credit, you're approved for a certain maximum amount and draw out the money on an as-needed basis, accruing interest only on the amount of money you take from the account.

Keep in mind the difference between secured and unsecured loans and lines of credit and don't put assets at risk that you can't afford to lose. For example, don't use your home or car as collateral. Ideally, the only collateral you should use to qualify for a secured loan is the inventory you're using the borrowed money to purchase.

Several financial-technology (fintech) companies (for example, Payability.com, Kabbage.com, and Fundbox.com) specialize in small-business loans and lines of credit and even offer them specifically for purchasing inventory. However, even though these companies typically make it easy to apply and qualify for loans and lines of credit, their interest rates may be higher than those charged by more traditional lending institutions.

TIP

Research and compare these companies and the financing options they offer so you fully understand the potential risks and the financing costs before signing any agreements. Also, look at what traditional lending institutions, such as one or more local banks or credit unions, have to offer.

4

Taking Your Business to the Next Level

Harness the power of additional Amazon Seller features and functionality to simplify tasks and improve your business — from tracking your Amazon account's performance to collecting and paying sales tax and generating business and inventory reports.

Decide whether to build your own brand and, if you choose to do so, find out how to create and trademark your brand and find private-label products.

Explore third-party services designed to simplify your life as an Amazon Seller, including tools for finding potentially profitable products, managing inventory, streamlining order management, and automating feedback and reviews.

Expand sales by marketing and selling your products to shoppers in other countries via Amazon Global and business-to-business (B2B) sales.

IN THIS CHAPTER

» Keeping tabs on your performance as an Amazon Seller

» Getting Amazon to handle sales tax for you

» Reviewing your business and inventory reports

» Staying in good standing with Amazon

» Obtaining and using the Amazon Seller Mobile App

Chapter **16**

Putting Additional Amazon Seller Tools to Work for You

A mazon Seller Central provides all the tools you need to list and sell products on Amazon, manage your inventory and orders, and advertise products. In this chapter, we introduce you to some additional tools for monitoring your account's health and performance, calculating the amount of sales tax you owe in different states (in the United States), and generating reports. We also provide guidance on how to obtain and use the Amazon Seller Mobile App for your smartphone, so you can continue to serve your customers while you're on the road or on vacation.

Tracking Your Account's Health and Performance

To a certain degree, Amazon's success hinges on the performance of its third-party sellers. To ensure consistent product quality and customer satisfaction across all sellers, Amazon sets performance targets and policies and provides sellers with tools for evaluating and improving their own performance. You can access the tools from Seller Central via the Performance menu to provide guidance. The following sections examine these tools in greater detail.

Checking your account health

Open the Performance menu and choose Account Health to access an overview of how well you're doing in terms of complying with Amazon's performance targets and policies (see Figure 16-1). Overall account health is reflected by three metrics: customer service performance, product policy compliance, and shipping performance, as we explain in the following sections.

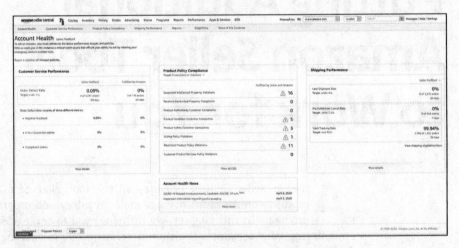

FIGURE 16-1:
A sample Account Health page.

Customer service performance

Customer service performance is measured in terms of *Order Defect Rate (ODR)* — the percentage of total orders that result in negative seller feedback, an A-to-Z Guarantee claim that's not denied, or a chargeback. (A *chargeback* is a reversal of a credit card payment initiated by the bank that issued the card.)

Amazon sets a target order defect rate for all sellers of less than 1 percent. Here you can view your order defect rate broken down by Seller Fulfilled versus Fulfilled by Amazon orders and by the three metrics: negative feedback, A-to-Z Guarantee claims, and chargeback claims.

REMEMBER

See the later sections "Reviewing customer feedback," "Monitoring and managing your A-to-Z Guarantee claims," and "Monitoring and managing your chargeback claims" for guidance on how to obtain additional details about the factors that impact your customer service performance rating.

Product policy compliance

Amazon has a long list of policies it expects its sellers to comply with, as we explain in Chapter 1. Even a single violation of one of Amazon's policies places your seller account at risk of suspension. To determine whether you have a clean record, check the Product Policy Compliance section of the Account Health page. Product compliance complaints include the following:

- » Suspected intellectual property violations
- » Received intellectual property complaints
- » Product authenticity customer complaints
- » Product condition customer complaints
- » Product safety customer complaints
- » Listing policy violations
- » Restricted product policy violations
- » Customer product reviews policy violations

Amazon sets a target of zero product policy complaints or violations. If you receive a performance notification from Amazon indicating that you're guilty of a violation or that someone has filed a complaint against you, respond immediately to address the issue. See the later section "Accessing Amazon's performance notifications" for guidance.

Shipping performance

Amazon gauges shipping performance by late shipment rate (with a target of under 4 percent), a pre-fulfillment cancellation rate (with a target of under 2.5 percent), and a valid tracking rate (with a target above 95 percent). You're responsible only for orders you fulfill. Amazon is responsible for Fulfillment by Amazon performance.

TIP

When filling orders yourself, underpromise and overdeliver. Promise a delivery window you're fairly certain you can beat by a day or two and try to get your products delivered a day or two early to impress your customers.

Reviewing customer feedback

The Account Health page includes a section for negative customer feedback, but if you're looking for additional customer feedback metrics, open the Performance menu and choose Feedback.

The Feedback Manager page appears (refer the Figure 16-2), displaying your overall customer feedback rating and breaking it down into periods of 30, 90, 365, and Lifetime. Metrics are broken down into percentages of positive (four or five stars), neutral (three stars), and negative (one or two stars). This page also includes all the feedback you received along with a set of actions (on the far right) for responding publicly to the feedback or requesting its removal if you think it violates Amazon's feedback policy.

FIGURE 16-2:
A sample
Feedback page.

REMEMBER

The Feedback Manager page also has an option to download your feedback report.

Monitoring and managing your A-to-Z Guarantee claims

Amazon's A-to-Z Guarantee ensures customer satisfaction when they buy from third-party sellers by guaranteeing that products are delivered on time and in good condition. If a customer contacts you about a problem with a product or its timely delivery, and the two of you are unable to resolve the issue, the customer can file an A-to-Z Guarantee claim to seek resolution from Amazon.

REMEMBER

Amazon requires that customers contact the seller prior to filing an A-to-Z Guarantee claim, either via Buyer-Seller messaging or by submitting a return request. If the customer isn't satisfied within 48 hours of filing the request, she can file an A-to-Z Guarantee claim. Amazon notifies you upon receipt of the claim, and you have 72 hours to respond. If you don't respond, Amazon grants the claim, refunds the customer's payment, and takes the money out of your account. Worse yet, because A-to-Z Guarantee claims are a key component of your order defect rate (ODR), which needs to be below 1 percent, not handling a claim increases your ODR, jeopardizing your account.

To monitor and manage your A-to-Z Guarantee claims, open the Performance menu and choose A-to-Z Guarantee claims. The resulting page includes four tabs for filtering your A-to-Z Guarantee claims: Action Required, Under Review, Option to Appeal, and All. You can also search for a claim by order number.

TIP

When a customer contacts you about an order, respond promptly and do your best to resolve any issues, even if you must take a loss on a transaction. You certainly shouldn't give into scammers who just want free products, but be open to resolving any issue that seems remotely legitimate. Depending on the A-to-Z Guarantee claim and how it's resolved, it may or may not add to your ODR. See Chapter 13 for details.

Monitoring and managing your chargeback claims

A chargeback typically occurs when a disgruntled customer is unable to resolve a dispute with a seller or service provider and turns to her credit card company for help. If the credit card company investigates the transaction, can't resolve the issue with the seller/service provider, and determines that the customer is right, the company may reverse the charge.

REMEMBER

As seller on Amazon, you want to avoid chargebacks, because they negatively impact your ODR and overall customer service performance rating.

To check whether you have any chargebacks and to manage any chargeback disputes, open the Performance menu and choose Chargeback Claims. The Chargebacks page appears, showing any chargeback claims that customers have filed against you. You can click the Action Required tab to view only active chargeback claims or the All tab to view a list of all chargeback claims.

Accessing Amazon's performance notifications

If Amazon's performance metrics indicate any issues that may negatively impact your account health or ability to sell, Amazon sends you a performance notification via email and stores a copy of it for reference. To access your performance notifications, open the Performance menu and choose Performance Notifications. To view the contents of a performance notification, click its subject line.

WARNING

To avoid having your account suspended, read all performance notifications and reply to any that indicate a response is expected.

Gaining additional insight via the Voice of the Customer feature

Voice of the Customer is a customer experience (CX) dashboard that uses statistical analysis to identify potential issues with product listings. Behind the scenes, Voice of the Customer analyzes your product listings and product and listing feedback from customers and uses the results to rank your listings as very poor, poor, fair, good, or excellent. You can then dig down to review issues with specific listings and address them to improve the customer experience.

To access Voice of the Customer, open the Performance menu and choose Voice of the Customer. Figure 16-3 shows a sample of the opening Voice of the Customer dashboard. Near the top of the dashboard is a CX Health breakdown of your listings, showing the total number of very poor, poor, fair, good, and excellent ratings. Below that is a table that shows CX details for each product you've listed.

FIGURE 16-3:
A sample Voice of the Customer dashboard.

Pay special attention to the details in the following columns:

>> **NCX Rate** is a percentage of orders that received negative feedback out of the total number of orders.

>> **CX health** is an indication of the average customer experience ranked from very poor to excellent.

>> **Last updated** is the most recent date a sale was made or an NCX was received.

If you just listed a product and haven't sold any yet, the product won't have an NCX or CX rating.

Improving your performance via Seller University

The one item on the Performance menu that seems to be out of place is Seller University, which would seem better suited for a Help menu. However, its placement on the Performance menu reflects how valuable Amazon believes Seller University can be in helping sellers quickly optimize their performance.

Seller University is a collection of brief video clips designed to bring sellers quickly up to speed on the process of selling on Amazon and using Amazon tools and applications to their advantage. (See Chapter 4 for more about Seller University.)

Dealing with Sales Tax

As an online retailer, you're required to collect and pay sales taxes in any state in the United States where you meet the following two criteria:

>> You have a *sales tax nexus* (a significant connection) to the state, such as a physical presence — a store, warehouse, or even inventory in the state. In many states, having inventory stored in an Amazon fulfillment center in the state qualifies as a sales tax nexus. Therefore, if you use FBA, several states require that you to collect and pay sales tax.

>> The product you're selling is taxable in the state in which you're selling it. For example, in several states, food items are not subject to sale tax.

Generally speaking, if you're storing your own inventory and fulfilling your own orders, you're required to collect and pay sales tax only on sales of products in your own state. However, most states have enacted *marketplace facilitator* legislation requiring marketplaces, such as Amazon, eBay, Walmart, and Etsy, to charge, collect, and remit sales tax on all sales, regardless of whether the marketplace (for example, Amazon) or a third-party seller (like you) made the sale.

If you have a sales nexus in a state with marketplace facilitator legislation, you don't have to calculate, collect, or remit sales tax to the taxing authority in your state, but you may need to register for sales tax with the state and submit quarterly sales/sales tax reports. If you have a sales nexus in a state without marketplace facilitator legislation, you're responsible for calculating, collecting, remitting, and reporting sales tax; if you're a Professional Seller, you can use Amazon's Tax Calculation Service (TCS) to calculate and collect sales tax for you in those states.

WARNING

To ensure compliance with sales tax laws in all states, consult a tax expert. Although Amazon is required to collect, remit, and report sales tax paid in each state where marketplace facilitator legislation is in force, it's not responsible for doing so in other states where you may be selling products or on sales made through other channels. In addition, you may be required to register for sales tax and file quarterly sales tax reports in some states even though Amazon is collecting and remitting the taxes in those states.

To ensure compliance with state sales tax laws and ease the burden on third-party sellers, Amazon provides two services: Marketplace Tax Collection (MTC) and Tax Collection Service (TCS), which we cover in the following sections.

Grasping the basics of Marketplace Tax Collection

For all items you sell on Amazon, it serves as your marketplace facilitator in all jurisdictions (state, county, city, and district) that have legislation requiring it to do so. In all these jurisdictions, Amazon is responsible for calculating, collecting, remitting, and reporting sales tax and processing the refunds of any sales tax on returned items. In essence, Amazon becomes the taxpayer in these jurisdictions. As of this writing, Amazon MTC covers the following states:

Alabama	Illinois	New Jersey	Texas
Alaska	Indiana	New Mexico	Utah
Arizona	Iowa	New York	Vermont

Arkansas	Kentucky	North Carolina	Virginia
California	Maine	North Dakota	Washington
Colorado	Maryland	Ohio	West Virginia
Connecticut	Massachusetts	Oklahoma	Wisconsin
District of Columbia	Michigan	Pennsylvania	Wyoming
Georgia	Minnesota	Rhode Island	
Hawaii	Nebraska	South Carolina	
Idaho	Nevada	South Dakota	

Amazon calculates each product's taxability using the product category and item description you specify when creating your product listing. If you assign a product tax code (as we explain in the next section), Amazon ignores it when making this determination.

Using Amazon's Tax Calculation Service (TCS)

For any products sold to customers in non-marketplace facilitator jurisdictions, and/or where MTC isn't implemented, you're responsible for your sales tax calculation, remittance, and reporting obligations. To help, Amazon offers its Tax Calculation Service (TCS) to Professional Sellers in the United States and Canada and Value Added Tax (VAT) Calculation Service (VCS) for sellers in the European Union and Japanese marketplaces.

Based on the tax calculation settings you enter and any other relevant information you provide Amazon, it calculates your sales and use taxes, collects the taxes, and remits the amounts to you, so you can remit them to the taxing authorities in the jurisdictions in which you sell products. You pay Amazon 2.9 percent of all sales and due taxes and other transaction-based charges it calculates, and it retains those fees to cover any refunds on related transactions.

Amazon provides a list of product tax codes and related product taxability rules. For each product, you assign the appropriate tax code. If you don't assign a code for a product, TCS doesn't calculate or collect taxes for it. You must also provide Amazon with your tax registration number for each jurisdiction in which you want TCS to calculate and collect taxes.

When you upgrade from Individual seller to Professional Seller for the first time, you have the option to enroll in TCS. After enrolling in the service, you must configure your tax calculation settings, but before you do, take the following steps:

1. **Review the Amazon tax methodology document at** `sellercentral.amazon.com/tax/nexus/methodology` **to find out how Amazon will calculate your sales and use taxes.**

2. **Review Amazon's list of product tax codes at** `sellercentral.amazon.com/tax/nexus/settings/ptc`.

3. **Obtain a state tax registration number for each state where you want to collect taxes.**

Follow these steps to enter or adjust your tax calculation settings:

1. **In Seller Central, open the Settings menu (upper right) and click Tax Settings.**

2. **Click the View/Edit Your Tax Obligations and Shipping & Handling and Gift Wrap Tax Settings.**

3. **Scroll down to where you enter your configuration settings, open the Use Default Product Tax Code box, and select the PTC you want to use whenever you don't specify a PTC in a product listing.**

   If you don't specify a PTC here or in a product's listing, no tax will be collected. Consider using A_GEN_TAX as your default PTC to ensure that every item you sell is taxed at the basic rate for each state if you forget to specify a PTC in one or more product listings.

4. **Take one of the following steps to select the state where you want to collect taxes:**

   - To configure tax settings for a new state, add the state from the drop-down box.

   - To modify existing state configurations, locate the state in the configuration box.

   If a state listed shows "For all shipments to this state, Amazon manages sales and use taxes," Amazon MTC handles tax collection (see the previous section) and you won't be allowed, in Step 6, to choose jurisdictions.

5. **For each state you selected, enter your state tax registration number.**

6. **For each state, select the jurisdictions (state, county, city, district) you want the system to calculate taxes for.**

7. **For each jurisdiction, select either or both of the following boxes if the jurisdiction taxes the cost of these services:**

   - Shipping & Handling

   - Gift Wrap

8. **If desired, enter a custom sales tax rate (as a percentage) for any of the states you're configuring.**

   Enter a custom sales tax rate only if necessary to override the rate supplied by Amazon's service provider if that rate is in error for some reason.

WARNING

9. **To enroll in the Amazon tax exemption program, select the box next to Enroll in the Amazon Tax-Exemption Program.**

10. **Scroll to the bottom of the page and click Save Settings.**

REMEMBER

If you sell in countries outside the United States, you may need to comply with different tax laws, such as the value added tax (VAT) in countries that are members of the European Union and the goods and services tax (GST) levied in India. Consult a tax specialist who has knowledge of the tax laws of international marketplaces in which you sell products to ensure compliance with all laws.

Generating Business and Inventory Reports

Fulfillment by Amazon (FBA) business reports provide data and summaries that can help you gauge the health and performance of your Amazon ecommerce business. Amazon provides a broad selection of FBA business reports broken down by type, as we present in the following sections.

Sales reports

Sales reports provide insights into which products are selling best and where, how pricing and promotions impact sales, how your various sales channels are performing, and much more. Amazon features the following sales reports:

>> **Amazon Fulfilled Shipments** presents product-level details on FBA orders only. Details include purchase price, quantity, tracking, and shipping information. To access this report, open the Reports menu, select Fulfillment, and in the Sales section select Amazon Fulfilled Shipments.

- » **All Orders** presents product-level details on FBA and seller-fulfilled orders. Details include order status, fulfillment and sales channel info, and product details. To access this report, open the Reports menu, select Fulfillment, and in the Sales section select All Orders.

- » **Customer Shipment Sales** presents product-level details on shipped FBA orders. Details include price, quantity, and destination. To access this report, open the Reports menu, select Fulfillment, and in the Sales section select Customer Shipment Sales.

- » **Promotions** presents special offers, such as Super Saver Shipping, applied to orders. To access this report, open the Reports menu, select Fulfillment, and in the Sales section select Promotions.

- » **Sales Tax** presents details including delivery destination, tax jurisdiction, and sales tax collected by revenue type. To access this report, open the Reports menu, select Fulfillment, and in the Sales section, select Customer Taxes.

- » **Your FBA Sales Lift** compares sales on products fulfilled by Amazon to those fulfilled through other methods. To access this report, open the Reports menu, select Business Reports, and then Your FBA Sales Lift. (Note that this option is available only when FBA sales lift data is available.)

Inventory reports

Amazon features a broad collection of reports that provide insight into the status of your inventory and facilitate inventory management. Inventory reports include the following:

- » **Stranded Inventory** calls attention to products in Amazon fulfillment centers that have no active listing on Amazon. To view this report, open the Reports menu, select Fulfillment, and in the Inventory section select Stranded Inventory.

- » **Bulk Fix Stranded Inventory** creates a stranded inventory file you can use to relist stranded products in bulk. To view this report, open the Reports menu, select Fulfillment, and in the Inventory section select Bulk Fix Stranded Inventory. This report is available only to Professional Sellers.

- » **Reserved Inventory** highlights products set aside to fulfill an existing order, to move to a different fulfillment center, or to be used to complete some other task, so they're currently unavailable for purchase. To view this report, open the Reports menu, select Fulfillment, and in the Inventory section select Reserved Inventory.

>> **Inventory Reconciliation** helps you analyze inventory movement into and out of Amazon fulfillment centers, including products sold, returned, removed/disposed of, damaged, lost, and found. To view this report, open the Reports menu, select Fulfillment, and in the Inventory section select Inventory Reconciliation.

>> **Amazon-Fulfilled Inventory** presents a near real-time accounting of all your products in Amazon fulfillment centers. To view this report, open the Reports menu, select Fulfillment, and in the Inventory section select Amazon Fulfilled Inventory.

>> **Daily Inventory** presents a daily accounting of all your products in Amazon fulfillment centers, including quantity, location, and disposition. To view this report, open the Reports menu, select Fulfillment, and in the Inventory section select Daily Inventory History.

>> **Monthly Inventory** presents a monthly accounting of all your products in Amazon fulfillment centers, including quantity, location, and disposition. To view this report, open the Reports menu, select Fulfillment, and in the Inventory section select Monthly Inventory History.

>> **Received Inventory** shows which products have passed through the receiving process at Amazon fulfillment centers. To view this report, open the Reports menu, select Fulfillment, and in the Inventory section select Received Inventory.

>> **Inventory Event Detail** breaks down details about inventory receipts, shipments, adjustments by SKU, and fulfillment center. To view this report, open the Reports menu, select Fulfillment, and in the Inventory section select Inventory Event Detail.

>> **Inventory Adjustments** shows changes to inventory related to damages, lost products, discrepancies between shipping and receiving records, inventory transfers, and more. To view this report, open the Reports menu, select Fulfillment, and in the Inventory section select Inventory Adjustments.

>> **Inventory Health** presents an overall assessment of your sales, your current sellable and unsellable inventory, inventory age, weeks of cover remaining, and more. To view this report, open the Reports menu, select Fulfillment, and in the Inventory section select Inventory Health.

>> **Manage FBA Inventory** presents current listing details, including condition, disposition, and quantity. These details facilitate daily inventory management tasks. To view this report, open the Reports menu, select Fulfillment, and in the Inventory section select Manage FBA Inventory.

>> **Inbound Performance** provides details about issues encountered with products you've shipped to Amazon fulfillment centers. To view this report, open the Reports menu, select Fulfillment, and in the Inventory section select Inbound Performance.

Payments reports

Amazon automatically processes payments from your Amazon Seller account to cover various Amazon fees. Several reports are available to help you keep track of where your money is going, including the following:

>> **Long-Term Storage Charges** presents details about any recent long-term storage fees broken down by stock keeping unit (SKU), including condition of items, quantity, size, and total fee per SKU. To access this report, open the Reports menu, select Fulfillment, and in the Payments section select Long-Term Storage Fee Charges.

>> **Reimbursements** presents details of any payments made to you for missing or damaged inventory that Amazon is responsible for. To access this report, open the Reports menu, select Fulfillment, and in the Payments section select Reimbursements.

>> **Statement View** enables you to create a custom report of sales and fees for a specific date range. To access this report, open the Reports menu, select Payments, and select the Statement View tab.

>> **Transactions View** presents a list of all transactions between you and Amazon from the previous settlement date until the previous day's closing. To access this report, open the Reports menu, select Payments, and select the Transactions View tab.

>> **Fee Preview** presents estimates of your Amazon selling and FBA fees for your current FBA inventory. To access this report, open the Reports menu, select Fulfillment, and in the Payments section select Fee Preview.

Customer concession reports

Customer concession reports enable you to track product returns and exchanges processed by Amazon. Two customer concession reports are available:

>> **Returns** shows a list of items returned by customer, the reason given for each return, and the returned product's condition. To view this report, open the Reports menu, select Fulfillment, and in the Customer Concessions section select FBA Customer Returns.

>> **Replacements** shows a list of replacement items sent to customers for returned products, including the reason the replacement was sent. To view this report, open the Reports menu, select Fulfillment, and in the Customer Concessions section select Replacements.

Removal reports

Removal reports provide information about inventory stored in Amazon fulfillment centers. Three removal reports are available:

>> **Recommended Removals** informs you of any FBA inventory that will be subject to long-term storage fees at the next inventory cleanup date. To access this report, open the Reports menu, select Fulfillment, and in the Removals section, select Recommended Removal.

>> **Removal Order Details** provides details of removal orders, including the removal type (returned to you or discarded), the status of the removal order, and any fees charged for the removal. To access this report, open the Reports menu, select Fulfillment, and in the Removals section, select Removal Order Detail.

>> **Removal Shipment Details** presents the carrier and tracking number for any removal shipment to help you track items returned from FBA inventory to you. To access this report, open the Reports menu, select Fulfillment, and in the Removals section, select Removal Shipment Detail.

Managing Your Amazon Seller Account with the Mobile App

Success as an Amazon seller relies on providing superior customer service 24/7/365. It requires being responsive to customer questions and complaints whether the customer tries to contact you during or outside business hours and even when you're on vacation with your family.

To stay in close contact with Amazon and your Amazon customers, consider downloading and installing the Amazon Seller app on your smartphone. With this free app, you can do the following:

>> Receive Amazon notifications and address critical issues when you're away from your office

>> Snap, edit, and save product photos using your mobile device

>> Scan products with or without a bar code using visual search, so you can easily create product listings for new products

>> Conduct sale analysis and track your sales growth

>> Manage orders, inventory, and advertising and promotional campaigns

>> Contact Amazon Seller support when you need help

>> Share the app with your team to become even more responsive to customers and have more eyes on opportunities and critical issues

Getting the Amazon Seller Mobile App

The Amazon Seller Mobile App is currently available for iOS (Apple) and Android devices, and it's free to install and use. To get the app, go to the app store for your device, search for "amazon seller," and, when the Amazon Seller app appears, press the Install button. You can find the Amazon Seller app at any of the following App Stores:

>> Apple's App Store

>> Google Play

>> Amazon App Store

After installing the app, press the button to run it and then select your primary marketplace (country). When prompted to log on, enter your login credentials (username and password), just as you would do to log on to your Amazon Seller account from a computer.

Navigating the Amazon Seller Mobile App

The Amazon Seller Mobile App has many of the same features and functionality as are built into the version you access via your computer's web browser; everything is just presented a little differently. Most of the opening screen is dedicated to displaying your recent sales performance over the past seven days (as in Figure 16-4). Just above the main area is a bar you can swipe left or right to view key information, such as today's total sales (in dollars and units), your current Amazon balance, when you can expect your next payment from Amazon, and your customer feedback rating.

In the upper-left corner of the screen is a menu button you can tap to view a list of options for returning to the Home page, managing inventory, viewing orders, communicating with customers or Amazon staff, getting help, signing out, and more. Near the bottom of the opening screen is another menu with options for performing common tasks, such as adding a product listing, managing orders, and checking your Amazon account health.

TIP

Tap the camera icon in the upper-right corner of the screen to scan a product, using its bar code or just a snapshot of the product, and create a product listing from it. This technique is a great way to add listings for specific products when you encounter a product anywhere that you want to start selling.

Camera

Sales performance

FIGURE 16-4:
The Amazon
Seller Mobile App.

» **Building a brand from the ground up**

» **Protecting your brand via trademarking**

» **Creating a brand around private label products**

Chapter **17**

Building Your Own Brand (or Not)

A mazon offers brand owners the option of joining the Amazon Brand Registry and listing their own branded products. As a member of the Brand Registry, you have control over the listings for your branded products; the listings you post and any updates you make to them are what shoppers see when they view your products. If other sellers on Amazon list your branded products, your product description and images are what shoppers see.

Brand Registry also unlocks benefits and tools available exclusively to Registry members, including Seller Central's Brand Dashboard, Sponsored Brands, A+ Content (see Chapter 11), a branded Amazon Store (Chapter 14), and tools for protecting your brand against unauthorized or improper use.

To join Amazon's Brand Registry, you need to be a brand owner. In this chapter, we present the pros and cons of creating a brand and adding it to Amazon's Brand Registry, provide guidance on how to build a brand and trademark it, and explain how to add your brand to the Brand Registry. Near the end of the chapter, we discuss how to create your own brand using private label products. (A *private label product* is made by a third-party manufacturer and sold under a retailer's brand name.)

REMEMBER

You must be registered as a Professional Seller to register your brand in Amazon's Brand Registry.

Deciding Whether Branding Is Right for You

To brand or not to brand? That's the question many sellers ask themselves. In some cases, the answer is easy — if you already have a well-known brand and you want to maximize the sales of your branded products on Amazon, then, yes, you want to brand. On the other hand, if you're just selling a variety of products on Amazon, branding may or may not be necessary or desirable; you can list and sell products on Amazon regardless of whether you're a brand owner or belong to the Amazon Brand Registry.

If you're on the fence about branding, consider the following benefits of owning a brand and adding it to Amazon's Brand Registry:

» **Brand identity gives your products market recognition.** *Market recognition* is customer awareness of a company's products and services, which drives sales in and of itself. Strong brand identity creates a readily recognizable image in the minds of shoppers.

» **Branding builds trust.** An established brand shows consumers that the business is legitimate, stands behind its products, and plans to be around for a long time. Customer trust leads to higher conversion rates.

» **Branding increases customer loyalty.** Customers identify closely with certain brands. A brand's identity may not only reflect a customer's identity but also influence it.

» **Branding communicates the authenticity of a product.** Customers buy brand-name products knowing that the manufacturer invested more in materials, manufacturing, and quality control to protect the brand's reputation.

» **A brand name and logo are valuable advertising assets.** Branding simplifies the task of advertising your business, products, and unique identity. You can use your company name, logo, and the tag lines on everything from products to packaging to increase your market recognition.

» **Bigger brands command bigger valuations.** Increased brand recognition raises the value of a company beyond its products, inventory, and infrastructure.

» **Branding inspires your team!** People like to work for well-known brands and take pride in doing so. A strong brand can inspire and energize a team, boosting innovation and productivity.

» **Successful branding drives positive word of mouth.** When customers are excited about a brand, they share that excitement with their friends, family members, and associates.

>> **A strong brand is a competitive advantage.** In a crowded marketplace, a strong, positive brand image makes a product stand out among competing products.

>> **Branding provides access to Amazon's Brand Registry.** Membership in Amazon's Brand Registry unlocks the doors to Amazon's most powerful marketing tools, including A+ pages, Amazon Vine, and Sponsored Brand ads.

Creating Your Own Brand

Before you can register a brand in Amazon's Brand Registry, you need a brand to register. To create a brand, first do some soul searching to discover your brand's appeal and personality and then unleash your creativity to figure out how to effectively communicate your brand's appeal and personality conceptually. In this section, we lead you through the process of creating a recognizable brand.

Discover your purpose

Every business starts with an idea that's usually inspired by an unmet need or desire in the marketplace. Your brand's purpose is to fulfill that need or desire. To identify the purpose behind your effort to create a new brand, ask yourself the following questions:

>> **What's the driving force behind my business and products?** Have you identified an unmet need or desire in the marketplace? Are you developing the brand or product with a certain person in mind, such as a friend or relative? Will your products help solve a certain problem?

>> **What's motivating me to create this business or this new line of products?** Do you have a passion for helping the average person become more fit and trim? Are you committed to helping people express their personality through what they wear? Are you full of ideas for improving experiences in the kitchen?

>> **What products and services am I offering to consumers?** List the products and services you offer. This exercise often reveals a theme or concept that's common to a line of products or services. Doing so may also help you identify products that don't fit with your desired brand concept.

>> **How will my products and services impact the lives of consumers?** Think less about the great features of your products and services and more about how these features will benefit your customers. How will their lives be better or different as a result of your products and services?

>> **What makes my products and services best suited to fill a certain gap in the market?** What makes you and your products uniquely qualified to serve consumers' unmet needs or desires? How are you and your products and services different from and better than the competition?

TIP

To discover your brand's purpose, make your customers your central focus. Your brand's goal should be to solve their problems, offer better solutions, or make their lives fuller or more enjoyable or pleasant in some way. As you conceptualize your brand, think about how the brand can most effectively communicate its purpose.

Analyze your competition

A key component of effective branding is differentiation. Your brand must communicate what makes you and your products and services uniquely different and better than what's already out there in the marketplace.

Identify and examine the competition closely, assessing them based on the following factors:

>> Product quality

>> Creativity

>> Brand message and consistency

>> Marketing strategies

>> Reputation

A careful examination of the competition often reveals not only what they're doing but what they're not doing to win customers and expand their market share. Whatever they're not doing provides opportunities for you to increase and communicate how you're different from and better than the rest.

Identify your target market

Ultimately, your brand must meet the needs or fulfill the desires of customers, but not all customers have the same needs and desires. As you develop your brand, think about your *target market* — the people who are most likely to benefit from the products and services you offer.

Define your customers and study their lifestyles. Are you looking to meet the needs of weekend athletes who are facing fitness challenges? Single moms struggling to raise their children? College students looking for ways to become more productive? Narrow your target market and create a customer profile that reflects your ideal customers and their personality. Your customer profile should include the following:

>> Age

>> Gender

>> Location

>> Education

>> Income

>> Aspirations and goals

>> Hobbies and affinities

A deeper understanding of your customers provides the insight that drives effective brand creation.

Identify your brand's key benefits

Many businesses make the mistake of making their brand all about themselves, focusing the brand solely on the business's personality or the products it offers. However, customers care more about how the brand will benefit them. They want to know how products are going to make their lives easier or better or more enjoyable.

When you're developing a brand, keep your customers' needs and desires front and center. Ask yourself, "What's in it for them?" Here are a few examples of benefits that may be conveyed through a brand:

>> Healthy, organic

>> Environmentally friendly

>> Fun

>> Exciting

>> Reliable

>> Relaxing

Write a slogan

A *slogan* is a short, memorable phrase that conveys the essence of a product, service, or brand. When creating your brand, try to express its essence in just a few words that will resonate with customers in your target market. Here are a few examples:

>> From single mom to Super Mom

>> Crafting innovation into your life

>> Every athlete's best friend

>> Healthy food, healthy body

>> Because your family deserves a break

Visualize your brand

Every successful brand has a readily recognizable look and feel. McDonald's has its golden arches. Nike has a swoosh logo shaped as a wing of the Greek goddess of victory (named Nike). Apple has an apple. Target has a bull's eye. Starbucks uses a mermaid. Many companies have stylized text-based logos, such as IBM, Google, eBay, Coca-Cola, 3M, FedEx, and VISA.

Close your eyes and imagine what your brand would look like as a logo. What colors would it be? What image or font would capture and convey the essence of your brand? What would stick in the minds of consumers?

Work it: Reinforce your brand

After defining your brand and creating brand assets (slogan, logo, color scheme, and so on), use those assets to imprint your brand on the minds of consumers. Brand your website and blog, social media properties, webstores (including your Amazon Store), mobile app, packaging materials, company T-shirts, marketing and advertising content, and more. You want consumers to see your brand everywhere they turn.

REMEMBER

To increase your brand recognition, be clear and consistent in all your messaging, whether you're communicating in text, graphics, or both. Align everything from your slogan to your logo and your mission statement to reinforce your brand in the minds of consumers.

Trademarking Your Brand

A *trademark* is a symbol, word, or words legally registered or established by use as representing a business and the unique products and services it offers. The brand you create is a trademark. After creating your brand, register your business name and all associated brand assets to protect them against unauthorized use by other businesses or individuals.

In this section, we lead you through the process of registering your trademark. You can register it with the United States Patents and Trademark Office (USPTO) via its website or by using Amazon's Intellectual Property (IP) Accelerator. We provide guidance for both of these options. You also need to register your brand with Amazon's Brand Registry so Amazon can help protect your brand in specific marketplaces.

REMEMBER

Trademark registration protects only the brand name and logos used for a business and its products and services. To protect other intellectual property (IP) rights, you need to apply for a patent (for inventions) or copyright (for literary works) or domain name (for websites and blogs).

Registering your trademark on USPTO.gov

The United States Patent and Trademark Office maintains its own website, where you can find out all about trademarks, patents, and copyrights. The website provides step-by-step instructions for registering a trademark, along with a collection of links and a number of videos that provide additional information and guidance. We encourage you to visit the site at uspto.gov and select Trademarks in the menu bar near the top of the opening page to access a collection of links for complete information and instructions.

Here's a general rundown of the process:

1. **Prepare for the application process by doing the following:**

   - Decide on the type of mark — a word, design, or sound mark.

   - Identify the goods and/or services for which the trademark applies.

   - Search the USPTO trademark database at www.uspto.gov/trademarks-application-process/search-trademark-database to see whether anyone else has already registered the same or a similar mark.

   - Determine the filing basis for the application, such as "for use in commerce."

   - Hire a trademark attorney if desired or necessary. An attorney is necessary only if you're not a U.S. resident.

2. **File your trademark application using the Trademark Electronic Application System (TEAS).**

   You can set up your USPTO.gov account and log in to the system to file your trademark application at www.uspto.gov/trademark/login.

3. **Monitor your application status through the Trademark Status and Document Retrieval (TSDR) system at tsdr.uspto.gov.**

WARNING

   Check the status at least once within six months of filing your application so you don't miss any deadlines. If you change your email address, be sure to update it in the system to ensure that you receive any important notifications or updates.

4. **Work with the USPTO-assigned examining attorney to complete the process.**

   The attorney can do one of the following:

   - Refuse the application and send you a letter listing the reasons for refusal. You then have six months from the date of the letter to respond.

   - Approve the application, in which case your trademark is published in the USPTO's weekly gazette. If the USPTO doesn't receive opposition to your trademark request within eight weeks, it issues you a trademark registration certificate.

REMEMBER

USPTO is responsible only for registering the trademark. In the event of a trademark violation, you're solely responsible for enforcing your rights. The USPTO doesn't police the use of trademarks.

Streamlining the trademark registration process with IP Accelerator

As we explain in the previous section, getting your trademark registered through the USPTO is a process that can take months before you receive your trademark registration certificate. This long wait can, in turn, delay the process of adding your trademark to Amazon's Brand Registry. To streamline the process of getting your trademark into its Brand Registry, Amazon features IP Accelerator.

IP Accelerator connects sellers with qualified and curated IP law firms that provide high-quality trademark services at competitive rates. These firms simplify the process of applying for trademark registration, but they don't necessarily help you obtain your trademark registration certificate any faster. Instead, as soon as you complete the application process with the connected law firm, Amazon invites you to enroll in the Brand Registry, which immediately provides trademark protection in the Amazon marketplaces of your choice. You don't have to wait for your trademark registration certificate from the USPTO.

To register your trademark using IP Accelerator, go to brandservices.amazon.com/ipaccelerator, press the Get Started button, and follow the on-screen instructions.

Adding your trademark to the Amazon Brand Registry

If you have an approved trademark, you can create an Amazon Brand Registry account and add your trademark to the Brand Registry, assuming you meet the following program requirements:

>> You have an active trademark that appears on your products and packaging.

>> You can verify that you're the owner of the trademark. (You have a trademark registration certificate from the USPTO or you applied for trademark registration through Amazon's IP Accelerator.)

>> You have an Amazon Brand Registry account, which you can create using your existing Seller Central credentials. See the later section "Adding your brand to Amazon's Brand Registry" for instructions on how to create an Amazon Brand Registry account.

In the following sections, we list the benefits of having your brand registered on Amazon and provide instructions on how to add your brand to Amazon's Brand Registry.

Recognizing the benefits of Amazon Brand Registry

Amazon's Brand Registry delivers several benefits to brand owners, including the following:

>> **Accurate brand representation:** The listings you create for your branded products are the listings shoppers see. You're the only seller who can change the content of your branded product listings.

>> **Brand protection:** Amazon prohibits other sellers from using your brand and provides you with search and report tools to identify potential infringements and report them to Amazon. In addition, Amazon's predictive protection mechanisms identify and remove any content that's suspected of infringing on your brand or providing inaccurate content about your branded products.

>> **24/7/365 support:** As a registered brand owner, you have access to Amazon support teams 24 hours a day, 7 days a week, and 365 days of the year to answer questions and address concerns.

>> **Brand-building tools:** Registered brands have access to Amazon's brand building tools including A+ Pages, Sponsored Brands, Stores and the Brand Dashboard. (See Chapter 11 for guidance on creating A+ Pages and Chapter 14 for more about building and managing your own store on Amazon.)

Adding your brand to Amazon's Brand Registry

When you're ready to add your brand/trademark to Amazon's Brand Registry, take the following steps:

1. Go to brandservices.amazon.com and press the Get Started button.

2. Review the eligibility requirements and press the Enroll Now button.

3. Select the country-specific marketplace where you want to enroll your brand.

4. After the Tell Us About Your Business page appears, enter the requested details about your business and press the Create Account button.

5. From the Amazon Brand Registry page, press the Enroll a New Brand button.

    Amazon asks you to confirm your brand eligibility, as shown in Figure 17-1.

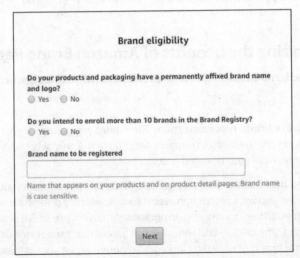

Brand eligibility

Do your products and packaging have a permanently affixed brand name and logo?
○ Yes   ○ No

Do you intend to enroll more than 10 brands in the Brand Registry?
○ Yes   ○ No

Brand name to be registered

Name that appears on your products and on product detail pages. Brand name is case sensitive.

[Next]

FIGURE 17-1:
Confirm your
brand eligibility.

6. **Answer the following questions and press the Next button:**

- Do your products and packaging have a permanently affixed brand name and logo?

- Do you intend to enroll more than ten brands in the Brand Registry?

- Do you have a brand name to be registered?

After you click the Next button, the Intellectual Property page appears, as shown in Figure 17-2.

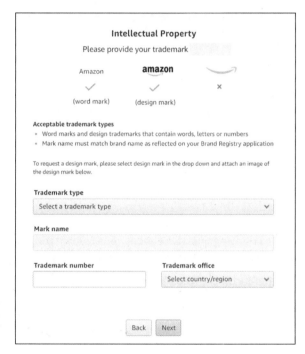

FIGURE 17-2:
Enter details about your trademark.

7. **Enter the requested information, as follows, and press the Next button:**

- **Trademark type:** Open the list and select Word Mark or Design Mark.

- **Mark name:** Click in the box and type the mark name as it appears on your trademark registration certificate.

- **Trademark number:** Click in the box and type the trademark number that appears on your trademark registration certificate.

- **Trademark office:** Open the list and select the country or region from which the trademark registration certificate was issued.

After you click the Next button, the Tell Us More About page appears, as shown in Figure 17-3.

Tell us more about

Do your products have UPCs, ISBNs, EANs, or other GTINs?
Each product sold on Amazon uses a unique identifier such as UPCs, EANs, ISBNs or GTINs to connect it to a brand. You can still list products that do not have UPCs, EANs, ISBNs or GTINs by submitting a GTIN Exemption Request. **Please note:** Brand Registry does not grant GTIN exemption and you will only be able to list products after you are approved through the GTIN Exemption process.
◯ Yes   ◯ No

If you sell your products online, let us know where (optional)
Why is this important ⌄

Seller and Vendor account information
Why is this important ⌄
Does your brand have an existing Seller or Vendor relationship with Amazon?
◯ Seller
◯ Vendor
◯ Both
◯ No, my brand does not have an existing Seller or Vendor relationship with Amazon

Manufacturing and licensing information
Why is this important ⌄
Does your brand manufacture products?
◯ Yes
◯ No

Does your brand license trademarks to others who manufacture products associated with your intellectual property?
◯ Yes
◯ No

Where are your brand's products manufactured?
[Select country/re... ⌄] [Add country/region ✚]

Where are your brand's products distributed?
[Select country/re... ⌄] [Add country/region ✚]

[Back] [Submit application]

FIGURE 17-3:
Describe additional trademark characteristics.

8. **Answer the following questions about your trademark, products, seller and vendor accounts, and manufacturing and licensing:**

   ● Do you products have UPCs, ISBNs, EANs, or other GTINs?

   ● If you sell your products online, let us know where (optional).

   ● Does your brand have an existing relationship with Amazon? If it does, specify your role: Seller, Vendor, or Both. Otherwise, choose No, my brand doesn't have an existing seller or vendor relationship with Amazon.

   ● Does your brand manufacture products?

   ● Does your brand license the trademarks to others who manufacture products associated with your intellectual property?

   ● Where are your brand's products manufactured? Select your answers from the lists provided.

   ● Where are your brand's products distributed? Select your answers from the lists provided.

9. **Press the Submit Application button.**

   Amazon sends an email message with the case ID and another with a verification code to the contact you specified on your trademark application (you or your attorney). If you don't receive these messages, ask your attorney to forward them to you.

10. **Log in to Seller Central and scroll down to the Manage Your Case Log section.**

11. **Open the case message that applies to your adding your brand to the Brand Registry and choose the option to reply to the message.**

12. **Type or paste the verification code into your reply and choose the option to send the message.**

   The Amazon Brand Registry support team completes the brand registration process and notifies you of its completion within one or two days.

Building a Brand with Private-Label Products

One way to create your own brand is to source generic products from a manufacturer, stick your own brand name and logo on them, and sell them to consumers as brand-name products. With your own private label products, you have control over your product listings and access to Amazon's enhanced marketing and advertising tools.

REMEMBER

Building a brand with your own private label products isn't a quick and easy way to earn a buck. You need to do everything right — research products and competitors, find reliable and affordable suppliers, create great product listings, leverage the power of Fulfillment by Amazon (FBA), and deliver superior customer service. In addition, you need to brand your products.

Here's a quick step-by-step approach to building a brand with private-label products:

1. **Research products to find items with great sales and profit potential, as Chapter 6 discusses.**

2. **Research competitors who are selling the same or similar products you discovered in Step 1 to identify their weaknesses and find ways to outsell them.**

   Again, turn to Chapter 6 guidance on how to check out the competition.

3. **Find a reputable, reliable, and affordable supplier that makes the products you want to sell and allows private labeling.**

   See Chapters 7 and 8 for details on finding and working with suppliers.

4. **Brand the products with your own brand name, logos, and other brand assets.**

   You may need to create your own branded labels and packaging.

5. **Choose one or more fulfillment methods to ensure speedy delivery of products to your customers, as we explain in Chapter 10.**

6. **Create great product listings for your branded items, as we discuss in Chapter 9.**

7. **Market and advertise your products to generate sales.**

   See Chapters 11 and 12 for details, and be sure to take advantage of A+ Content to reinforce your brand identity.

8. **Focus on delivering superior customer service, as we explain in Chapter 13.**

   Customer service is especially important when you're trying to build a positive brand image.

REMEMBER

As a registered brand owner, you have access to Amazon's powerful brand-building tools, including A+ Content (for telling a compelling brand story), Sponsored Brands (for creating brand-centric advertising campaigns), Amazon Vine (for obtaining product reviews from the most influential reviewers on Amazon), and Amazon Store (where you can list all your products in one place). As you capitalize on the sale of private-label products, don't overlook these powerful branding tools.

Chapter **18**

Taking Advantage of Third-Party Tools and Service Providers

Seller Central is packed with features that enable you to list products, manage orders and inventory, advertise and promote your products, build and manage your own ecommerce store, monitor your performance, and generate a variety of business reports. However, developers and service providers outside the Amazon marketplace offer additional tools and services that can simplify many tasks, automate or outsource complicated or time-consuming activities, and enable you to make well-informed business decisions, such as choosing which products to sell.

In this chapter, we provide guidance on tools and services you may find valuable in boosting sales and profits and growing your ecommerce business within and beyond the Amazon marketplace. We also introduce you to Amazon's Service Provider Network (SPN), where you can connect with trusted local service providers to find the tools and expert assistance you need regardless of your level of experience.

TIP

We recommend two types of software solutions for your ecommerce business — one for conducting product research and another for managing the backend of your business. (The *backend* of an ecommerce business is everything that goes on behind the scenes, including processing orders and payments, managing inventory, and tracking shipments and returns.) A third software solution you may want to consider is one for automating the process of managing customer feedback.

The first three sections of this chapter cover these three software solutions. The last section introduces you to Amazon's Service Provider Network.

Taking Product Research to the Next Level

As we explain in Chapter 6, you can perform some basic product research on Amazon by checking out Amazon's Best Sellers and the product details page of any product you're thinking of selling. The Amazon Seller Mobile App is an even better product research tool, delivering additional information, including whether you're eligible to sell a specific product and how much you can expect to profit from a product after covering all your costs. (See Chapter 16 for more about the Amazon Seller Mobile App.)

However, Amazon's product research tools pale in comparison to the third-party products that are now available. For example, with JungleScout, one of the more popular Amazon sales analytics tools on the market, you can do the following:

» Access sales and revenue data for specific products on Amazon.

» Track a product's sales performance over time to identify trends.

» Filter through hundreds of millions of products to get ideas for products to sell.

» Identify potentially profitable niche markets.

» Search Amazon for products and instantly access valuable details about a selected product, including its sales and revenue potential, opportunity score, product demand, and competition.

Many software solutions marketed primarily as product research tools have additional features, including the following:

» Keyword optimizer to help you identify the search words and phrases shoppers most commonly enter to find a specific product

>> Supplier database, which you can search after you find a product of interest to locate a wholesale supplier from which you can source the product

>> A performance dashboard that enables you to track sales, profits, and costs and analyze a product's sales and profitability

Managing the Backend of Your Ecommerce Business

Many of the more complicated and time-consuming aspects of managing an ecommerce business are related to the backend of the business — what your customers don't see, such as order and payment processing and inventory management. If you sell on multiple ecommerce platforms such as Amazon, eBay, Walmart Marketplace, and Shopify, backend operations also include coordinating your activities across all your platforms.

Numerous software solutions are available for simplifying the many tasks associated with backend operations. These solutions provide a single interface through which you manage all backend operations for all your sales channels. Typical core functions of backend ecommerce management systems include the following:

>> Multi-channel integration

>> Order management

>> Inventory management

>> Automated repricing

In the following sections, we discuss these core functions in greater depth.

We don't recommend any specific ecommerce backend management solutions, but some of the more popular ones you may want to check out are Brightpearl, ecomdash, Orderhive, Sellbery, Sellbrite, and TradeGecko.

REMEMBER

Backend ecommerce management systems are often marketed to highlight one core function in particular. For example, a certain software package may be marketed as a multi-channel integration system, another as an order management system, and another as an inventory management system. However, most of these solutions are all-in-one systems for managing product listings, orders, inventory and suppliers, sales analytics, and more across multiple sales channels. Many of these solutions are also cloud-based, so you can access them anytime, anywhere using any Internet-enabled device.

Handling multi-channel integration

If you're selling the same products across a number of ecommerce marketplaces, multi-channel integration can simplify the process by providing a single interface through which you can list, sell, reprice, and ship items across Amazon, eBay, Walmart Marketplace, Shopify, and other ecommerce marketplaces. Specifically, with multi-channel integration, you can save time, money, and effort by doing the following:

» Create and post product listings one at a time or in bulk to all your ecommerce marketplaces.

» Receive warnings about any restricted items you're about to list on Amazon, eBay, or other marketplaces to maintain compliance with marketplace policies and keep you out of legal trouble.

» Reprice items according to simple rules to remain competitive and maximize sales and profits as market conditions change. Some systems use machine learning and artificial intelligence to determine optimal price points.

» Consolidate orders to create your own pick lists and save shipping costs.

» Increase the speed at which you process orders from all your ecommerce marketplaces anywhere in the world.

» Keep inventory levels in sync across all ecommerce marketplaces to help avoid overselling a product and running out of stock.

» Simplify the process of creating and tracking FBA shipments.

» Streamline the order fulfillment process with courier integration.

» Integrate with popular accounting software.

» Manage transactions in different currencies.

» Analyze sales performance across all channels.

Multi-channel management functionality may also include integration with suppliers, enabling you to find competing suppliers, compare prices, identify restricted items before you place an order, and automate inventory replenishment.

REMEMBER

Compare software solutions carefully and be sure the solution you choose provides integrations for all your ecommerce marketplaces, couriers, suppliers, your accounting software, and more. Also, if you plan to sell in other countries, be sure the solution can handle your global ecommerce needs, such as managing payments in different currencies.

Streamlining order management

An *order management system (OMS)* provides a single interface for tracking sales, orders, inventory, and fulfillment to ensure customers receive the products they ordered when promised and prevent you from running out of stock. An OMS should also integrate payment processing and collection and manage orders across all ecommerce channels (see the previous section for more about multi-channel integration). Here's how an OMS functions during typical sales transactions in the following order:

1. **Tracks orders.**

   When a customer places an order, the OMS captures the order details, including customer name and address, payment information, and items ordered.

2. **Locates and updates inventory.**

   The OMS finds the warehouse or distribution center nearest the customer that has the item(s) in stock and updates the quantities in stock to account for items removed from inventory to fulfill the order.

3. **Fulfills orders.**

   Prepares and prints pick lists and shipping labels; tracks packing and shipping progress; coordinates with couriers; and tracks package from pickup to delivery.

4. **Processes payments.**

   Records and verifies payment information and updates the accounting system.

5. **Manages returns and exchanges.**

   Tracks returns and exchanges, issues refunds, and updates the accounting system.

REMEMBER

Order management is a core function of multi-channel integration systems, which we discuss in the previous section.

Simplifying inventory management

If you're selling products only on Amazon and have all your inventory stored in Amazon fulfillment centers, Seller Central's inventory management features, as we explain in Chapter 15, are probably sufficient for your needs. However, if you sell products in a number of ecommerce marketplaces (and perhaps from your own webstore) or need to manage inventory stored at two or more locations, third-party inventory management software can greatly simplify the task while improving efficiency and reducing costs. Here are some common features of inventory management software that can ease the burden of inventory management:

>> Ability to manage your entire supply chain from suppliers to customers

>> Ability to scan product bar codes into the system

>> Inventory forecasting and optimization to maintain just the right levels of inventory for each product without overstocking or understocking items

>> Inventory alerts to warn you when you're running low on a product or when products have been sitting in inventory for too long

>> Integration with your suppliers to facilitate automated inventory replenishment

>> Integration across multiple warehouses and sales channels

>> Sales analytics to help you identify products that are selling well and those that aren't

>> Integration with the accounting software you use

WARNING

In your search for software to help manage the backend of your ecommerce business, you may encounter dedicated inventory management solutions, such as Fishbowl, which are geared more toward manufacturing. Steer clear of these solutions. Although they're great for manufacturing, they don't provide the features and functionality for managing retail operations.

Automating price changes

Repricing automation software enables you to implement pricing strategies to remain competitive and achieve your sales goals without having to adjust prices manually for each and every one of your products. You choose a pricing strategy or set rules or metrics to govern how prices are adjusted, and the software automatically reprices products accordingly.

TIP

Start by setting a minimum price (so you're never taking a loss on a sale) and a maximum price (so you're not gouging customers). You can then set rules based on the minimum and maximum prices. For example, you can create a rule to offer the lowest price in a certain marketplace down to your minimum price and to charge your maximum price when you're the only one who has the product in stock.

Here are a few pricing strategies you can execute using repricing software:

>> **Win the buy box:** Suppose you want to win the buy box on Amazon. Your strategy may consist of always offering the lowest price (within a certain price range) among FBA Sellers. You create a rule that reflects your strategy, and whenever a competing FBA Seller lowers his price for the product, your repricing software lowers your price a few pennies below that price. (By specifying only FBA Sellers, you avoid competing against non-FBA sellers who may offer a significantly lower price because they charge for shipping.)

REMEMBER

Sophisticated repricing software accounts for the total price a competitor charges, including the price of the product and shipping, in which case you wouldn't need to specify FBA-only sellers.

>> **Compliance pricing:** Some marketplaces, such as Walmart, feature a lowest-price guarantee. If your product isn't being sold for the lowest price compared to its price in other marketplaces, such as Amazon, Walmart may not display your product listing. With repricing automation software, you can always ensure that you're offering the lowest price available.

WARNING

If you're competing to offer the lowest price, be sure you set a minimum, unless you're willing to take a significant loss on a product.

>> **Pricing to a target profit margin:** You can create a rule that targets a specific profit margin (percentage or amount). The repricing automation software will increase the price when your costs rise and lower the price when your costs drop.

>> **Velocity pricing:** With velocity pricing, you set a sales goal for a certain period of time. The repricing software adjusts prices automatically to meet that goal while maintaining a specified profit margin.

REMEMBER

Most all-in-one ecommerce backend management systems support repricing automation, but before you choose a solution, check to make sure. You can also find stand-alone software solutions that specialize in automatic repricing, such as RepricerExpress, RepriceIt, Sellery, and SellerRepublic.

Automating Feedback and Reviews

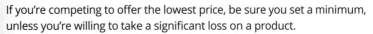

Your seller rating and feedback scores have some influence over where Amazon places your products in a shopper's search results and over your chances of winning the buy box. Plenty of high ratings and positive customer feedback equate with higher product search rankings and a greater chance of winning the buy box. Better yet, you may be able to win the buy box even when your prices are higher than those of your competitors, thus enabling you to increase both your sales and profit margins.

Unfortunately, few customers are inspired to rate and review sellers or post product reviews unless they've had a remarkable shopping or customer service experience. They often need to be coaxed into leaving feedback, and that's where feedback automation software comes into play. Whenever a shopper makes a purchase, the software captures the person's contact information, and then a few days after the order is confirmed, it contacts the customer via the marketplace's messaging system or via email, requesting product or seller feedback (or both).

WARNING

Amazon and other ecommerce marketplaces have strict rules that govern what sellers are permitted and prohibited from doing in regard to soliciting feedback from shoppers. Read and comply with all customer feedback policies.

Some feedback automation systems include templates to help you compose messages that resonate with customers. Templates may be available to automated responses to different situations, such as, if a customer requests a refund or exchange or leaves negative feedback.

Many feedback automation systems also include a feature that notifies you when customers leave low ratings or negative feedback. You can choose to receive these notifications via email or as text messages to your mobile device so you can follow up with customers in near real time to address concerns or complaints.

REMEMBER

We don't recommend any specific feedback automation solutions, but a couple of the most popular ones are FeedbackExpress and Feedback Genius. Bqool is another option that includes feedback automation, automatic repricing, and product research.

Finding Help through Amazon's Service Provider Network

Selling products on Amazon is simple, but building a successful ecommerce business on Amazon isn't easy. As competition heats up and you expand your operations, you may encounter certain operations that are beyond your pay grade or that you simply choose to outsource so you can shift attention to more enjoyable endeavors. Whatever the reason, Amazon's Service Provider Network (SPN) can connect you with trusted local providers who specialize in the following areas:

>> **Amazon account management** to help with your day-to-day Seller Central operations and provide guidance on how to grow your business on Amazon.

- **Accounting services** can help you integrate your accounting system with Amazon, analyze products for profit potential, reconcile payments with orders, and manage your accounting for you.

- **Advertising services** can help you create and manage your advertising and promotional campaigns to increase sales and profitability.

- **Cataloging services** can help you create and optimize your product listings.

- **Compliance assurance providers** conduct testing, inspections, certifications, audits, and quality control to ensure your products comply with the laws and regulations of the countries in which they're being sold.

- **A+ Content services** help you develop rich, creative content for branded products, including enhanced product descriptions, professional product photos and videos, detailed product specifications, and interactive media.

- **FBA preparation services** include bagging and tagging products, conducting quality checks, bundling products, shipping products to Amazon fulfillment centers, and *kitting* — moving products from their country of origin to a different country.

- **Imaging services** provide high-quality photos, graphics (such as logos and illustrations), and videos that you can include in your product listings to increase conversions.

- **International shipping and returns services** provide expertise in shipping products to customers or to Amazon fulfillment centers in other countries and accepting returns from buyers and shipping them to another buyer or bundling them and shipping them back to you.

- **Storage services** provide warehousing alternatives (both domestic and foreign) to FBA to facilitate faster delivery to customers.

- **Tax specialists** can help you meet your tax obligations in the various jurisdictions you do business, including other countries. These providers may also help collect and remit taxes to the various taxing authorities.

- **Trainers (Amazon certified)** provide guidance on how to list and sell products on Amazon and how to take full advantage of the features and functionality built into the Amazon marketplace and Seller Central.

- **Translation services** facilitate the process of listing and selling on Amazon in countries where you don't know the language.

REMEMBER

For additional details about SPN, including guidance on how to become a credentialed Amazon service provider, click in the Search box near the top of Seller Central, type **service provider network**, press Enter, and explore the search results to find the information you're looking for.

Chapter **19**

Expanding Your Operations: B2B and Global Sales

When you're comfortable selling products to retail shoppers in your own country and you've achieved the desired degree of success, you may want to consider different ways to expand your operations and increase sales and revenue. Well, you've come to the right place. In this chapter, we introduce you to opportunities that extend beyond what's available to sellers on Amazon. Specifically, we explain how to sell products to Amazon as a vendor, sell products to businesses, and expand your sales to customers in other countries.

REMEMBER

As a seller on Amazon you can usually get the most bang for your buck by investing your time and effort exploring ways to increase sales to retail shoppers in your own country. The opportunities and techniques that we present in this chapter are off the beaten path and are more advanced than most sellers want or need. The exception is the section on business-to-business sales, which may be relevant to certain sellers, such as those who sell computers or office supplies on Amazon.

Selling Products to Amazon as a Vendor

You can make money on Amazon selling products as a seller or as a vendor. A seller has a third-party (3P) relationship with Amazon, selling products to consumers. A vendor has a first-party (1P) relationship with Amazon, selling products directly to Amazon, which then sells the items to consumers. As a seller, you're a retailer. As a vendor, you're a wholesaler.

Unfortunately, you can't simply choose to become a vendor. The opportunity is available by invitation only; Amazon must invite you to become a vendor. Invitations are typically extended to well-recognized brands that have a product with significant potential for sales and profitability. Amazon commonly chooses brands with products that are already selling well on Amazon, but Amazon recruiters may also discover candidates at popular tradeshows.

Weighing the pros and cons of selling to Amazon as a vendor

Whether you've been invited to become an Amazon vendor or are considering pursuing that opportunity, weigh the pros and cons before making a final decision.

Here are the pros:

>> **Less work for you:** As a vendor, your primary responsibilities are filling purchase orders and billing Amazon. Filling purchase orders involves labeling and packing products and delivering them to Amazon fulfillment centers, so they're ready to be picked, packed, and shipped to customers. Amazon takes care of all the labor-intensive and sometimes aggravating tasks associated with selling directly to consumers, including customer service.

>> **Higher sales volume:** Products you sell to Amazon are obviously going to get special treatment, including better product placement. In addition, the items will be listed as "sold by Amazon," which removes any doubt from the shopper's mind as to whether she'll get the product on time and whether the seller will stand behind the product.

>> **Greater promotional support:** Through Vendor Central, you can access all the marketing tools available to brand owners, including A+ Content Manager, Subscribe & Save (Amazon's subscription service), and Amazon Vine.

>> **Few or no fees:** Vendors typically don't pay seller fees, such as referral and fulfillment fees.

Here are the cons:

>> **Low profit margin:** When selling your products as a retailer, you get to mark up the price and maximize your profit margin. When you sell to Amazon, you get wholesale prices, and Amazon is very aggressive when negotiating prices. You want to be sure that the increase in sales volume you get from being "sold by Amazon" is worth the decrease in profit margin.

>> **Strict inventory policies:** When a product is sold by Amazon, running out of stock can result in penalties, including chargebacks and possibly losing your Amazon vendor status.

>> **60- to 90-day net payment term:** Waiting 60 to 90 days to get paid may create a cash flow problem. Amazon does offer a 30-day payment option, but it deducts 2 percent for early payment.

Increasing your chances of getting invited to become a vendor

Amazon has teams of recruiters who attend tradeshows and monitor products being sold on Amazon. The company is always on the lookout for products with great sales and profit potential. When Amazon spots a product that meets its criteria, Amazon contacts the brand owner or manufacturer and invites them to become Amazon vendors. The best way to increase your chances of getting invited to become a vendor is to offer products that are or likely will be in high demand and that are or likely will be highly profitable.

TIP

You may be able to contact an Amazon recruiter to express interest in becoming one of its vendors. You can use the Contact Us link on Vendor Central, try tracking down and contacting a recruiter (vendor manager) via LinkedIn, or try connecting with a recruiter at a tradeshow or exhibition. Just be sure you have a product with significant sales and profit potential before pitching it to a recruiter; otherwise, you'll be wasting the recruiter's time as well as your own.

Selling to Other Businesses

The Amazon Business Seller Program is a feature set you can choose to add to your existing Amazon Professional Seller account to extend sales to members of Amazon Business, its business-to-business (B2B) marketplace, and adjust your listings to make your products more appealing to business customers. After joining the program, you access Business Seller features via Seller Central.

One of the main incentives to becoming a Business Seller is that Amazon's B2B marketplace is large and diverse, claiming as its members 55 of the Fortune 500 companies, more than 50 percent of the 100 biggest hospital systems in the United States, and more than 40 percent of the 100 most populous local governments. Globally, it accounts for more than $10 billion in sale annually, more than half of which is attributed to third-party sellers.

REMEMBER

Amazon Business can also help to maintain stable revenues when retail sales slump.

In addition to gaining access to Amazon's B2B marketplace, you benefit from the following features:

>> **Business pricing and quantity discounts** enable you to sweeten the deal for business customers.

>> **Business-only offers** allow you to offer certain products exclusively to business customers.

>> **Business-only selection** enables you to list certain products and in certain categories made available only to business customers.

>> **Enhanced content** allows you to upload additional content, such as user guides and material safety data sheets (MSDSs) in several categories.

>> **Seller credential program** gives you the option to claim certain credentials relevant to your business, such as quality, diversity, and ownership.

>> **Enhanced seller profile** enables you build a business profile with enhanced content, such as a logo, year established, business type, and more.

>> **Business reporting** provides access to a number of reports that provide useful data, such as when business customers placed orders and the number of businesses you serve.

Getting up to speed on performance standards and rules

Compared to Seller Central, Amazon Business has more stringent performance standards, as shown here:

Seller Central	Amazon Business
Order defect rate 1 percent or less	Order defect rate 0.5 percent or less
Pre-shipment cancellation rate 2.5 percent or less	Pre-shipment cancellation rate less than 1 percent
Late shipment rate 4 percent or less	Late shipment rate less than 1 percent

In addition, if you're going to sell on Amazon Business, you have a few extra rules to follow:

>> You must participate in the Amazon Business Seller program to offer special pricing to business customers.

>> If you use Amazon's tax calculation services, you must honor the customer's tax exempt status.

>> You must provide a tracking number for every business order and a packing slip and purchase order number for every package.

To join the Business Seller program, you must be an Amazon Professional Seller, as we explain in Chapter 1. To become a Business Seller, type Amazon Business in the Search bar near the top of Seller Central and press Enter. Click Amazon Business Overview and then Learn More About the Amazon Business Seller Program. Scroll down the page, press the Register for ABS button, and follow the on-screen instructions.

Managing business pricing and quantity discounts

For all stock keeping units (SKUs) eligible for business sales, you can offer a business price or quantity discount:

>> **Business price** is a discounted price available only to Amazon Business customers regardless of the quantity of the product they purchase.

>> **Quantity discounts** are tiered discounts also available only to Amazon Business customers based on the quantities of items purchased.

If you already have a product listing for the item you want to sell to Amazon Business customers, you can simply add the business price and quantity discounts using a feed file or by making changes through the Manage Inventory page, as the next two sections explain. If you don't have a listing for the product, create a product listing first (refer to Chapter 9).

Adding business pricing and discounts via the Manage Pricing page

The easiest way to add a business price or quantity discounts is through the Manage Pricing page. Take the following steps:

1. In Seller Central, open the Pricing Menu and select Manage Pricing.

2. The Manage Pricing page appears; if you don't see the Business Price column, click Preferences and select the Business Price box.

3. Click in the Business Price field for the product whose price you want to change, type the business price, and click the Save button.

4. To add quantity discounts, select Add Quantity Discounts for the desired product and then select either Percent off Business Price (to offer a percentage discount) or Fixed Prices (to set the price per item as a dollar amount).

5. In the At Least box, enter the minimum order quantity required to qualify for the first tier business discount.

6. In the For box, type the price per item or percentage discount for this tier.

7. To add more discount tiers, click the Add More Price Breaks button and enter the minimum order quantity and per item discount for the next discount tier.

REMEMBER

You can add up to five discount tiers. The bigger the quantity, the bigger the discount, so each subsequent tier should save the customer more per item. If you're following a fixed-price model, the dollar amount per item should decrease from one tier to the next. If you're using percentages, the percentage discount should increase from one tier to the next.

8. Click the Save Prices button.

9. Repeat Steps 3 to 8 for any additional products you want to offer to business customers at a special price or quantity discount.

Using a feed file to add business pricing and discounts

If you have several product listings you want to modify to offer business pricing or quantity discounts, consider using the Business Price/Quantity feed file to make the changes all at once. A feed file is an Excel spreadsheet you download from Seller Central, complete, and then upload. Take the following steps:

1. **In Seller Central, open the B2B menu and select B2B Central.**

2. **The B2B Central page appears; scroll down to the Selling on Amazon Business section, where you can find directions to download feed files, and select Set a Business Price or Quantity Discount.**

3. **Open the downloaded file and save it to a location where you'll remember it's stored.**

4. **In Excel, open the spreadsheet file you just saved, and click the Price Template tab to display the Price worksheet.**

   The column headings on this worksheet identify fields into which you type your desired entries. Each row is dedicated to a specific product or SKU.

TIP

   The leftmost tab of the spreadsheet file contains detailed descriptions of the fields on the Price sheet along with instructions on what to type in each column and sample entries.

5. **In the first SKU field, type the product's SKU number.**

6. **In the Business-Price field, type your business price, which must be lower than your standard price, or your business price will be deactivated.**

   The business price is a required entry. Offering discounts is optional.

REMEMBER

7. **To offer quantity discounts, type the desired entries in the following fields:**

   - In the Quality-Price-Type field, choose Dollar or Percentage to specify the discount as a fixed dollar amount or percentage.

   - In the Quantity-Lower-Bound1 field, type the minimum quantity that must be ordered to obtain the discount.

   - In the Quantity-Price1 field, type the discounted price as a dollar amount or percentage. If you're specifying dollar amounts, type the per-item price. If you're using percentages, type the percentage off per item.

   You can add discount tiers by typing the desired entries in the additional Quantity-Lower-Bound and Quantity-Price fields. You can add up to five price breaks, but each lower-bound quantity must be higher than the previous lower bound quantity — for example, 50 in the first Quantity-Lower-Bound field, 100 in the second, and 200 in the third. Likewise, discounts must be greater for each subsequent tier. If you're using dollar amounts, the dollar amount per item must be less for each subsequent tier. If you're using percentages, the percentage discount must be greater for each subsequent tier.

8. **Enter any additional details for the product in the designated fields.**

WARNING

   If you're an FBA seller, leave the Quantity and Leadtime-to-Ship columns blank. These fields are used for merchant-fulfilled network (MFN) listings, and entering a value in them will convert your offer to an MFN offer.

9. Repeat Steps 5 to 8 to enter business prices, discounts, and additional business offer details for any additional SKUs.

10. Use the File, Save As command in Excel to save the file as a Text (Tab-Delimited) file.

11. Return to Seller Central, open the Inventory menu, and select Add Products via Upload.

12. In the Upload File section, open the File Type list and select Price & Quantity File.

13. Click Choose File and use the resulting dialog box to select the feed file you just completed.

14. Click the Upload button.

Seller Central displays a confirmation message indicating whether the upload was successful. (If the upload wasn't successful, check the Upload Inventory Status table for clues to troubleshoot why it wasn't successful.)

Creating business-only offers

Business-only offers are product listings available only to Amazon Business customers, not retail customers. This option may come in handy in the following situations:

» The manufacturer restricts the sale of the product to businesses.

» The project is fragile and is likely to break or fail if the customer doesn't have the training or expertise to properly handle or install the product.

» The product is a specialty item that could injure a customer who doesn't have the training or expertise to properly handle or install the product.

To create a business-only offer, take the following steps:

1. If you already have a listing for the product with a retail price, delete the listing.

If the product doesn't have an existing listing, proceed to Step 2.

WARNING

If you delete a listing for one of your FBA products, any stock you have stored in FBA inventory may be stranded, but creating a new listing for the product, in Step 2, should fix the problem. However, to be sure, check for and fix any stranded inventory; open the Inventory menu, select Manage Inventory, and click the Fix Stranded Inventory tab. This page displays reasons any inventory is stranded and solutions (on the right).

2. **Create a new listing for the product, as we explain in Chapter 9, but leave the Standard Price field blank.**

3. **Open the Pricing Menu and select Manage Pricing.**

4. **The Manage Pricing page appears; if you don't see the Business Price column, click Preferences and select the Business Price box.**

5. **In the Business Price field for the product whose price you want to change, type the business price.**

   Leave the Standard Price field empty.

   If you add the standard price in the future, the product will be available to retail customers and will no longer be a business-only offer.

REMEMBER

6. **Click the Save button.**

   Your new listing is now a business-only offer.

Enrolling in Amazon's tax exemption program

Nonprofit businesses can choose to register for the Amazon Tax Exemption Program (ATEP) to make tax-exempt purchases. If you choose to participate in ATEP, Amazon automatically records and processes the tax exemption for you. More importantly, when business customers search for products and filter the results to show only products from sellers who offer tax exemptions, your listings are eligible to appear in the search results, whereas nonparticipating sellers' products aren't included.

As a business seller, you're automatically enrolled in ATEP as soon as you enter your tax info. To check whether you're enrolled and to opt out or opt in to the program, take the following steps:

1. **In Seller Central, select Settings (top right).**

2. **Scroll down to the Amazon Tax Exemption Program (ATEP) section.**

3. **Select the box next to Enroll in the Amazon Tax Exemption Program to opt in to the program, or remove the checkmark to opt out.**

4. **Select the box next to the option showing that you agree to the terms of the agreement.**

5. **Press the Save Settings button.**

If you opt out of the program, a tax-exempt business buyer can still buy your product and then contact you to request a tax-only refund. For FBA orders, Amazon customer service issues the tax-only refund after receiving the necessary supporting documents from the buyer.

Negotiating business prices

Amazon allows business buyers and sellers to haggle over pricing via its Negotiated Pricing feature. After you and the buyer agree to a pricing agreement (via Amazon's messaging service or over the phone), you can add the buyer to your account and provide the buyer with the agreed-upon price list.

Before you begin, obtain the business customer's Amazon Business identification number. Also, be sure you have a listing for each product you've agreed to sell at a discount.

To add your business customer to your account and submit a negotiated price list to the customer, take the following steps:

1. **In Seller Central, open the Pricing menu and select Negotiated Pricing. The Negotiated Pricing page appears.**

2. **Press the Add Customer button, enter the customer's Amazon Business ID, and press the Search button.**

    Seller Central displays the customer's information.

3. **Press the Add button.**

    Seller Central adds the customer to your account and returns you to the Negotiated Price page.

4. **Press the Upload Price Sheet button.**

5. **After the Upload Price Sheet page appears, click the Download New Template link, download the new price sheet template to your computer, and save or move it to a location on your computer you'll remember.**

6. **Open the new price sheet template and follow the instructions on the first worksheet of the template to add the required pricing details.**

7. **Use the File, Save As command in Excel to save the file as a Text (Tab-Delimited) file.**

8. **Return to the Upload Price Sheet page in Seller Central, press the Browse button, find and select the new price template file, and press the Open button.**

    You're returned to the Upload Price Sheet page, which now displays the name of the file you selected.

9. **Type the price sheet details in the appropriate text boxes: Version Description (descriptive name for this price sheet), Price Start Date, and Price End Date.**

10. **Press the Upload Price Sheet button.**

   Your price sheet is uploaded, and Seller Central displays the account page for this customer showing that the pricing update is "In Progress." The customer will be notified that the new price sheet is available and be instructed to review and approve it. The new prices will be available after the customer approves the new prices until the specified price end date.

To manage your price sheets from Seller Central, open the Pricing menu and select Manage Pricing. The Manage Pricing page enables you to add, delete, or replace price sheets.

Expanding Your Operations Globally

Amazon provides you an opportunity to expand sales into international markets, giving you access to millions of addition shoppers. You have the option to participate in the following international selling programs:

>> **FBA Export** provides an easy way to sell your products to customers in more than 100 countries.

>> **Global Selling** enables you to pick and choose the countries in which you want to sell.

In the following sections, we describe these two programs and explain how to take advantage of them.

Simplifying the process with FBA Export

FBA Export enables you to ship your products to customers in more than 100 countries in which Amazon has distribution centers. Here's how FBA Export enables you to go global:

>> International customers from more than 100 countries can shop on Amazon and access millions of products eligible to ship to their countries.

>> FBA Export is available at no extra cost to you; international customers pay shipping, customs, and any other fees. (You may pay extra if you use FBA to fulfill orders from other sales channels outside the Amazon marketplace.)

>> You can choose which products and countries to exclude. Amazon helps you identify products eligible for FBA Export.

>> Amazon FBA fulfills orders for you, handling the complexities of customs inspections other international commerce issues.

>> Amazon FBA decides which products are eligible for returns and handles all returns and refunds for you.

REMEMBER

Oversize products aren't eligible for FBA Export. Also excluded from the program are media products.

In the following sections, we explain how to enroll in FBA Export and how to exclude countries and products, if desired.

Enrolling or unenrolling in FBA Export

To participate in FBA Export, you must be enrolled in the program. Most FBA sellers are enrolled by default. You can check whether you're enrolled and choose to enroll or unenroll by taking the following steps:

1. **In Seller Central, select Settings (upper right) and then Fulfillment by Amazon.**

2. **Scroll down to the Export Settings section and press the Edit button in that section.**

   The Export Settings page appears.

3. **Select the desired option: Disabled or FBA Export.**

4. **Scroll to the bottom of the page and press the Update button.**

Finding out which of your products are eligible for FBA Export

Certain products are ineligible for FBA Export for a variety of reasons, including export and import restrictions of various countries and transportation and logistics restrictions. To find out which of your products are eligible for FBA Export, take the following steps:

1. **In Seller Central, select Reports and then Fulfillment.**

2. **In the navigation bar on the left, under Inventory, select Show More.**

3. **Scroll down the list of inventory reports and select Exportable Inventory.**

   The Exportable Inventory report appears, showing which of your products are eligible for export.

Excluding countries or products from FBA Export

FBA Export gives you complete control over the countries in which you choose to conduct business and the products you choose to sell. By default, you're set up to sell all your eligible products in all available countries, but you can choose to exclude individual countries or products.

To exclude countries, take the following steps:

1. **In Seller Central, select Settings (upper right) and then Fulfillment by Amazon.**

2. **Scroll down to the Export Settings section and press the Edit button in that section.**

3. **In the Shipping Restrictions section, press the Edit button.**

4. **After the Countries/Regions Excluded from FBA Export dialog box appears, select the box next to each country you want excluded.**

5. **Scroll to the bottom of the dialog box, and press the Save button.**

To exclude products from FBA Export, take the following steps:

1. **In Seller Central, select Settings (upper right) and then Fulfillment by Amazon.**

2. **Scroll down to the Export Settings section and press the Edit button in that section.**

3. **In the Shipping Program section, next to the FBA Export option, select the Exclude Products link.**

4. **After the FBA Export: Exclude Countries/Regions per Product page appears, follow the on-screen instructions to download, complete, save, and upload the FBA Export exclusion file.**

TIP

   The FBA Export exclusion file is an Excel workbook. The first page of the workbook contains detailed instructions for filling out the Exclude Products from Export worksheet. After reading the instructions, click the Exclude Products from Export tab to access the worksheet you need to fill out.

Expanding your operations into other countries using Amazon Global Selling

Amazon Global Selling enables you to list and sell products in any Amazon marketplace in North America, Europe, and Asia, as well as any international markets that Amazon will enter in future.

REMEMBER

Before you register to sell in a particular marketplace, research the market and become familiar with its regulations and taxes. This process varies from one market to the next and is beyond the scope of this book.

Before you can list and sell products in another country, you need to create a separate Amazon Seller account in that country. Notable exceptions to this rule are that if you have an existing seller account in North America, you can sell in Canada, the United States, and Mexico, and if you have a seller account in a European country, you can list and sell products in other European marketplaces. Some restrictions apply to specific marketplaces:

>> During the writing of this book, Amazon India wasn't accepting sellers from outside countries.

>> Amazon Italy is in Italian, so you need to register by contacting the support team.

>> During the writing of this book, Amazon's Chinese marketplace (Amazon.cn) was closed.

To create a new seller account for a country in which you want to be able to list and sell your products, take the following steps:

1. **Click in the Search box near the top of Seller Central and search for** Amazon Global.

2. **In the search results, select the Amazon Global Selling link.**

3. **Scroll down to the Amazon Global Selling section and select the Register and Launch with Amazon Global Selling link.**

4. **Select the Setting Up Your Amazon Global Selling Account link.**

5. **Scroll down the page to find links for specific countries and click the country in which you want to list and sell your products.**

6. **Follow the on-screen instructions to complete the process.**

To simplify the process of listing and selling in different marketplaces, link your existing accounts by taking the following steps:

1. **In Seller Central, select Settings (upper right) and select Global Accounts.**

2. **After the Global Accounts page appears, press the Linked Accounts button.**

3. **After the Linked Accounts page appears, select Add Additional Accounts and follow the on-screen instructions to complete the process.**

5

The Part of Tens

Discover ten ways to improve product search ranking, boost sales, and get the most bang for your advertising buck.

Explore ten techniques for taking your customer service to the next level without letting customers push you around.

Boost sales and profit margins by following ten product selection tips that set you apart from the competition.

Chapter **20**

Top Ten Advertising Tips

Whenever an Amazon shopper searches for a product, sponsored products appear at the top of the list. These items represent keyword-targeted advertisements that sellers bid for. Sellers who bid higher are more likely to have their listings appear near the top of the search results.

However, advertising success involves more than merely paying a premium for better product positioning. In this chapter, we present ten tips for optimizing the results of your advertising efforts, most of which are free.

Get to Know the Different Ad Types

Before you pay for any advertising on Amazon, familiarize yourself with the different ad types, so you can choose the most effective ad type for your desired outcome:

» **Sponsored product ad:** You select the product you want to advertise and the keywords to target (or allow Amazon to automatically target keywords it deems relevant). You also specify a total budget and a per-click bid amount. You pay only when a shopper clicks your ad. Ads may be displayed at the top of, alongside, or within search results and on product detail pages.

>> **Sponsored brand ad:** With sponsored brand ads, you can have your brand's products placed higher than those of competing brands when a shopper searches for a relevant product or even a competing brand. You can also use a sponsored brand ad to promote multiple products with a custom headline or logo. Ads drive customers to a product detail page or to your Amazon Store.

>> **Display ad:** Display ads provide a more flexible format for presenting media-rich advertisements to reach prospective customers on and off Amazon, using Amazon layout tools or your own custom content. You can link a display ad to an Amazon product detail page, your Amazon Store, a custom landing page, or an external website.

>> **Video ad:** These multimedia ads enable you to combine text, images, audio, and video to promote your brand to prospective customers on and off Amazon. You can even embed a video ad into a display ad. You can link a video ad to an Amazon product detail page, a website, or another Internet destination.

REMEMBER

Amazon advertising is available only to certain business entities. For example, sponsored product ads are available only to Amazon Professional Sellers, vendors, book vendors, Kindle Direct Publishing (KDP) authors, and agencies. Sponsored brand ads are available only to Amazon Professional Sellers who are brand owners and to retail vendors. Display and video ads are for all businesses, regardless of whether they sell products on Amazon.

Test the Market with Automatic Targeting

Although you probably want to target your Amazon ads manually by entering your own custom search terms, consider testing the market first with Amazon's automatic targeting to gather some ideas for search terms you may want to use.

When you set up your Amazon ad, choose automatic targeting instead of manual targeting and specify a low budget and maximum bid: for example, a \$10 budget with a maximum bid of \$0.25. Let your ad run for a few days and then check the results. You can then use some of the search terms identified by Amazon in a new manually targeted ad campaign.

Make the Most of Manual Targeting

When you create an Amazon ad, you have the option of choosing automatic or manual targeting. Automatic targeting is great for saving time and for testing the market (as we explain in the previous section). However, when you choose manual targeting, you can do much more than merely specifying your own search terms, including the following:

>> **Specify a bid adjustment.** To influence how often your products will appear at the top of search results on the first page, enter a bid adjustment of up to 900 percent to increase your base bid as needed to win a top placement.

>> **Target an entire product category.** Expand the reach of your ad by targeting an entire product category or subcategory. After choosing your products, select the product categories or subcategories you want to target. You can also narrow your reach by specifying brands, price ranges, or star ratings within the selected categories or subcategories.

Find Your Long-Tail Search Terms

Long-tail search terms are longer, more specific search phrases that shoppers are more likely to use when they're looking for a highly specific product and when using voice search. For example, instead of a simple keyword such as "chainsaw," a long-tail search term may be something like "Oregon battery-powered chainsaw." Using long-tail search terms in your product listings and ads, you can reduce the competition and earn a higher position in the search results when a shopper searches specifically for this phrase.

If you've used Amazon ads, you can download a search term report to gain insight into possible long-tail search terms that may be effective by following these steps:

1. **Head to Seller Central, click the Reports tab, and click Advertising Reports.**

2. **Open the All Campaigns list and click Sponsored Products.**

3. **Open the Report Type list and click Search Terms.**

4. **In the Report Name box, type a name for the report.**

5. **Open the Report Period list, click Customized, and enter a date range to view the past 60 days of your Amazon ad activity.**

6. **Click the Create Report button.**

7. **Click the Download link and follow the on-screen cues to download the report file.**

You can now open the report in Excel or another spreadsheet program that supports Excel files and sort the report by number of orders for each search term. This will help you identify effective search terms and possibly some long-tail search terms that can improve your search rank by avoiding some of the competition.

TIP

If you haven't used Amazon ads, consider using a third-party keyword tool to identify long-tail search terms. See Chapter 9 for more about researching search terms.

Research Your Competitor's Search Terms

Before you list or advertise a product, check out the search terms used by the top sellers of the product on Amazon. You can find plenty of third-party applications for researching search terms, including Viral Launch's Amazon Keyword Research Tool (https://viral-launch.com/keyword-research.html), Helium 10's Cerebro (www.helium10.com/tools/cerebro/), Sonar (http://sonar-tool.com/us/), and Amazon Keyword Tool (https://keywordtool.io/amazon).

Most Amazon keyword research tools enable you to research by search term or Amazon Standard Identification Number (ASIN) reverse lookup; you look up a product by its ASIN, and the tool provides insight into which keywords are used by competitors and, depending on the tool, how successful specific keywords are in terms of search rank and sales.

After you identify which search terms are most effective, create an ad campaign using those search terms.

TIP

Targeting effective keywords can be costly, because you have to outbid your competitors. A more effective approach, in some cases, is to use slightly less effective keywords in your pay-per-click advertising, so you can keep your costs down while increasing your product's search rank for specific terms.

Write Copy Specific to Your Product

When preparing product listings, you may be tempted to copy and paste a manufacturer's product description, but this approach doesn't give you a competitive advantage.

A better approach is to compose an original product description and other copy tailored specifically to the product — something that highlights both the product's features and its benefits. You may be better at writing marketing copy than anyone the manufacturer has on staff. If that's the case, take full advantage of your skills.

TIP

The same tip is true for product images. If you're a skilled photographer, consider snapping your own original product photos, especially if you can illustrate the value of the product more creatively than the manufacturer has done.

Avoid These Common Search Terms Mistakes

As you research and assign search terms to your product listings and Amazon ads, avoid the following common mistakes:

>> **Targeting only the most popular search terms:** Although you should certainly include popular search terms, competition can be stiff for the most popular ones, which can be costly if you're targeting them in your PPC advertising. Consider competing for less popular search terms until you build some traction.

>> **Choosing keywords that are overly broad:** A keyword that's too broad may get your product ranked in more searches, but if your product isn't relevant to what shoppers are looking for, they won't click it. Even worse, they may click it without buying it, which can cost you money if it's a sponsored ad.

>> **Targeting the plural instead of the singular:** For big-ticket items such as computers, smartphones, and home appliances, shoppers are only looking for one, so stick with the singular for of the search term.

>> **Using vague search terms:** Some words have different meanings in different contexts; for example, "memory" can refer to a memory-enhancement supplement, computer memory (RAM), memory foam, a memory card (for a camera), and so on. Be specific.

>> **Measuring search term success in clicks instead of conversions:** When choosing search terms for your products, more isn't necessarily better. More search terms may help your products appear in more searches with higher rankings and draw more clicks, but they don't necessarily result in more sales. Be selective. Focus more on conversions than on clicks.

Specify Negative Search Terms

Negative search terms are words or phrases that tell Amazon to exclude a certain product from the search results when a customer's search includes those terms. If you don't specify negative keywords, you're likely to suffer the following consequences:

>> Paying for ads that don't lead to conversions and, as a result, having less money to pay for ads that do lead to conversions

>> A lower click-through rate (CTR), which may hurt your product's search rank overall

>> Search-term cannibalization, which occurs when you have two products competing for the same search term

As you monitor your PPC ad performance, look for the following signs of negative keywords:

>> Low CTR (lots of impressions with few or no conversions)

>> High-spend or high-click ads with few or no conversions

To specify negative keywords in an ad campaign or ad group, take the following steps:

1. **Log in to Amazon Seller Central.**

2. **Navigate to the desired campaign or ad group.**

3. **Click the Negative Keywords tab.**

4. **Select the desired match type:**

   1. **Negative phrase** prevents the ad from appearing in any search queries that contain the specified words in the specified sequence (with allowance for plurals and minor misspellings); for example, if the negative search phrase is "prewashed jeans," the ad won't appear when the search query is "men's prewashed jeans" but will appear for "men's relaxed fit jeans."

   2. **Negative exact** prevents the ad from appearing only if the search query matches the specified phrase exactly (with allowance for plurals and minor misspellings); for example, if the negative search phrase is "prewashed jeans," the ad won't appear when the search query is "prewashed jeans," but will appear for "women's prewashed jeans."

5. **Type your negative search terms, each on a separate line, in the box below Match Type.**

6. **Click Add Keywords.**

7. **Click Save.**

Always Test and Track

Launching an advertising campaign isn't the end; it's the beginning. The key to success lies in measuring results, testing changes, and fine-tuning your ads to improve results.

To track the success of your ads, log in to Seller Central, click Advertising, then click Campaign Manager. Check the following metrics:

>> **Spend:** The amount you've spent on clicks

>> **Sales:** Total product sales generated from clicks on your ads

>> **Advertising cost of sales (ACoS):** The percentage of sales spent on advertising

>> **Return on advertising spend (RoAS):** The dollar amount produced in sales divided by the dollar amount spent on advertising

Don't Rush! Good Advertising Takes Time

After creating an ad, give it time to work. Set a relatively low budget for the ad to reduce the risk of spending too much on an ineffective ad while you await the results. You can always increase the budget for an ad when you're happy with its performance.

TIP

Test changes, one change at a time, to determine the impact of each change on the ad's success. If you make several changes at once, you won't know which change impacted the outcome.

> » Responding to customers quickly, honestly, and empathetically

> » Exceeding your customers' expectations

> » Understanding an issue before taking action

> » Adding a personal touch to your customer correspondence

Chapter **21**

Ten Tips to Deliver Awesome Customer Service

mazon takes customer satisfaction very seriously, and it expects its sellers to do so as well. After all, every seller interaction with a customer reflects back on Amazon. Therefore, a large part of your success on Amazon is tied to customer satisfaction. Satisfy your customers, and you'll be rewarded with higher search rankings and more sales. If you disappoint or upset customers, you'll be punished with lower search rankings, decreased sales, and perhaps even a suspended or canceled Amazon Seller account.

As a seller on Amazon, your goal should be not only to satisfy customers but to wow them — to deliver products and customer service that exceed their expectations. Achieve that goal, and you'll be rewarded accordingly — by both your customers and Amazon. In this chapter, we provide ten tips for exceeding your customers' expectations.

Follow Amazon's Rules and Updates

Prior to selling anything on Amazon, read and understand its selling policies and seller code of conduct. The seller code of conduct stipulates the following do's and don'ts:

- » Do provide accurate information to Amazon and its customers.

- » Do act fairly.

- » Don't misuse Amazon's features or services.

- » Don't attempt to damage or abuse other sellers or their listings or ratings.

- » Don't attempt to influence customers' ratings, feedback, or reviews.

- » Don't send unsolicited or inappropriate communications.

- » Don't contact customers except through Buyer-Seller Messaging.

- » Don't attempt to circumvent the Amazon sales process.

- » Don't operate more than one Selling on Amazon account without Amazon's permission.

In addition to this code of conduct, Amazon has specific policies related to category, product, and listing restrictions; product detail pages; prohibited seller activities; prohibited content; condition guidelines; drop-shipping; ASIN creation; supply chain standards; standards for selling brands in the Amazon Store; imaging and video services; and the Japanese Consumption Tax.

REMEMBER

With any rule change, Amazon sends an email notification to its sellers. Read all Amazon correspondence to familiarize yourself with any rule changes.

Respond in a Timely Manner

Amazon expects sellers to respond to all customer inquiries within 24 hours, but in today's era of on-demand information and instant text messaging, customers expect to hear back within minutes or seconds. Although within-24-hours is the requirement, set your goals much higher to impress your customers and keep the folks at Amazon happy.

Follow Amazon's lead. For example, when Amazon FBA handles a return for a Prime customer who pays with a credit card, the customer receives a return shipping label almost immediately upon submitting the return request and a full refund within minutes of dropping off the package at the local UPS or USPS return shipping location.

Be Honest

Customers understand that businesses have certain limitations and sometimes make mistakes, and they're generally understanding and forgiving as long as the business is honest and open. If you drop the ball, admit it, apologize, and, if possible, offer something of value to make amends. Being honest and open helps you reap the following benefits:

- >> Increased trust
- >> Increased customer loyalty
- >> Positive word of mouth
- >> Fewer returns
- >> Higher customer ratings

When providing customers with advice or guidance, focus on the person, not on the sale. You may lose the sale or have to issue a refund, but establishing a reputation as a retailer who cares about your customers pays handsome dividends.

Be Empathetic

Empathy involves imagining how another may think or feel in a given situation. When interacting with a customer, think first about what that customer may be thinking or feeling. Then, let the customer know that you understand by saying something like, "I certainly understand why you're upset . . . ." or "I would be upset, too, if I thought . . . ."

Sometimes, customers simply need to have their feelings validated. As soon as you show empathy, you're no longer the enemy — instead, you're sharing and alleviating the burden of the customer's psychological or emotional pain. You can then have a more rational discussion of how to resolve the issue fairly.

REMEMBER

You can't argue with feelings, even if the customer has no basis for feeling a certain way, so don't try to deny a person's feelings. Accept that your customer feels the way she does, regardless of the reason, and work toward bringing her to a better place.

Go the Extra Mile

Going the extra mile means exceeding customer expectations. Look at going the extra mile as something fun to do — just as you would go the extra mile for family or friends to brighten their day and make them feel appreciated. The goal is to pleasantly surprise your customers, so they're inspired to leave positive feedback and tell everyone they know about their positive shopping experience. Here are a few examples of going the extra mile:

>> If you sell jewelry, pack it in a gift box instead of in a plastic bag.

>> Use decorative tissue or packing paper instead of plain brown paper.

>> Offer tips on how to use the product or suggest a creative way to use the product.

>> Provide a refund and let the customer keep the product.

WARNING

Don't ask a buyer for a positive review or ask her to change or remove a review. Whatever you offer a customer as part of your going the extra mile is a gift; don't request or even expect anything in return.

Ask Questions

Prior to responding to a customer, be sure you fully understand the issue. If a customer contacts you and is obviously upset but isn't clear regarding what she's upset about, ask questions until you have a clear idea.

Also ask questions when you're trying to resolve an issue with a customer. For example, if you find out that a product the customer ordered wasn't shipped, ask whether the customer would like a refund or to have the product shipped overnight. Consider asking a disgruntled customer, "What can we do to make this right and keep you as a customer?"

Personalize Your Responses

Most disgruntled customers simply want to know that someone is listening, hears and understands the source of their dissatisfaction, and cares. One way to demonstrate all of this is to personalize your responses to customers, even when answering a question for the thousandth time:

» Address the person by name, if possible.

» Reply in a conversational tone.

» Acknowledge the cause of the customer's concern or complaint to demonstrate understanding and empathy.

» If you made a mistake, admit it.

» Offer a solution (if the solution is clear) or ask the customer what you can do to rectify the situation.

WARNING

When personalizing messages, avoid making any "you" statements that could be interpreted as accusatory. Try wording your responses with "I" or "we." For example, instead of replying with "You may have misread the product description," consider replying with, "I understand how the product description can be confusing."

Stay Calm

Customers can be unreasonable and even abusive, but you must remain calm, cool, and collected at all times. Don't take it personally, and don't launch a personal attack of your own. If a customer is getting to you, shift your focus from the customer to the issue and try your best to resolve the issue, even if it means letting the customer keep the product, giving a full refund, and still getting negative feedback. Let it go, and look forward to the next sale.

TIP

If a customer is being particularly difficult, consider offering to discuss the situation over the phone. Customers often find it easier to be abusive via email or text messaging than over the phone. Also, you may have better luck calming a customer over the phone.

Remain Positive

Positivity can make an unpleasant customer experience pleasant. Avoid negative words and phrases, such as "no," "not," "can't," and "don't." Use positive words instead, as shown in Table 21-1.

TABLE 21-1

Replace Negative with Positive Expressions

Instead of . . .	Use . . .
No:	Another option would be to . . . .
I don't know.	I'll check with the manufacturer and let you know the answer within the next two hours.
Calm down.	I understand how you must feel.
I'm sorry.	We can resolve this issue.
That's not possible.	That may be out of my control. Let's explore our options.
I can't	I can . . . .
I'm sorry, that's our policy.	That's our policy, but in your case, let's see what we can do.
There's nothing we can do.	I really wish we could solve this problem for you.
No problem.	I'm glad I could help.

Think Long Term

When you're dealing with a challenging customer, you're living in the present, and not in a good way. That one difficult customer or situation can eclipse all the good you've experienced in the past and all your visions for future happiness and prosperity. Even worse, it can cast a shadow on your daily activities and on your transactions with other customers.

As we explain in the previous section, your success hinges, in part, on your ability to remain positive in the midst of negative circumstances. When you notice your-self becoming upset over anything, envision a rosy future in which your sales are through the roof, all your customers are happy and leaving positive reviews, and you have more than enough money to finance your dreams. Then, believe it. The resulting attitude will energize you, will be projected to everyone you encounter, and will result in more positive outcomes.

REMEMBER

Your circumstances don't control your mind or heart; on the contrary, what you think and how you feel can have a tremendous influence over experiences and outcomes. Even better, you have complete control over your thoughts and emotions. Use that power to build the reality you envision.

> » **Being unique to avoid stiff competition**
>
> » **Checking out what your competitors are selling and how well they're doing**
>
> » **Improving your profit margins with higher priced products**
>
> » **Picking products with low return rates and few or no legal issues**

Chapter **22**

Ten (Plus One) Tips to Find Best-Selling Products

A major key to success as a seller on Amazon is product selection. You need to choose high-quality products that are in high demand and won't get you into trouble with Amazon or legal authorities. Because Amazon has millions of products offered by hundreds of thousands of sellers, you must choose products that sell and sell big. In this chapter, we provide ten tips for choosing great-selling, profitable, worry-free products.

Recognize Key Product Selection Criteria

As you scour the market for product ideas, keep the following product selection criteria in mind:

» **Solid profit margin:** Make sure you can sell a product for a profit that makes your time and effort worthwhile. When estimating your profit margin, be sure to account for all fees, commissions, and other costs you're likely to incur.

» **Popular in online searches:** Choose products that match commonly searched for words and phrases. Use keyword research tools such as Google Ads to identify keywords that are popular in terms of monthly search volumes and relevancy.

» **Small and light:** The smaller and lighter a product, the cheaper it is to store, pack, ship, and return. Avoid large, heavy products that can destroy your profit margin in shipping costs alone.

» **Heavily advertised:** Look for products that are heavily advertised on Amazon and other marketplaces and on the Internet in general. If you find a significant number of advertisements for a certain product, you know that a lot of sellers are betting on the product's salability.

TIP

Explore social media and discussion forums to gather ideas for additional products that meet these criteria. You can often identify opportunities by tuning into the problems people are having or the topics they're discussing.

Find a Niche

Instead of trying to sell every imaginable product on Amazon, consider choosing a product category or even a subcategory to specialize in, such as lawn and garden, home entertainment, beauty products, silver jewelry, books, cellphones, or sports. The more specific it is, the better. For example, you can start with a general category such as Clothing, Shoes, Jewelry, & Watches, narrow that down to Women, and then Jewelry, and Rings. You can always expand your scope to other subcategories within the selected category as demand for other items grows.

Choosing a niche offers several benefits, including the following:

» You can become an expert on a specific product type, which enables you to write better product descriptions and offer shoppers better guidance on how to select products that meet their needs and desires.

>> You spend less time and resources than if you were to try to compete on a broader selection of products.

>> You face less competition.

>> You can more easily establish yourself as a leading seller in your niche market, increasing your visibility.

TIP

A product that doesn't have a product video posted by a competitor on YouTube may be a good candidate to offer as a niche product because you can create a YouTube channel around the product. Cornering the market with a popular video can make a huge impact on sales, increasing your visibility both on YouTube and among search engines. (Chapter 12 discusses more specifically how you can use YouTube to market your products.)

Sell What You Know and Love

The best salespeople know their product and love it so much that they feel compelled to get it into the hands of everyone they know. They're excited to show it off to everyone, knowing that their customers' lives will be better or more enjoyable as soon as they start using the product.

When choosing products to sell, think about the products you have or wish you had, activities and hobbies you enjoy, and products you know a lot about, whether it's power tools, haircare products, jewelry, drones, home entertainment systems, personal fitness equipment, dietary supplements, or educational toys.

WARNING

Don't sell products you know little or nothing about. For example, unless you're at least a weekend mechanic, don't sell tools or supplies for repairing and maintaining vehicles.

Do Your Own Thing

Amazon is overcrowded with me-too sellers. Too many sellers look at the competition and want to be just like them. They list the same products with the same copy and photos for about the same price, trying to ride the competitors' coattails of success.

To be highly successful in the retail industry, be unique. Amazon isn't the place to blend in. Be yourself. Have fun in every aspect of your business, from selecting your product to composing product listings to delivering customer service. Let your personality shine, and express your enthusiasm over the products you're selling. When you're unique and having fun, people will be drawn to *you* and be more likely to buy from you than from other, run-of-the-mill sellers, even if you charge a little more.

TIP

"Do your own thing" can also mean manufacturing your own products to sell on Amazon. When you design your own product, patent it, and produce it, you eliminate the competition and reap several benefits, including the following:

>> The freedom to price the product to sell at whatever margin you desire and the market will support.

>> The ability to brand your products. As brand owner, you can claim additional benefits on Amazon, including the following:

- The ability to create brand pages, promote your brand, and engage with the customers more effectively.

- Amazon's protection against counterfeit products, assuming you own the patent and trademark rights. Amazon will come to your rescue if anyone tries to sell knock-offs of your popular brand.

>> The opportunity to define the market through product innovation and perhaps even create an entirely new line of products around your ideas.

>> Control over the quality of the product, thus improving customer satisfaction leading to increased sales.

Refer to Chapter 7 to find out more about manufacturing and selling your own merchandise.

Don't Expect Seasonal Products to Sell Year-Round

Seasonal products are great for boosting sales and profits at specific times of the year, but don't expect seasonal items to sell year-round. Seasonal items are those that sell well during only certain periods of the year, such as the following:

>> Holidays, including Christmas, Hanukkah, Easter, and Halloween

>> Fashion items (such as winter boots and coats or swimming suits and flip-flops)

>> Recreation and leisure activities (such as swimming and boating)

>> Back to school

>> Winter (shovels, ice-scrapers, space heaters)

Carrying some seasonal inventory is fine, but be sure your inventory includes mostly products that sell year-round.

Though some experienced sellers do well selling seasonal products, they usually have built-in alternatives to accommodate off-season sales slumps. As a new seller, you'd be hard-pressed to achieve success with seasonal-only products.

Decide Whether to Pursue Best Sellers

One strategy for increasing sales on Amazon is to list products that are in high demand on Amazon. Amazon encourages and facilitates this strategy by highlighting its 100 Best Sellers in every category and subcategory. These lists are updated hourly based on real-time sales data.

To find Amazon's best sellers, go to Amazon.com and click Best Sellers in the menu bar near the top of the page. Amazon displays a list of Departments on the left and a list of Best Sellers in currently popular departments on the right. Use the Department list to navigate to the desired product category and subcategory. When you select a category or subcategory on the left, its Best Sellers are displayed on the right.

WARNING

Pursuing Amazon Best Seller may not always be a wise move. Whenever a product becomes popular among Amazon customers, Amazon Sellers swarm to it to get their share of the sales and profits. If it's a big enough seller and has a high enough profit margin, chances are good that Amazon will start to sell it, too, and perhaps even create its own Amazon brand equivalent. As competition stiffens, profit margins tend to drop.

Capitalize on Low Competition

For sellers on Amazon, the holy grail is a high-demand product with a great profit margin that few, if any, other people are selling. To find your holy grail, start by searching for products that are popular or are growing in popularity. Here are a few places to look:

>> **Amazon Best Sellers:** Go to Amazon.com and click Best Sellers, in the menu bar near the top of the page. Use the Any Department list on the left to see the Best Sellers in specific product categories or subcategories.

>> **Pinterest:** Search Pinterest for a product category or subcategory. The top search results are likely to show the most popular products in the specified category or subcategory.

- **AliExpress:** Go to AliExpress.com, choose the desired product category or subcategory, and choose Sort by Orders. This presents the products in the selected category by the number of items sold.

- **Amazon product finder:** Use an Amazon product finder, such as JungleScout (www.junglescout.com) or Helium 10's Black Box (www.helium10.com/tools/black-box) to research products.

- **Google Trends:** Go to Google Trends (trends.google.com), search for the desired product category or subcategory, and scroll down the page to view a list of popular search terms in the category. For example, if you search for "fashion," you're likely to see a currently popular new fashion, such as camp style (which regards clothing that's appealing because of its bad taste).

After finding a popular product, size up your competition on Amazon. Search for the product on Amazon to determine how many Amazon Sellers list the product. If nobody is selling it, you've struck gold. If others are selling it, check out their reviews, as we explain in the later section "Check Competitors' Reviews." If one or more sellers have only a few (or no) reviews, you've found a product with relatively low competition. On the other hand, if one or more sellers have lots of reviews, you may be wise to pass on this product. See Chapter 6 for additional guidance on how to conduct product research.

Focus on Products That Sell for More than 20 Bucks

Selling low-priced products on Amazon is a loser's game. Even if you have a markup exceeding 300 percent, if you buy a product for $3.25 and sell it for $10, you're lucky if you break even and very likely to sell at a loss. Shipping costs and Amazon fees will gobble up any profits.

REMEMBER

Choose products that sell for more than $20 and comply with the 3x Rule. The *3x Rule* is a method estimating whether a product will be profitable. Assuming you want to double your money, aim to triple it, figuring that your costs will eat about a third of your profit; for example, if you buy a product for $10, sell it for $30, and subtract $10 for costs, your net profit is $10 or 100 percent.

Consider selling a product that sells for $2 with net profit margin of 50 percent earning $1 every sale. Even though product margin is very good, you need to sell a lot of that product to generate a considerable profit. On the other hand, you can sell a product that costs $40 with a net profit margin of 30 percent, earning you about $13 every sale. You sell one item to earn $13 instead of having to sell 13 of a lower priced product.

Check Competitors' Reviews

Prior to listing a product, search for it on Amazon to find out if other sellers list the product. If they do, check the product reviews for the following criteria:

» **Number of reviews:** If a product has hundreds or thousands of reviews, the seller is probably very well established, and you'll have a tough time competing. Number of reviews and number of sales are closely related; so unless you're sure you can compete with the top sellers on the number of reviews, you probably won't be able to compete on sales.

» **Number of negative reviews:** If a product has dozens of negative reviews, you may be looking at a dud or an opportunity. If the negative reviews highlight defects or shortcomings in the product, you may want to steer clear of it. However, if the negative reviews point to problems with customer service, you may have success selling the product by offering superior customer service.

TIP

Use an Amazon product research tool, such as JungleScout (www.junglescout.com) or Seller App (www.sellerapp.com), to conduct your research. With such a tool, you can usually search for a specific product and then sort the list by number of sales and number of reviews.

Reduce Returns

Amazon has a liberal return policy, especially for its Prime customers, who pay nothing for return shipping. However, some products, such as clothing and shoes, have a higher return rate than others, such as books, DVDs, and mobile phone accessories. Obviously, returns increase your costs, especially when a customer returns an item in a condition that prevents it from being resold.

Here are a few suggestions for lowering your return rate and return costs:

» Choose products with lower return rates.

» When selling clothing, offer guidance on how to choose the right size.

» Create detailed product descriptions, so the customer can make a well-informed purchase decision.

» When listing a product, use great product photos and include images of the product being used or worn.

- » Inspect your product packaging before shipping products to FBA fulfillment centers.

- » Negotiate with your suppliers to replace items returned for being defective or damaged.

REMEMBER

You can add a restocking fee (and include it as part of your product listing) to discourage returns, but this fee will also discourage some shoppers from buying the product from you.

Avoid Legal Issues

WARNING

When selecting products, steer clear of those that have a high risk of presenting legal issues, which can be very expensive and time-consuming, not to mention harmful to your relationship with Amazon.

Make sure products or brands you're planning to sell have no exclusive trademark deals, distribution agreements, or patents. If you want to sell such products, obtain written authorization in advance from the patent, trademark, or brand owner.

Index

About the Authors

Deniz Olmez is an Amazon consultancy that specializes in search engine optimization, new account setup and management, Fulfillment by Amazon, and branding services. Deniz established Amazon Consulting Services in 2012 following seven years' experience with top e-commence platforms to help online and multi-channel retailers and brand manufacturers succeed on Amazon and other global marketplaces by analyzing competition, developing key marketing, Amazon SEO solutions, advertising strategies, and customizing business plans. He advises everyone from start-ups to global brands and retailers. He currently provides Amazon consultancy services and project management to clients in the United States and abroad.

Joe Kraynak is a freelance writer/editor who has authored and co-authored numerous books, including *Flipping Houses For Dummies* and *Bipolar Disorder For Dummies* both published by Wiley, and *Take the Mic: The Art of Performance Poetry, Slam, and the Spoken Word.*

Joe graduated Purdue University with a B.A. in Creative Writing and Philosophy and an M.A. in English Literature. For three years, he wrote for Training Specialists, Inc., where he interviewed machine operators in manufacturing plants and prepared task-analysis training manuals for Indiana's Training for Profit (TfP) job-training program.

He spent the next five years working in-house at Macmillan Computer Publishing, where he edited and wrote books on a variety of computer topics for beginning computer users.

Joe has been freelancing for more than 30 years, collaborating on writing projects for some of the top publishers in the industry, including John Wiley & Sons, Macmillan, Penguin, and Pearson.

Publisher's Acknowledgments

Senior Acquisition Editor: Tracy Boggier

Project Editor: Chad R. Sievers

Proofreader: Debbye Butler

Production Editor: Siddique Shaik

Cover Image: © Maxx–Studio/Shutterstock

Leverage the power

Dummies is the global leader in the reference category and one of the most trusted and highly regarded brands in the world. No longer just focused on books, customers now have access to the dummies content they need in the format they want. Together we'll craft a solution that engages your customers, stands out from the competition, and helps you meet your goals.

Advertising & Sponsorships

Connect with an engaged audience on a powerful multimedia site, and position your message alongside expert how-to content. Dummies.com is a one-stop shop for free, online information and know-how curated by a team of experts.

- Targeted ads
- Video
- Email Marketing

- Microsites
- Sweepstakes sponsorship

20 MILLION PAGE VIEWS EVERY SINGLE MONTH

15 MILLION UNIQUE VISITORS PER MONTH

43% OF ALL VISITORS ACCESS THE SITE VIA THEIR MOBILE DEVICES

700,000 NEWSLETTER SUBSCRIPTION TO THE INBOXES OF

300,000 UNIQUE INDIVIDUALS EVERY WEEK

# of dummies

Custom Publishing

Reach a global audience in any language by creating a solution that will differentiate you from competitors, amplify your message, and encourage customers to make a buying decision.

- Apps
- Books
- eBooks
- Video
- Audio
- Webinars

Brand Licensing & Content

Leverage the strength of the world's most popular reference brand to reach new audiences and channels of distribution.

For more information, visit dummies.com/biz

PERSONAL ENRICHMENT

Staying Sharp — 9781119187790 — USA $26.00 — CAN $31.99 — UK £19.99

Facebook — 9781119179030 — USA $21.99 — CAN $25.99 — UK £16.99

Guitar — 9781119293354 — USA $24.99 — CAN $29.99 — UK £17.99

Investing — 9781119293347 — USA $22.99 — CAN $27.99 — UK £16.99

Beekeeping — 9781119310068 — USA $22.99 — CAN $27.99 — UK £16.99

Digital Photography — 9781119235606 — USA $24.99 — CAN $29.99 — UK £17.99

Meditation — 9781119251163 — USA $24.99 — CAN $29.99 — UK £17.99

Pregnancy — 9781119235491 — USA $26.99 — CAN $31.99 — UK £19.99

Samsung Galaxy S7 — 9781119279952 — USA $24.99 — CAN $29.99 — UK £17.99

iPhone — 9781119283133 — USA $24.99 — CAN $29.99 — UK £17.99

Crocheting — 9781119287117 — USA $24.99 — CAN $29.99 — UK £16.99

Nutrition — 9781119130246 — USA $22.99 — CAN $27.99 — UK £16.99

PROFESSIONAL DEVELOPMENT

 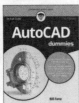     

Windows 10 — 9781119311041 — USA $24.99 — CAN $29.99 — UK £17.99

AutoCAD — 9781119255796 — USA $39.99 — CAN $47.99 — UK £27.99

Excel 2016 — 9781119293439 — USA $26.99 — CAN $31.99 — UK £19.99

QuickBooks 2017 — 9781119281467 — USA $26.99 — CAN $31.99 — UK £19.99

macOS Sierra — 9781119280651 — USA $29.99 — CAN $35.99 — UK £21.99

LinkedIn — 9781119251132 — USA $24.99 — CAN $29.99 — UK £17.99

Windows 10 All-in-One — 9781119310563 — USA $34.00 — CAN $41.99 — UK £24.99

SharePoint 2016 — 9781119181705 — USA $29.99 — CAN $35.99 — UK £21.99

Fundamental Analysis — 9781119263593 — USA $26.99 — CAN $31.99 — UK £19.99

Networking — 9781119257769 — USA $29.99 — CAN $35.99 — UK £21.99

Office 2016 — 9781119293477 — USA $26.99 — CAN $31.99 — UK £19.99

Office 365 — 9781119265313 — USA $24.99 — CAN $29.99 — UK £17.99

Salesforce.com — 9781119239314 — USA $29.99 — CAN $35.99 — UK £21.99

Coding — 9781119293323 — USA $29.99 — CAN $35.99 — UK £21.99

dummies.com

dummies®
A Wiley Brand

Learning Made Easy

ACADEMIC

9781119293576
USA $19.99
CAN $23.99
UK £15.99

9781119293637
USA $19.99
CAN $23.99
UK £15.99

9781119293491
USA $19.99
CAN $23.99
UK £15.99

9781119293460
USA $19.99
CAN $23.99
UK £15.99

9781119293590
USA $19.99
CAN $23.99
UK £15.99

9781119215844
USA $26.99
CAN $31.99
UK £19.99

9781119293378
USA $22.99
CAN $27.99
UK £16.99

9781119293521
USA $19.99
CAN $23.99
UK £15.99

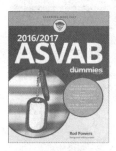

9781119239178
USA $18.99
CAN $22.99
UK £14.99

9781119263883
USA $26.99
CAN $31.99
UK £19.99

Available Everywhere Books Are Sold

dummies.com

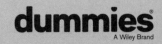